LIVES OF THEIR OWN

The Individualization of Women's Lives

Charles   Lorna   Lorne
Jones   Marsden   Tepperman

TORONTO
OXFORD UNIVERSITY PRESS
1990

Oxford University Press, 70 Wynford Drive, Don Mills, Ontario, M3C 1J9

Toronto   Oxford   New York   Delhi   Bombay   Calcutta   Madras   Karachi
Petaling Jaya   Singapore   Hong Kong   Tokyo   Nairobi   Dar es Salaam
Cape Town   Melbourne   Auckland

and associated companies in
Berlin   Ibadan

CANADIAN CATALOGUING IN PUBLICATION DATA

Jones, Charles L.
Lives of their own

(Studies in Canadian sociology)
Includes bibliographic references.
ISBN 0-19-540789-X

1. Women – Canada – Social conditions. 2. Women –
Social conditions. 3. Women – Employment – Canada.
4. Women – Employment. 5. Women – Education –
Canada. 6. Women – Education. I. Marsden, Lorna R.,
1942-   . II. Tepperman, Lorne, 1943-   .
III. Title. IV. Series.

HQ1453.J66 1990   305.4'0971   C90-093224-4

1 2 3 4 - 3 2 1 0
Printed in Canada

Contents

Acknowledgements

We should like to express our gratitude to colleagues at the the University of Toronto, and particularly to Clayton Mosher, Vappu Tyyska, and Antonia Maughn. We also thank Gordon Turpin and Sandra Badin. For assistance with the manuscript preparation we also thank Carolyn Hume. Sally Livingston and Richard Teleky of Oxford University Press provided invaluable editorial advice. We are also indebted to Prof. Jacques Zighera of the Université de Paris X-Nanterre à Nanterre, to Drs Robert Wright and Andrew Hinde of the Population Studies Centre, University of London, and to Dr Kathleen Kiernan of The City University, London. Institutions that have helped us include the Centre for Urban and Community Studies and New College, University of Toronto. Many of our data resources were originally set up by Statistics Canada. The Ontario survey of Women's Employment Histories was funded by the Social Sciences and Humanities Research Council of Canada (Strategic Grants Division). Our research has also been funded by the University of Toronto, by Labour Canada, and by Health and Welfare Canada under the Demographic Review Programme. Any errors are our own.

Introduction

Have you noticed how different, how variable and unpredictable women's lives are today? No two lives seem quite the same. Even two women who graduated from the same high school on the same day—even if they were best friends and similar in many ways—will be living very different lives a decade or two later. Sally is married with three children; Judy is divorced with one child (or perhaps she never married). Sally works part-time in a library; Judy manages dress stores for a major clothing chain. Sally is taking recreational courses at the university and dreaming about a full-time job in management. Judy doesn't have time for much of anything recreational, and dreams about taking a year off to travel or study a foreign language. These are the kinds of women who might have been best friends ten or twenty years ago.

All three of us teach sociology at a large urban university in central Canada. The cross-sections of students we see are probably similar to those in the greater Toronto, Montreal, Edmonton, Halifax, or Vancouver areas. We have been working here long enough to notice some major changes in the students we teach; for in fact, our university is a miniature version of Canadian society. Everything important that is happening 'out there'—all of those changes in women's lives we just mentioned—is also happening 'in here', in what some people mistakenly call the Ivory Tower.

That's why university students today are quite different from the way they were fifteen or twenty years ago. Today our students come from a wider variety of social, ethnic, and economic backgrounds. They are older, on average, than students were in the past. They come with a richer, more complex first-hand history of personal experiences. And they come with a wider variety of on-going responsibilities and social relationships.

In all of these respects, our female students are more varied than our men students. Consider the following women—fictionalized, to be sure—who represent scores of actual women we have taught in the last few years:

SUZY: age 18, just out of high school, a straight-A student, who does not yet know what she wants to study but feels confident she will make the right decision and do well;

BRENDA: age 18, also just out of high school, a B-student who is taking easy courses and waiting until she gets married to someone she expects to meet at university;

DIANA: age 22, who is graduating this year and does not know what she wants to do. She's scared stiff by everything sociology has taught her about job discrimination against women and the probabilities of marital breakdown;

CARLA: age 25, who has done brilliantly in her undergraduate and MA studies, but is having trouble deciding whether to continue working towards a doctorate, move to the west coast with her husband, have a baby, or just take a job and relax for a while;

GAIL: age 27, who did very well in her BA and MA studies, took time off to work but then found there were so many BAs out there that she needed another degree in order to get a 'reasonable' job. She's back at school;

ANNA: age 33, who dropped out of university over a decade ago to follow her man across the continent. Now she's on her own again, back after doing a variety of jobs (among them, driving a bus, delivering mail, doing rough carpentry) to finally get a degree;

ROSA: age 37, a graduate scientist, divorced with two children, who was a housewife for almost a decade. Now she is trying to get a law degree and achieve economic independence;

MARGARET: age 50, a public-school teacher who is taking one or two courses a year towards a BA, but finds it tough going. Her husband and daughter will not help out with household chores and other family responsibilities. When her old aunt broke a hip, Margaret was late getting in all her class assignments.

These are just a few of the 'kinds' of women we see at the university. The Suzies and Brendas have always been around; but the other women—the Carlas and Gails, Annas and Rosas and Margarets—are much more numerous than in the past. We believe this is because women's lives have changed a lot while we have been teaching. So far, too little is known about the how, the why, and the 'what next?' of it. But while our women students are often different from the ones we knew twenty years ago, so are many of our men students. Even though their lives may not be so different, the women with whom they are involved have changed, and many men are as interested in those changes for personal reasons as we are for sociological ones. Now, it may be that most of our men students will study, get jobs, marry, have children, and eventually retire. But many more men are finding it difficult to understand the women they meet. FRANK is typical. Approaching his fortieth birthday, he is back at university to complete a degree he abandoned twenty years ago. He works for the government in a middle management position, and all around him women are moving into jobs traditionally held by men. Recently divorced, he is not hostile, but confused and wanting to understand. In the same class with Frank you might find LES, who came straight to university from high school. He has noticed that women seem to have richer relationships than he can have with the jocks in the dorm. LES doesn't want to be different from the other men, but he does actively inquire about women's feelings and women's lives. Sometimes he feels that men are getting the short end of the stick in our society. Sometimes he gets impatient with sociological data showing that women earn less than men. Sometimes he feels embattled in classroom debates. But above all he wants to understand himself, his friends, and his future.

Sociology has fallen behind the rapidly changing real world; this book is an attempt to catch up. As teachers, we need to understand our students better. As sociologists, we need to understand the world around us better. So the writing of this book is justified by concerns that grow out of our experiences as teachers and sociologists. In fact, though, it actually began as a fairly 'pure' research project, funded by Labour Canada and by the Social Sciences and Humanities Research Council. It then became an exercise in demographic research for the government of Canada when the Department of Health and Welfare decided to conduct a multi-disciplinary 'review of demography' intended to help legislators understand the most pressing population issues in Canadian society: questions about immigration, the aging of the population, the availability of trained workers, the reasons people migrate from one part of the country to another, the effects of ethnic and racial differences, and so on.

As part of this review, Jones and Tepperman completed a study of changes in adult women's lives, and their findings comprise the core of the present book. But to write it required that we add and subtract a great deal, and set current changes in women's lives against a backdrop of historical development and debates in the fields of sociology, economics, and women's studies. This is where Marsden, who for years has been teaching and writing in the area of women's studies and labour markets as they affect women, came in. The result is a book that should not only help legislators determine what policies will ensure an adequate supply of labour in

Canada's future, but also alert undergraduate readers to some very dangerous gaps between fantasy and reality.

The real worlds of marriage, parenting and career are *not* what you may have thought, even wished, they might be. A great many people just like you—for example, Gail and Anna and Rosa and Frank—are having to change their lives because when they were younger, they did not know what to expect and how to plan ahead. This book is about what *you* should expect.

Growing up, getting married and entering the world of work today is not what it was in your parents' time. Your parents probably can't tell you much about how to plan your future; their own experience is simply too far out of date. You will live your adult life in a society unlike the one your parents knew, one that will be changing dramatically from decade to decade. Fortunately, there is a pattern to these changes, and that is what our book is about: a pattern that we call 'individualization'.

By 'individualization' we mean the process by which each generation of women is now involving itself in work and education in ways unlike those of earlier generations. Increasingly, women's lives will be quite different not only from the lives women lived in earlier generations, but from the lives other women are living in their own generation. Diversity will continue to increase.

Fifty years ago male and female adult lives differed in simple ways. Men completed their formal education, then entered full-time paid work, in which they continued—unless interrupted by serious illness—until they retired, after which they were at leisure. Women, on the other hand, completed their formal education and then entered either full-time housework or full-time paid work. If the latter, they would continue working for pay until either the birth of a child or retirement. After that, in either case, they would spend the rest of their lives engaged in the complex, highly skilled activity that is housework.

Even fifty years ago, women's life patterns, though simple, were more complex than men's. Whereas men typically held only one work status, women commonly held two, one after the other or at the same time, as full-time wage-workers and/or full-time houseworkers. What has happened in the last fifty years is a further increase in the complexity of women's lives.

I

CAUSES OF CHANGE
IN WOMEN'S LIVES

1

Changes in
Women's Personal Lives

The 1960s saw the beginning of many important changes, especially for women. These changes gave rise to strains in the existing
institutions regulating sexual behaviour, marriage, and divorce.
With hindsight, we can see the year 1968 as a watershed in
women's personal lives: that was when omnibus federal legislation took the Canadian government 'out of the bedrooms' of
Canadians, freeing up sexual behaviour, and made getting a
divorce easier than it had ever been before. These changes in
personal relations reflected the dramatic changes already under
way in the character and stability of marriage, in decisions about
children, and in the spousal division of labour. In turn, the legal
changes led to more need for spousal economic independence.
That, together with a demand for workers, especially women
workers, and an ever-rising cost of living, led to a two-income
family. Combined with reduced child-bearing and increased job
opportunities, these changes led women's work lives to
'individualize'.

1968: THE TURNING POINT

It was in the 1960s that birth-control technology became safe,
sophisticated, and easy for the average woman to obtain; higher
education became more accessible to all Canadians (benefitting
women among others); birth rates continued to fall after peaking
around 1957; and two incomes became a necessity for most middle-class urban families. These changes set in motion three processes we shall consider at length below: (a) a rapid and prolonged
rise in divorce rates; (b) a reduction and compression of child-
bearing; and (c) a stronger career commitment among women. (A
fourth process, the change in labour-market demands for female
labour, will be discussed in the next chapter.)

What were the results of these interlinked changes in women's personal lives? Taken altogether, they increased not only the risk in adult women's lives, but also the flexibility, at least in the public sphere of work, while they may have reduced flexibility in the private sphere of domestic life. These two spheres are a theme that this book will address time and again; the present chapter will make only a beginning toward that goal.

We shall see that the coming of easier divorce let loose an explosion of divorces, which has only recently peaked and shows little sign of decreasing significantly. One can scarcely overstate the consequences of this divorce explosion for women planning their educations, careers, and families. It has redefined adult life in Canada.

So has the coming of safe, predictable contraception. The new contraceptive pills and diaphragms made it possible for women to plan how many children they wanted and, equally important, *when* they wanted them to arrive. This made planning for education and career advancement easier and more certain than it had ever been in the past. Having a particular kind of education, career, and family now lay within the grasp of many more Canadian women than before.

Along with the decreasing reliability of marriage and increasing reliability of contraception came growing opportunities for higher education and entry into traditionally male jobs and careers. Now it was feasible for women to consider becoming doctors, lawyers, architects, and engineers. This new feasibility was supported by a more active 'women's liberation' movement which encouraged female independence and started to break down the institutional barriers to gender equality. Still, what was needed was a revolution in domestic relations to allow women a better balance between family and career commitments. This takes us back to the new instability in marital relations: the divorce explosion.

THE COMING OF EASY DIVORCE

It may be impossible today to talk about a typical family or typical marriage. Major trends in family life include declining family sizes, increasing numbers of lone-parent families, increasing numbers of families created by remarriage, more multiple-earner families, and more people living alone. The old-style 'monolithic family' model (Eichler, 1981)—with a single male 'breadwinner' and a stay-at-home wife who looks after two or three children—no longer describes the majority of Canadian adult lives.

In 1986, both spouses earned an income in 60 per cent of Canadian families. Only 40 per cent of families followed the 'traditional' pattern, with the husband as sole breadwinner (Employment and Immigration, 1989: 10). Data from the Canadian Survey of Consumer Finances (Wolfson, 1986) show a rise in the proportion of unattached individuals and of 'empty nests'. From 1965 to 1983, there was a one-quarter drop in the proportion of family units that were 'traditional' husband-wife families with children, and a one-third increase in the proportion of single-parent families.

Rates of first marriage have fallen to an all-time low in Canada. This falling national marriage rate has been led by large declines in Quebec, which 'has not only the lowest rate of all the provinces but one of the lowest rates in the world' (Statistics Canada, 1987c: 19). The trend among younger people towards opting for common-law unions over marriage partly explains this decline. But there is also evidence that people are merely delaying, not rejecting, marriage, so that the average age at first marriage is increasing.

Late marriage has historically been associated with high proportions of the population's never marrying (Hajnal, 1965). Both patterns are common in periods when economic conditions may make marriage and child-bearing seem too risky for some. People who delay beyond a certain age appear to lose interest in ever marrying; they become accustomed to the single life, and, for women, child-bearing becomes riskier or impossible. So both increased common-law cohabitation and delayed marriage reflect a temporary (if not permanent) flight from marriage and predict that lower percentages of people will ever marry.

Only one type of marriage is growing much more common: remarriage. The number of marriages in which at least one of the spouses was previously married has more than doubled since 1968, when divorces became easier to get. With the numbers of first marriages dropping, the increasing remarriages have come to represent over twice as high a proportion of all marriages in 1985 as in 1968 (Statistics Canada, 1987c: Table 5). Recently, three marriages in ten were remarriages for one or both partners. This tendency of the divorced to remarry is one main source of evidence that marriage remains a desired state.

Risks of marriage breakdown are high

Statistics Canada (1982: 4) data show that rates of divorce remained fairly steady at about 200 divorces per 100,000 married women aged 15 and over each year from 1952 through 1968. With law reforms that made divorcing a spouse easier after 1968, the rates shot up five-fold, to 1000 divorces per year per 100,000 married women, by 1978. Rates levelled off in the 1980s, and then started to fall (Statistics Canada, 1987c: 22).

The recent decline in marital breakdowns may be more apparent than real. Some couples may have been waiting for recent amendments to the Divorce Act before starting proceedings. Others may be breaking up and forming new (common-law) unions without going through the formalities of divorce. By 1984, when Statistics Canada conducted a national Family History Survey (Burch, 1985), one man in ten and one women in eight who had ever been married had divorced at least once.

These statistics should be interpreted with some care, because the risk of marital breakdown varies widely among people from different regions of the country and different educational levels. Divorce rates are much lower than average in the Atlantic provinces and Quebec, and much higher than average in British Columbia (Burch, 1985: Table 19). Likewise, people who have completed a post-secondary education are about half as likely to ever divorce as those with no more than a secondary-school education (Burch, 1985: Table 20). Nonetheless, household dissolution is very common. Estimates of future divorce rates over the life course, which assume that present age-specific rates will continue to prevail, range anywhere from 30 to 40 per cent, with a few even higher.

Alternatives to marriage are increasing

New housing patterns make living together easier than ever for unmarried people (Miron, 1988: 33). By 1984, roughly one adult respondent in six had been in a common-law partnership at one time or another (Burch, 1985: Table 4A). Among young people aged 18 to 29, the proportion was much higher: about one man in five and one woman in four. 'On Census Day in 1981 approximately 6 per cent of the couples enumerated were not legally married, and half of the 704,000 or so persons involved were between 20 and 30 years of age' (Statistics Canada, 1987c: 25).

The 1984 Family History Survey reveals that just under half of the people ever in a common-law union ended up marrying their common-law partners. The percentages are even higher for younger respondents: for example, of people aged 30 to 39 in 1984 who had ever been in a common-law relationship, 52 per cent of males and 50 per cent of females married their common-law partners. The high and growing likelihood of marrying a common-law partner suggests that, increasingly often, common-law unions serve as trial marriages. This 'trial marriage' interpretation is supported by evidence (Burch, 1985: Table 4A) that the vast majority of people ever in a common-law partnership have been in only one.

Today there is wide and growing recognition of the pitfalls of early marriage. 'The divorce rate among such young marriages is estimated at from two to four times that among persons who marry after 20 years of age. The divorce rate is related to low educational levels, low economic levels, premarital pregnancies, and possibly to personality difficulties' (Leslie and Korman, 1985: 396). For all these reasons, early-marrying males

> have rates of marital instability more than 50 per cent higher than men marrying on time or relatively late. It seems likely that men who marry early are relatively immature at the time of marriage. Their choice of a marriage partner might be ill-considered because of this immaturity, or problems associated with the sudden entry of an immature man into a marital union may produce strains that result in marital discord (Hogan, 1981: 204-6).

Young women who marry and/or procreate before their education is complete pay an even heavier price. Data from the 1984 Family History Survey (Pool and Moore, 1986: 49) suggest that female lone parents are more likely than others to have become parents too soon, before getting enough education and job skills to make themselves economically independent. The authors continue, 'In the longer run, this lack of job-related resources may have limited their power within a marriage or union and, thus, may have predisposed its termination.'

Increasingly, the problems of marriage arise from the fact that both partners are pursuing careers. There is little evidence that husbands are giving their wives the support and co-operation they need at home to make the dual-career family work effectively, especially where children are present (Michelson, 1985a, Chap. 5). Women are necessarily changing their conception of marriage in

significant ways. They are equipping themselves for independence. Even women who are married are placing less importance on that arrangement in the overall scheme of their lives
(Baruch, Barnett, and Rivers, 1983: 294).

As we have seen, the risks of marriage breakdown are high.
Under these circumstances, it would be foolish to build one's life
around the prospect of a single, lifelong marriage. Moreover, the
alternatives to marriage are increasing. Single life is more viable
than it has ever been, although single parenthood remains very
difficult, especially for women. Yet certainly our culture has come
to accept single status as common and blameless. Increasingly,
people will spend more of their adult years in the single status,
whether or not they have ever been married. As well, more people
are spending more of their adult lives in cohabitation arrangements of various durations, rather than legal marriage.

Both marriage and cohabitation can bring the benefits of two
incomes in a single household. Cohabitation has the advantage of
easier dissolution of the relationship. Above all, people seem to
want their freedom and fear making a commitment that may
produce children; for child-bearing brings enormous economic
and emotional consequences in its wake.

THE COMPRESSION OF CHILD-BEARING

Low levels of fertility have gone hand in hand with major increases in both divorce and remarriage over the past two decades.
The odds are stacked against a young woman's raising three or
four children and staying at home to do it, with a husband providing the family's only income.

A recent analysis of the events in women's lives (Balakrishnan
and Grindstaff, 1988) shows that the pattern has gone largely
unchanged: for most women, it is still education, then marriage,
then child-bearing. Women's age at first birth is a critical predictor
of subsequent life-events. In particular, early childbirth is a strong
predictor of divorce. One-sixth of first births now take place
outside marriage entirely, but within marriage the two-child norm
remains strong.

The decline in family size goes back a century or more. Around
1871, marital child-bearing in Europe and North America began
a significant fall that was never to be reversed. Since 1871, it has
almost steadily decreased to a current level that, in Canada and

many other developed countries, is well below replacement (i.e., the number needed to equal the size of the parental generation).

Reduced infant mortality together with industrialization made large families unnecessary, even a liability. To merely maintain a family over generations, parents needed only two children, not the four or more that were needed when many children died before reaching adulthood. Increasingly, urban middle-class parents decided that their children would do better in life if there were fewer of them, so that each could receive more of the family's care, encouragement, and financial support (Banks, 1954). Further, the reduced child-bearing meant five to ten years less of close child-care on the part of wives and thus the potential for greater and longer participation in the labour force.

Anatole Romaniuc (1986) reports that Canada began its own decline in fertility a century ago. Since then, the total fertility rate has fallen from an average of six births per woman to 1.7 in 1985, which is below the level required to replace or maintain the Canadian population. This trend has been interrupted only twice: by the Great Depression of the 1930s, which produced far fewer births than one might have expected, and the 'baby boom' of the 1950s and 1960s, which produced far more.

This progression to smaller family sizes has been punctuated by phases of fast and slow decline. Even the enormous 'baby boom' and subsequent 'baby bust' are mere deviations from a steady downward trend. As well, a pattern of older child-bearing is emerging. More women are having their first child after the age of 30. The youngest birth cohorts—Canadian women born after 1952—may not bear enough children to replace themselves, but some are merely delaying, not denying, parenthood. Even Quebec's fertility rate, for a long time Canada's highest, has fallen; indeed, it is now Canada's lowest, at 1.4 births per woman. Although this accords with Quebec's lowest-in-Canada rate of marriage, views differ on precisely why Quebec women have changed so radically.

Special tabulations from the Canadian Labour Force Survey over the years 1976-87 show a general increase in the proportion of women without dependent children. Even if, ideally, children are the mutual responsibility of both parents, in our society they remain largely the day-to-day responsibility of mothers. The fact that more of the population is past the child-bearing stage and that dependent children are fewer means that more women are able to enter the paid labour force. For the time being, it appears that women have more scope for non-family activities.

Most of the changes taking place in the family today work against child-bearing. Changes in marriage may well speed up the century-long downward slide in births. This would lead to a Canadian population in the twenty-first century very much smaller than today's, unless immigration increases dramatically or strong pro-natalist policies are undertaken. As noted earlier, fertility-enhancing patterns such as early marriage seem to require a sense of personal and marital security, but it is hard to see how such a heightened sense of security could come about. Roderic Beaujot (1985: 12) warns that 'greater proportions single or cohabiting, later marriage and increased marital interruption may well produce [even] more fertility decline'.

Accordingly, major changes in parenthood have already begun and are likely to continue into the foreseeable future (Gee, 1986: 277). For example, whereas in earlier generations women typically bore their children over a period of ten to fifteen years, today they do so in five years or less. With this 'compression' of the child-bearing period, the number of years when one or more children are present in the home has dropped from thirty to twenty years. This, together with increasing longevity, means that instead of spending almost no time alone with a spouse in the 'empty nest', present wives can expect to average twenty or thirty years in that state.

Such compression means that a woman will have more non-domestic time in her life than earlier generations did. She may use this extra time earlier or later. For example, she may delay child-bearing until her thirties, or get it over with in her early twenties. Delayed marriage, delayed house purchase, and delayed child-bearing make up one set of choices. Another is to do all of these in one's twenties, so that the mortgage is paid off and all the children are gone by the time parents are fifty. Whichever pattern they follow, women will spend more years alone with their spouses than in the company of children: the opposite of what most married women have experienced in the past century and a half—perhaps for most of human history. To fully appreciate the significance of this reversal, we need to consider how the presence of children affects people's lives.

Parenthood changes life significantly

The onset of parenthood is a particularly trying time.

> Young parents are not more or less inclined than other people to express satisfaction with their life in general or with particular domains of life. There is a difference, however, in their perception of strain; both men and women express more feeling of strain at this stage than at any other period of their married lives. (Campbell, 1979: 187)

Raising small children also strains the marriage: disagreements become more common, and both husband and wife feel they get less companionship from their mate than they once did. Both marital satisfaction and enjoyment of parenthood are low or declining.

> Two out of five of these mothers of small children go so far as to admit they sometimes wish they could be free of the responsibilities of being a parent, a much larger proportion than is found among mothers of older children. (Campbell, 1979: 188)

In some ways, this period is the hardest. Once the mother takes a job, financial anxieties start to diminish; two-income parents feel less tied down, less strained or burdened by parenthood, and are more likely to enjoy it. With children in the age range 6 to 17,

> parents . . . disagree less often about spending money and they feel they understand each other better. But they do not regain the strong sense of companionship . . . they had as young couples until they reach the next stage of life when the children have grown up. (Campbell, 1979: 189)

A comparison of families by Lupri and Frideres (1981: 300) shows that, at all ages (and marital durations), married women without children are more satisfied with marriage than women with children. Employed wives reach a lower level of marital satisfaction than non-employed wives; conversely, the husbands of non-employed wives reach a lower level of marital satisfaction than the husbands of employed wives. In all cases, the low point occurs roughly when the children are adolescents. Parenthood hits employed wives harder than it hits their spouses because the dual responsibilities of work and parenthood are heavier for them.

On the other hand, husbands of non-employed wives will be harder hit than their spouses because the financial burden becomes heavier as the children enter adolescence. This greater need for money in middle age, at the very time when a husband's income has started to level off, is often called the 'life-cycle squeeze'. Two kinds of marital conflict arise as the children reach adolescence. A wife who does not work outside the home may start to feel more satisfaction with marriage at the very time when her husband, smarting under a greater financial burden, is feeling the least satisfaction ever. A wife who does work outside the home will feel declining marital satisfaction, because of pressures at home and on the job, at the very time her husband is starting to feel greater marital satisfaction.

How long these conflicts go on is determined by the length of time it takes all the children to pass through adolescence and leave home. The fewer the children and the more closely they are spaced, the shorter the period of minimal satisfaction for one or both spouses and the briefer the marital conflict that parenthood produces.

The sociological evidence leaves no doubt that parenthood strains the relationship between husbands and wives. For some couples this in itself may be a good reason for reducing or eliminating child-bearing, but it is not the only one. The decline in parenthood has been going on for over a century for other reasons: chiefly because it has become progressively harder to live a comfortable urban life with many children. Given the choice between more children and more disposable income, most people in the West have been choosing the latter for most of the last hundred years. With the economic recession of the 1970s and early 1980s, the motivation to further restrict child-bearing grew stronger. With the development of new contraceptive technology, the desire for a smaller family was easier to fulfil.

If, as we argue, child-bearing tends to increase marital tension and reduce satisfaction, then the decline in child-bearing should increase people's satisfaction with marriage and reduce the divorce rate. But for the time being, people are finding that raising children is increasingly difficult and expensive (particularly in the event of marital dissolution). Above all, it creates enormous strains on the two-income family, especially around the question of finding a balance between family and career. The responsibility for finding a balance falls most heavily on wives, and as working women become more committed to career advancement, they find it harder and harder to achieve.

This is illustrated by comments women made to interviewers in Jones's study of southern Ontario work lives. One woman remarked: 'Balancing child care and a career . . . It's an emotional conflict as to how much time you want to be with the child'. Another noted the difficulty of 'maintaining a good balance of home life and work': 'it is always stressful . . . I'd always wanted a challenging job [but it] might be too hard on one's home life . . . I couldn't continue working in a stressful job and look after home too'. Women have increasingly had to find a balance between new opportunities and traditional domestic duties. Even for couples who share the traditional domestic duties the situation is no easier, given the demands made upon men in the labour force, the lack of good-quality child-care, and the failure of our society to accept non-traditional roles for fathers.

PROBLEMS OF CAREER COMMITMENT

The 1960s and 1970s will be remembered as a time when educational spending made it possible for more young Canadians to get a post-secondary education than ever before. A commitment to equal educational opportunity meant that previously under-represented people—young women, working-class people, racial minorities, native people, the physically handicapped, and post-adolescents with full-time work or family responsibilities—could now get higher degrees that allowed them to dream ahead to more interesting, challenging jobs and financial independence.

But for women the situation has been further complicated by domestic responsibilities. As women—even highly educated women—have entered the labour force, they have come under ever greater pressure to balance their various domestic and occupational activities. In part, the problems are purely practical: how to do twenty-five hours' worth of activities in a twenty-four-hour day. But the problems are also cultural. All of us want the freedom and personal space to do what our hearts desire: that is the North American individualistic ethic. Desires for privacy, independence, and upward mobility have spread to everyone; male and female, child and parent all want more of each. But as historian Carl Degler (1980: 471) has said, 'Democracy, individualism and meritocracy, the values most closely identified with two centuries of Western history, are conspicuous by their absence from the family.'

Today family members are pursuing quite different, largely independent lives. To get everything done, families now must purchase many domestic services from 'outsiders', and still need to find better ways of integrating their very diverse interests and schedules. At present, wives still bear the heavier burden in the typical household. Sociologist Bill Michelson (1985a: 55) showed that full-time housewives average 436 minutes a day in housework and child-care, while women with part-time paid jobs average 356 minutes a day, and women with full-time paid jobs, 192 minutes a day. Husbands' home duties typically do not increase when their wives work full-time for pay. The standards of housekeeping and child-care simply drop, unless equivalent services are purchased from outsiders: nannies, cleaning ladies, fast-food cooks, and producers of pre-packaged meals for the microwave.

Some observers have called this transformation of household tasks into paid services 'the commodification of household labour' or the 'industrialization of housework' (Bergmann, 1986). Such services include housecleaning, grocery shopping, delivery of prepared meals, baby care, child supervision (and disciplining) and transport, and minor health care of children and the elderly. Mothers with full-time jobs work longer combined hours than husbands or any other kinds of wives: an average of nearly ten hours a day. This has been called the 'double day of labour'. Even when household services are purchased from outside or a servant is employed in the home, it is the mother who has the responsibility for organization. Working mothers have little free time during their waking hours.

Not surprisingly, then, employed mothers report a lot of tension in activities that would be easy if time were plentiful: activities like waking the children, getting them ready for school or day-care, caring for the baby, caring for the older children, preparing food, cleaning the house, and getting to work on time. Said one of Jones's respondents, 'I find I don't have enough energy for the children', while another confesses, 'My heart tells me a mother should be home with her children but my sanity knows I could never do it.' Further research should examine more objective indicators of hardship, such as the sickness and death rates of women with children.

Too little time means tension and marital conflict

Michelson (1985) also shows that the tension associated with an activity increases significantly when choice is lacking. Not only are women involved in more activities than men, but they generally have less choice about when and where they will spend their time, and suffer more tension as a result.

A prime tension-producer is daily travel. Many more female responsibilities—such as shopping for food or taking the child to and from day-care—require travel, and 'women often travel with less efficient resources and fewer choices' (Michelson, 1985b: 5). One of Jones's respondents reported: 'I have to get a job close by or one that provides transportation since the hours my husband works vary, so he can't drive me to and from work.'

Women often have less access to the family car and little choice over where daycare, shopping, and work will be located. Toronto women, for example, are about three times as likely as their husbands to use public transportation, especially for trips to and from work. The problems for most parents—especially mothers—are the strains of having too many duties, conflicts arising out of unequal parental arrangements, and financial concerns produced by increased reliance on paid child-care and housekeeping services.

Women find a number of ways to handle this problem (cf. Marshall, 1989). Some career-oriented women, particularly those in male-dominated careers, choose not to marry; others marry but choose not to bear children. As one of Jones's respondents admitted, 'If I had children I would not be able to do my job the way I do it now—I couldn't put the hours or the effort in. I probably wouldn't want to.' Another said: 'I don't have enough time left for anything else, because once you work, if you are a career-oriented person, you have to be totally involved in your job. [Having children] is too much work.'

Others still bear one or two children in a very short time, to limit the interruption of their careers. Many of these women leave full-time paid work to bear children, then return to it almost immediately. This pattern is most common among highly educated women who have career goals, not merely jobs, and salaries large enough to pay for high-quality child-care. Less educated or career-oriented women are more likely to leave the paid workforce until their children begin attending school full-time. Accordingly, labour-force participation is much higher for women with children over five years old than it is for mothers of younger children.

Part-time work: a solution or a problem?

A second and apparently growing solution to the problem of balance is part-time work, currently defined in Canada as less than 30 hours of paid work per week (Labour Canada, 1983: 17). In economies based on agriculture or fishing, activity is seasonal, and much work is part-year. Even today, industries such as agriculture, fishing, and service and retail trade have cyclical labour requirements. However, for much of this century the dominant mode of employment in urban economies has been full-time work. Most of the deviations from this dominant mode—part-time work, short-term contracts, self-employment, unpaid family workers, multiple job-holding—involve a marginal or 'fluid' attachment to the labour force.

Much part-time work is involuntary, resulting from an inability to get full-time work; and recent Canadian statistics (Akyeampong, 1987: 27) show that since 1975 involuntary part-time has become over twice as common a portion of all part-time work. Voluntary part-time also continues to grow as a portion of all paid work, especially among married women (Langlois, 1989). Labour unions generally oppose the expansion of part-time work because it may come at the expense of full-time work, may not be fully voluntary, and currently allows employers to avoid paying the fringe benefits that full-time workers typically receive.

Most female part-time workers aged 25 to 54 appear to want part-time, not full-time, work for a variety of reasons, among them the need to fulfil personal and family responsibilities (Labour Canada, 1983: 53). Said Jones's respondents:

> If a woman can combine the family and her career, that is great, but personally I feel better about working part-time only and spending more time with my family;

> It's difficult to work out a schedule to have a job and still meet the needs of the children.

Few female part-time workers want more hours of paid work per month than they already have (Labour Canada, 1983: 69). Part-time work allows enormous flexibility and many varied working and living patterns (Labour Canada, 1983: 67). Under the best circumstances the scheduling of work can almost be tailored to a worker's personal needs. Part-time work is ideal for meeting domestic obligations, especially when child-rearing makes a full-time job extremely difficult. Indeed, if part-time work becomes unionized, and pays benefits prorated to time spent on the job, it will become a more and more attractive option for both fathers and mothers. In Sweden, for example, part-time workers receive the same hourly wages as full-time workers, and they receive proportional non-wage benefits as well (Sundstrom, 1987).

Today highly educated professional and managerial women who seek part-time employment are not likely to be thought serious about their work. Even if given the part-time work they want, women may significantly hinder their prospects for major responsibility by allowing that impression to stand. This means that employed mothers, the main voluntary part-time workers, must weigh carefully whether they want to have careers and, equally important, be perceived as having them.

Even in the 1960s, British women employed full-time were much more likely than their husbands to prefer receiving more time off over more pay (Young and Willmott, 1975: 115). This fact has certainly not changed with time. As one of Jones's Ontario respondents said: 'I would prefer not to work so many hours. Everything I do for my family is very rushed; I have less time to do things for myself and for my family.' Moreover, employed women are more likely than their husbands to distance themselves from the thought of a career.

Even full-time female employees are half as likely as their husbands to report a link between their work and their leisure. Compared with their husbands, they are much less likely to say there is a 'career ladder' in their work, that they have 'a lot of say at work', or that they feel 'pressed' or 'sometimes pressed' at work, or to report doing overtime work during the previous week, or travelling more than ten miles to their jobs. Such differences are even greater between part-time female employees and their husbands (Young and Willmott, 1975: 116).

By and large, wives are less likely than husbands to hold jobs that interfere with their domestic duties. 'I can't give full-time dedication to a job,' said one respondent. When asked whether they wished to be promoted, quite a few said they were satisfied where they were, because going any higher would mean having to take more responsibility and they did not want the added pressure:

I'm happy where I am. I wouldn't want all that responsibility;

In this company there's nowhere to go except the boss's job; I don't want that—too much responsibility;

[I'm] not ready for any more responsibility;

There would be too much pressure;

[I don't want a promotion] because there is too much stress involved;

The higher you go the more you have to give up to the company, and I'm not willing to give that time or energy.

Avoiding interference with domestic life is easier in some jobs—clerical and manual, for example—than it is in professional and managerial work (Young and Willmott, 1975: 117). This suggests that highly educated mothers will be the most pressured women of all; they will have the greatest difficulty balancing parental and occupational duties. For these reasons, the employers of educated women face increasing demands for company-sponsored child-care and more flexible work schedules.

In addition, rising numbers of dual-income couples increasingly mean joint decisions about domestic task-sharing, work time, job transfer, and relocation. Child-rearing requires employer accommodation through 'flextime', part-time work, and more working at home. Goods and services to make housekeeping easier are increasingly demanded; to take a well-known example, the ready-to-serve food industry is growing more rapidly than most.

But without other institutional and societal changes to ease the burdens of motherhood, the flight from parenthood may continue and even accelerate. Said one of Jones's respondents:

The amount of assistance women get for children is very low, and in Canada they discourage having families. Canada is one of the countries with the least benefits for maternity leave. I think it's ridiculous that women having a child are only entitled to unemployment insurance. Most countries have full pay, whether it's shared by government or employer. There are countries where men get paid leave of absence to look after women who give birth.

Some solutions are economic, along the lines of the benefits provided to large families in France. One would be to provide more goods and services directly to the families of working women: more, better, and cheaper day-care, for example. Another would be to improve women's wages, enabling them to purchase the services they need. This would require legislation to prevent and remedy income discrimination against women, and to ensure that payment for part-time work is prorated against full-time pay and benefits.

A more contentious proposal is pay for housework. Said one respondent: 'I think women should be paid while they are staying home watching kids. I've tried to get some assistance from social services, and they refused me.' There is also the question of pensions. If women do not work for pay, they cannot contribute to the Canada Pension Plan and may be left impoverished in their old age. Of this, respondents said:

Pensions are a concern. Women should have a fairly decent pension. We are at a disadvantage as compared to men;

I believe homemakers should be able to contribute to Canada Pension Plan so that when they reach retirement age they can receive the benefits.

At present, the housework and child-care provided by wives are an unpaid benefit to their husbands' employers. They can rely on their male workers to show up for work regularly, in good health and well turned out, because wives do the unpaid work needed to ensure it. As one women said, 'a woman looking after her children and her husband contributes more for herself, her family and Canada's future than any outside job could do.' Some observers believe either that employers should pay their employees for wives' services by raising salaries, or that governments should pay wives from general tax revenues.

Resistance to all of these alternatives is strong. Most men still take for granted the services that wives and mothers provide, and devalue those services because they do not yield a cash income. Further, many oppose increasing services to employed women or paying wages for housework on the grounds that these actions would raise income taxes and/or the prices of goods and services. And while the rationale offered for opposition to these proposals may be cast in economic terms, traditionally men have been reluctant to lessen women's dependence on them. More modest proposals include improving public transportation to make employed parents' travel easier and faster; loosening zoning restrictions so that shopping and child-care will be closer to people's homes; allowing round-the-clock shopping for goods and services, to give employed parents a greater opportunity to do their household chores (e.g., food shopping) when most convenient; and increasing flextime to allow paid work (and work-related travel) to mesh more easily with domestic duties (Michelson, 1985b). Many of these changes also require public spending and/or impose new burdens on other workers. This means they will be resisted, at least in the short run.

Whether these changes are implemented or not, duties will have to be redistributed within the household if the current 'double burden' of mothers continues. Fathers in particular will have to become more involved in child-care and accept a greater share of the tensions associated with having too little free time. This will force men to spend less of their time and mental energy both on their work and on recreation that is not centred on the family.

Many women go to work out of necessity and would choose to stay home if they could afford to. Many others have the opportunity to work for pay or not work for pay; get married or not get married; bear children or not bear children. Among women who marry, the worst possible combination—heavy domestic and occupational demands—is widespread. It is not surprising that women are rethinking their options and acting differently: getting married later, if at all; bearing fewer children, and bearing them later, if at all; and organizing their work lives in ways quite different from the ways men do, so as to ensure some life-saving flexibility.

There is no guarantee that the present balance of forces will persist. Marriage may continue to decline as the most common adult status. Parenthood may continue to decline, perhaps to the point where Canada will require massive annual immigration to keep the population size constant. Perhaps the average woman of the future will spend few adult years as a wife and mother, and many more years getting educated and working for pay in a highly demanding career. Whatever happens, there seems little chance we shall return to the pre-1968 situation.

CONCLUDING REMARKS

Married Canadian women have always worked. Before 1968, however, most were likely to work outside the paid labour force. Their work was organized on the basis of home production and/or barter and exchange of services with other households—what we might call networks of reciprocity and obligation. In the aftermath of the Second World War, the industrial West was to attain unprecedented prosperity, yet governments and employers feared a return to the Depression years and a decline in fertility. These fears encouraged a cult of housewifeliness and suburban Arcadia.

The 1960s saw an upgrading of the educational system, as new recruits from the baby-boom generation began to roll into school. Technology triumphed; the television and the shopping mall introduced new ways of living and buying. But with new expectations of a high material standard of living came a diminishing possibility of having any kind of a good life without a large income.

Between 1960 and 1975, oral contraception came into wide use and was legalized. Marriage was increasingly delayed and cohabitation rates increased; family sizes got smaller and first births were postponed. We began to see more single mothers, perhaps because men no longer felt that love, sex, or even parenthood implied lifelong commitment.

Although mothers may still have much to teach their daughters about how to find a mate, traditional romantic ideas of marriage as lifelong commitment are no longer tenable. To be realistic, teenaged girls should avoid investing too much in the expectation that their marriage will survive—for example, working in a menial job to put boyfriend or husband through college. They should assume that they will have to work for most of their lives, and will need their own pension plans. Since they are likely to have one or two children, they will do best to get jobs that provide good maternity leave and maternity benefits.

Over the 1960s Canadian women's lives began to change very dramatically. These social changes were reflected in the easing of divorce laws. Today, demographers expect about one marriage in two to end in divorce. The development of safe, cheap contraceptives led to an unprecedentedly low level of child-bearing, and there is as yet no evidence that the 'flight from parenthood' has abated. Finally, the opening of educational and occupational opportunities has led to a rapid rise in labour-force participation by women, and some very difficult problems of time management. Men have yet to grant gender equality in the domestic workplace, and many women who work for pay are having enormous difficulties finding time to do everything they feel they have to.

That domestic work is becoming more burdensome—subjectively, at least—is indicated by a general decline in women's attitudes towards the homemaker's role (Glenn, 1987). Jones's respondents reflected these sentiments:

> I don't think that women who stay home with their kids get enough credit.

> It used to be that you were looked up to if you stayed at home with children but today you are looked down upon if you do.

> I think women with children should not be looked down upon if they want to stay home and be full-time mothers or home makers . . . I think parenting is probably harder than any other job I've done.

In addition, more women are worrying about having a nervous breakdown (Campbell, 1979: 130, 133). 'There is a persistently greater inclination among women (than men) . . . to report negative experiences—feeling depressed, worried or frightened' (Campbell, 1979: 131). Yet 'considering the countless inequities that women encounter in American life, the impressive fact is how closely their feelings of well-being resemble those of men rather than how they differ in some important respects' (Campbell, 1979: 143).

That working outside the home generally does provide advantages—income, security, psychic satisfactions—is indicated by many southern Ontario respondents in the Jones survey:

> I get depressed if I am at home too much;

> Work is fulfilling and keeps you in touch with other people—more connected to what is going on in society;

> I feel it is extremely important for me to work because my sense of self is dependent on meaningful work;

> I like going out to work. It makes me feel like I am doing something important with my time;

> It's boring at home. I need intellectual stimulation;

> I work for my own self-fulfilment and personal growth;

> I think women should work to have an identity;

> Some women see paid work as a source of power: you feel independent if you have your own source of income;

> You are more powerful if you work. You can support yourself—more independence—no matter what your husband does.

Yet women who remain in the home are apparently just as

satisfied (Campbell, 1979: 139), and this fact leads to several major conclusions. The first is that people tend to look for living and work arrangements that will give them the most life satisfaction. Second, people largely accommodate themselves to what their life demands, especially if they feel they have taken part in choosing it. Say Jones's respondents:

> Working is up to the individual person. In my case I felt I should be at home with my children because I wanted to, not because I was told to or circumstances made me do it. Five years from now . . . things may change.

> I prefer to stay home and look after my children and am very satisfied to do this.

Finally, adulthood is becoming more complicated and stressful for women, whichever adult role they choose to play. Today, a bare but growing majority (about 58 per cent in 1986, according to the census) of working-age women work for pay. Some of the remainder—especially older women or single mothers—depend on state support; but a substantial minority depend on their spouse's earnings. They remain dependent members of single-income or 'breadwinner' families.

The large-scale movement of women out of financial dependence on their spouses and into full-time participation in the labour force has occurred mainly within the last thirty years, although discussion of it began in the late nineteenth century (Sorensen and McLanahan, 1985). It is a dramatic social and economic change with important effects on the workplace, the marketplace, and the home. The next chapter considers how changes in the labour market encouraged women to change their life patterns and drew them into a more varied, idiosyncratic, and fluid relationship with work.

2

Changes in
Labour-Market Demand

The last chapter explored changes in women's personal lives, dating from about 1968, that had the effect of encouraging, and sometimes forcing, women to work for pay. In this chapter we explore the changes in the labour market that inclined employers to hire more women.

WORK IN THE DOMESTIC SPHERE

It would be convenient if the changes we need to discuss all started around the 1960s, but they did not. In fact, many of them began a century or more ago, so we must begin our historical analysis at least that far back. For the last few centuries, at least, women have always led more complex and, at the same time, more family-centred lives than men. Of women and the family in the United States since 1776, historian Carl Degler (1980: 434-5) writes:

> Compared with men the great majority of working women over the last century and a half have generally shaped their work around their family while, equally clearly, men have shaped their family life around their work ... Confronted with the social, psychological or emotional costs of being unable to have children and family if she chose a career, the wife chose to opt for family and a secondary job, rather than a career. That was a constrained choice, to be sure, but a choice nonetheless.

Degler's findings in the United States are supported by historical studies of working women in Europe. For example, Patricia Branca points out:

> Working class women as a group never chose to make employment a primary means of identification in their lives. They rejected it when it conflicted with family-centred goals and welcomed it when it could supplement not only earnings but also the diversity of personal experience. (Branca cited in Degler, 1981: 435)

Speaking of both peasant women and urban women in the nineteenth century, historians Joan Scott and Louise Tilly (1984: 56) make a similar point:

> The traditional role of a married woman, her vital economic function within the family economy, sent her into the labour force when her earnings were needed by the household budget. When the income of her husband and children was sufficient for the family's needs, she left the labour force. Mothers of young children would sometimes leave the labour force only after their oldest child went out to work.

Thus women's entry into paid work was not new in the twentieth century; nor was it a result of industrialization, nor a form of liberation from family obligation, nor the reflection of new, more democratic values. According to Scott and Tilly, women had always enjoyed respect and domestic power within the peasant and early urban family. They had always played a key economic role, whether their labour was paid or unpaid.

For the most part, women living before this century did a great deal of work of many kinds, if we recognize that work is no more (or less) than effort expended to advance someone else's well-being. Some of the work they did was in the household, and received no payment—call it 'family care'. Some of the work they did was in their own or someone else's household, for which they did receive payment—call it 'homemaking'. Some of the work they did was in the public sphere, outside the household, but it received no payment—call it 'charity' or 'exchanging favours'. We can call all of these types of work 'domestic work', for lack of a better name.

Before industrialization, most women spent most of their time in these three domestic work activities. Over their lives, the relative balance of the three components of domestic work would change in response to a variety of pressures and opportunities. Yet this pattern was the dominant and culturally legitimate form of work for women.

From time to time, women would leave these three kinds of work for a fourth kind: paid work outside the household, which we might call 'wage labour'. The transition between domestic activities and wage labour was also determined by a variety of pressures and opportunities. But by and large, wage labour was a less central form of work than domestic work. The shift of domestic activities from a central to a more peripheral role in women's lives happened very gradually, partly in response to progressive industrialization.

Industrialization only gradually transformed occupational opportunities. Old jobs persisted for many years alongside the new as women who married industrial workers and lived in cities imported old styles of behaviour into new contexts. Much of the work performed outside the home by married women was only temporary, so that even those women defined their role within the framework of the family economy. As Scott and Tilly (1984: 58-9) write:

> Long after their husbands and children had begun to adopt some of the individualistic values associated with industrialization, these women continued the self-sacrificing, self-exploitative work . . . that was characteristic of the peasant or household economy.

We can see these same behaviours among many immigrant women in Canada today, and even among their daughters. We can also observe a continuing commitment to the 'family economy' among women brought up in the working class.

It is possible to see three main periods in the history of women's lives since 1871. From 1871 to 1914, a very large proportion of Canadians lived on farms or in other kinds of primary production units (e.g., fishing, trapping). Industry was relatively undeveloped, and the nuclear family was typically the unit of production as well as of reproduction and consumption. As a result, there was a blurring of what we would today call the 'private' and 'public' spheres of activity. Although women were beginning to work in factories and offices—and an important debate developed in Canada regarding their 'proper sphere'—they were still the minority. The division of labour between men and women was fluid, did not segregate individual women from other men or women, and did not imply that women were less important economically than men.

In the second period, from 1914 to about 1968, the division of labour between men and women became increasingly sharp, pervasive, and entrenched. Now industrial manufacturing was well developed, and it was largely the preserve of men. The private and public spheres were sharply defined, with women holding primary or exclusive responsibility for the private or domestic sphere of activities—housekeeping, child-rearing, and domestic economic production, if any. This division of labour tended to segregate individual women from other adults and to imply that women were less important economically than men.

True, there was some variation over this period. For example, during the two World Wars women entered industrial production to take the places left vacant by men; with the end of fighting, they were forced to return to the household. In the Great Depression of the 1930s both men and women took whatever work was available, paid or unpaid, to keep food on the table. Moreover, the period did not end abruptly in 1968. But that year did mark a major shift, for reasons we made evident in the last chapter.

With the beginning of the third period, around 1968, women started entering the labour force in ever increasing numbers. This massive entry of women into the 'public' sphere of activity will probably continue until all women are working for pay during some part of their lives.

Sporadic labour-force participation is nothing new to Canadian women. Of the early twentieth century, historian Veronica Strong-Boag (1988: 42-3) writes:

> Women commonly entered paid employment in their teens or twenties, with those aged between twenty and thirty-four years showing a significant increase in participation from 1921 to 1941. By World War II, a period of waged work was a familiar stage in the life cycle, occupying many young women of all classes in the years between the classroom and marriage.

Indeed, 47 per cent of Canadian women aged 20 to 24 were working for pay, according to the censuses of 1931 and 1941 (cited in Strong-Boag, 1988: 343). But by age 35, over two-thirds of these women had slipped out of paid work and into domestic activities, and a majority were unlikely ever to return to it. This was a one-time-only movement into and out of wage labour.

Still, it marked the beginning of a major change in women's participation in paid work. Historical data show that Canadian women have been passing through what might be called an 'employment transition' process. This transition is incomplete in Canada, and more or less complete in other nations. It is characterized by a change in two key variables: the proportion of women working publicly for pay—i.e., outside domestic work—at a given moment (current participation [CURPAR]), and the proportion of women ever working for pay during their lifetime (cumulative participation [CUMPAR]).

Survey data show that in 1961 only 30 per cent of women were in the paid labour force; but about 50 to 90 per cent of working-age women born between 1901 and 1941 had held a paid job at some time in their lives. A mere twenty years later, in 1981, 54 per cent of women were in the paid labour force; and 75 to 95 per cent of working-age women born between 1921 and 1961 had held a paid job at some time in their lives.

These data also show that in the early part of the twentieth century, the rate of cumulative participation rose very rapidly. This rate of growth slowed down in the late 1960s, as rates of current participation started to increase rapidly. We graph these two processes against time in Figure 2.1 below.

Figure 2.1 THE FEMALE EMPLOYMENT TRANSITION
Size of Cohort Ever Entering the Labour Force and Number in Labour Force in Year Specified

Per 1000 Women

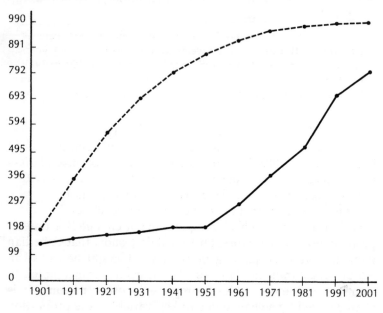

Censal Year

 Cohort entering per 1000   Number in lab. force per 1000

Over the course of the twentieth century, both of these proportions have increased, but they have done so at different speeds. About a hundred years ago only a minority of Canadian women—perhaps 10 per cent—worked outside the home for pay at a given time. A slightly larger minority of women alive at that time—perhaps 20 or 30 per cent at most—would have worked for pay at some time during their lives.

Canadian rates of labour-force entry may even have been lower than for comparable women in Victorian Britain, who made up '30 per cent of the workforce, almost all of them unmarried or poor or both' (*The Economist*, 1986, and Katz 1975: 273). At that time, Canada was much less urbanized than England: more an agricultural and manufacturing economy, and less a service economy. Therefore women were less sought-after for paid work, although many worked without pay in farm or family businesses.

By the time of the First World War, women were starting to enter paid work in larger, more rapidly growing numbers. This change was caused by the growth of cities and the kind of urban white-collar work (typically, light manufacturing, clerical, and sales jobs) that women could get. The departure of young men for the war may also have opened up opportunities in factory work, although such opportunities would have been far fewer than during the Second World War. At the same time, working-age women were immigrating to Canada and needed paying work in cities.

As a result, average women born after 1895—women in their early twenties around the time of the First World War—began to live somewhat differently from their mothers and sisters. They were more likely than their mothers to take paid work at some time in their lives. The proportion of women ever working for pay has continued to rise ever since, and it has reached more than 90 per cent for women born since 1940.

However, for most women throughout most of this century, paid work outside the home has merely punctuated major life changes. It has tended to coincide with major demographic events: marriage, the birth of a first child, the last child's entry into full-time schooling, or termination of marriage, to name only a few. Since 1945 have women begun to enter and leave the labour market much more readily than in earlier generations.

The increased push of women into the labour force, even for short periods, was spurred by several factors. One was the declining capacity of a single income to support a family or even a dependent wife; another was the related breakdown of the 'bread-winner ethic' and the rapid rise in marriage dissolutions through divorce (Ehrenreich, 1983). A third factor was the growth of feminism as an ideology encouraging female independence and equality. Combined with rising educational attainment, feminism increased the numbers of women who wanted to pursue careers. It also helped to provide institutional opportunities for such careers.

Other factors conspired to pull women into the paid labour force. In the United States between 1900 and 1960, for example, both pushes (supply factors) and pulls (demand factors) were important (Oppenheimer, 1979). However, the more important of the two was the demand for women to replace male workers in certain occupations (such as school teaching) and to fill jobs in the service industries, where interpersonal skills are particularly important. At first the demand was for young, educated women, but as the supply of those 'preferred' women declined, less desired (older, less educated, married) women were sought out as workers.

After the Second World War, job opportunities for women increased rapidly. Although traditional norms favoured female dependence, and a baby boom kept most women at home, as unpaid workers, through much of the 1950s and 1960s, eventually the expansion of poorly paying and non-unionized 'women's work' in the sales and service sectors provided new openings. These new opportunities for both part- and full-time paid work, together with the end of the baby boom, quickened the flow of women in and out of the labour market after 1965.

This final phase of the employment transition is still in progress. It combines a rapidly rising cumulative participation rate with a delayed but also rapidly rising current participation rate. The historical data suggest that at first women began to move more rapidly through a limited number of jobs, and then the number of jobs increased substantially. Before the employment transition began, women used to spend only a small portion of their lives in paid work; since then, that portion has kept growing. Cumulative rates of participation began to rise sooner (and faster) than current rates of participation. Instead of 10 to 20 per cent ever working for pay, and working more or less continuously, closer to 80 or 90 per cent of women have ever worked for pay today. But women are still holding jobs sporadically. If anything, interruptions of work are briefer and more frequent, work spells are shorter, and more women are working part-time than ever in the past.

The preliminary findings of the 1986 census of Canada offer dramatic evidence of this change in women's labour-force participation. Each succeeding generation of women has been more likely to work for pay than the one before it. As a result, younger women are quite different from older women in their work patterns and somewhat more like men.

For every ten men aged 15 to 24 in the labour force, there are more than nine working women of the same age. This gender equality falls off rapidly with age, so that women aged 65 and over are only a third as likely as men the same age to be in the paid work force. Though women who are young today will probably participate less in the labour force as they get older, it seems unlikely that as wide a gap will open up again between them and same-aged men.

Educational attainment also influences labour-force participation. For every ten men with a university degree who are in the labour force, there are nine women with a university degree also in the labour force. Participation rates drop to about 80 per cent of male rates among women with other post-secondary (i.e., non-university) qualifications; and gender inequality in participation rates is even higher for people with little or no high-school education. To some degree, this educational influence reflects the age difference we have just noted, for younger women are more highly educated (on average) than older ones.

Marital status influences female labour-force participation too. For every ten single or divorced men in the labour force, there are nine single or divorced women; but the number of female participants per hundred male participants drops to 83 for separated people, 70 for married people, and 60 for widowed people. Once again, these differences largely reflect age differences, with single people being younger and widowed people older.

If coming generations of women spend more of their lives outside marriage—whether single, divorced, separated, or widowed—they will spend more of their lives in the labour force. The combination of higher education, new norms of work behaviour, and less time spent in marriage will produce participation rates very different from those we have seen in the past. This chapter encapsulates a few of the major social and economic changes that have already occurred during this century, and particularly in the last two decades. Together, they represent a backdrop against which changes in the labour supply can be understood.

THE BIG CHANGE

In general, four main processes have increased the demand for women's labour over the last century. First was the historic growth in demand for nurses and elementary-school teachers, jobs that were thought compatible with women's caring role in the family. Later, the opportunity for women to do paid work was extended to occupational specialties in rehabilitation medicine, occupational therapy, and library science, among others.

Second, legislation and collective agreements have progressively made gender discrimination more difficult for employers and unions, especially in the face of clear economic need.

Third, and most recently, traditional barriers to married women's working for pay have been removed, and arrangements allowing part-time work have been formalized. Today, women can combine family responsibilities with paid work more easily than in the past.

Fourth are general trends that have led to the redefinition of certain jobs as being suitable for women. Although this applies especially to clerical work—to 'white-collar' and 'white-blouse' employment—more recently it has also applied to pharmacists, doctors, and lawyers. In all cases, such job redefinition accompanies a refinement of job descriptions within the occupation. Typically, women are allocated to more limited positions—some of which are today called 'mommy tracks'—within the occupation.

These changes have been part of a massive expansion in demand for clerical, sales, and service workers and a general increase in the size of work organizations, which in turn follow from what some have called 'The Big Change': the change from a rural society based on primary industries to an urban society based on service industries. This change is important enough to justify further discussion.

Since 1900, Western countries have been shifting first from an agricultural to an industrial base (to 1945), and then from industrial to 'post-industrial' organization. This shift is reflected in the numbers of people working in different industries. First agriculture loses people to manufacturing; then manufacturing shrinks while employment in private service industries and government expands. The expanding service industries provide more white-collar (and pink-collar, or white-blouse) positions, and require that their employees have more formal education than in the past.

This Big Change has been particularly important for women, since they have historically been considered unsuited for work in primary or manufacturing industries. Over the last forty years, however, it is precisely these 'blue-collar' industries that have been in decline, while government employment and service sector industries have been expanding. The industries that have expanded the most since the Second World War are community, business, and personal service, closely followed by wholesale and retail trade (Picot, 1986).

A century ago, more than half the work force was in primary occupations, and only one-tenth in service jobs. Today, less than a tenth of the work force is in primary work, but more than 40 per cent is in business and personal services alone—a Big Change indeed to have occurred in a mere hundred years. The percentage of the Canadian labour force in the entire service sector rose from 47 per cent in 1951, through 56 per cent in 1961 and 62 per cent in 1962, to 66 per cent in 1981.

Part of the increase in the number of service-sector jobs was due to an expansion of government employment. By the mid-1970s, however, government expansion had ceased to be a significant factor, while the service sector has continued to grow.

What's new?

Of course, women have always worked, often without being paid any money wage. In earlier times, wives and daughters worked on the family farm or in the family business as bakers or weavers, and did the myriad tasks involved in cooking, preserving food, looking after the house, and bringing up children. In Roman Catholic communities, a significant number of young women became members of religious orders, several of which had teaching or nursing vocations, and staffed schools and hospitals—for example, the Hôtel-Dieu hospital in Quebec City, founded and run by nuns. Midwives and nurses learned and practised their trades informally in rural areas.

Even in nineteenth-century cities, most people were from a rural background and lived close to the edge of poverty, so that they depended far more on their spouse's or children's economic contributions to the household than we do today. Consider Francesca F., a woman of 36 who lived in Vienna in 1853 and is described to us by historians Joan Scott and Louise Tilly. A cabinet-maker's wife with five children, Francesca sewed gloves at home for part of each day. This piece-work added to the family wage, and she could do it while minding her children and looking after the house. Francesca had a rural background and rural values. She had entered the Viennese working class via the common route of domestic service. In 1853 she was still able to combine domestic piece-work with married life, producing the equivalent of 125 full days' paid work in that year. But this opportunity was lost when glove-making was taken over completely by the factory system, which employed full-time workers.

The Canadian transition was not so very different, and historian Michael Katz's study of Hamilton, Ontario, shows how far Canadian women's lives changed between 1851 and 1961. In the middle of the last century, women's opportunities for paid work in Hamilton were very limited:

> In each year [1851 and 1861] most of the employed women did menial work: 72 per cent were servants in 1851 and 59 per cent ten years later; in both years about 14 per cent were dressmakers, seamstresses, or milliners, occupations suitable enough in terms of the ideology of female domesticity, but offering irregular work at low wages. Few women . . . could be positively identified as prostitutes, but undoubtedly there were very many more . . . In 1851, perhaps 4 per cent of the women might have been considered marginally middle-class (teachers, innkeepers, grocers, clerks, tax collectors): by 1861, that figure was 11 per cent, including even one physician. At the same time, women followed a somewhat greater variety of occupations, forty-one in 1851 and fifty-four in 1861. (Katz, 1975: 58)

Widows and abandoned wives with children often took in boarders. The census forms show that more than 70 per cent of Hamilton widows did this in 1851, though only 40 per cent did ten years later; others might take in washing or sewing. As Katz concludes, 'Most of these women must have lived in stark poverty.' The only independently successful women in Hamilton owned and managed brothels, but their financial success was not accompanied by social respectability.

Female factory workers could be found in certain mill towns, but not in Hamilton. Domestic service was at its height between 1850 and 1918: even a household of relatively modest means might be able to afford a live-in servant. In Hamilton in 1861, a third of all households had at least one in residence, and as in many other cities, domestic service was the most common job for women. Women servants commonly lived with their employers and could not have their young children living with them. If they became pregnant, they would have to find other employment or farm out their children to relatives.

With a decline in Hamilton's economy over the 1850s, a massive out-migration of young men resulted in rising numbers of households headed by spinsters and abandoned wives. It also opened up opportunities for women in a few higher-level occupations—innkeeping, storekeeping, teaching—if only slightly.

Women were kept out of most paid trades, except for domestic service and, in some towns, factory work. As a result, four out of every ten Canadian women working for pay in 1891 were in domestic service.

How have jobs and labour markets changed so that there is now a much greater demand for women in the paid labour force? Among the many changes occurring since 1851, the advent of compulsory education for children and the growth in the urban population were particularly important. Generally, there has been an enormous increase in the kind of white-collar jobs that could be done by either sex, but had previously been reserved for men.

For example, the teaching occupation started to expand, professionalize, and feminize a century ago. A key date is 1871, when Ontario established free public schools. The advent of compulsory schooling had tremendous significance for women. First, it removed school-age children from the labour market, thus depriving working-class families of a small but significant financial contribution. Second, it increased the demand for teachers.

Because of immigration and new legislation that made school attendance compulsory, school committees faced larger numbers of students. Budgets were unable to keep pace with this increased demand for services, and men would not work for lower wages. Female teachers therefore seemed particularly appealing: they were 'appropriate' for young children and even better, they were cheaper to hire than male teachers. Given budget restrictions and a reluctance to hire foreigners, women were the only remaining choice. But even so, female teachers were encouraged to leave teaching when they got married, and senior administrative positions stayed under the control of men.

Around the middle of the last century, school teaching and clerical work were largely male preserves. A doubling in the number of women teachers in Hamilton between 1851 and 1861 partly reflected the general trend to a feminization of the teaching profession. By the final quarter of the nineteenth century, women filled most of the teaching positions in Canada.

The expansion and feminization of office work

Around 1881, more than half of all Canadian workers were in primary occupations, and only one in ten was in a service job. In little more than a hundred years, this situation has turned around so that less than 10 per cent of the work force is in primary work today, and more than 40 per cent in business and personal services. The majority of workers do non-manual work.

Non-manual jobs have risen from 15 per cent in 1901 through 25 per cent in 1941 to 52 per cent in 1981. They include managerial, professional, technical, clerical, and sales positions. The last two of these have not only grown enormously since the beginning of the century, from 6 to just under 30 per cent of the work force, but have also been overwhelmingly filled by women.

Office work involves keeping records, typing letters, copying documents, balancing accounts, and in some cases dealing with the public. In the 1850s the people doing this kind of work were called 'clerks' and were usually men. They went to work wearing a collar and tie, earned more than manual labourers, and considered themselves superior to them. Working in the railways, banks, insurance companies, post offices and many other businesses, some clerks were more successful than others, but they all considered themselves to be middle class.

By the turn of the century, it was common for women to be employed as stenographers, typists, or operators of office machines in banking and other white-collar industries. But they were rarely given work involving much responsibility, such as making ledger entries or serving as tellers.

As Canada industrialized and became more urban, the demand for clerical workers increased rapidly. Employers began to hire unmarried women to fill these jobs, at 50 to 60 per cent of male wage-rates. Sociologist Graham Lowe (1980) has shown that, in the process, the jobs were redesigned. When it was a man's job, clerical work had required a general knowledge of the functioning of the office and assumed the possibility of a lifetime career. Once the job was redesigned for (unmarried) women, though, it was simplified—what Harry Braverman (1974) has called 'de-skilled'—and led nowhere.

Alison Prentice (1988) reminds us that by the First World War there were more women in white-collar jobs than in manufacturing. But just as a sudden demand for teachers set off the feminization of elementary-school teaching, so labour shortages during the First World War sped up the feminization of office work that was already under way.

An example is the banking industry. In the days before deposit insurance, its principle objective was to convince customers of the bank's soundness; that is why bank architecture of the time is so massive and impressive. For the same reason, well-spoken men were strongly preferred as tellers. Neither women nor men of humble social origin were thought capable of maintaining public confidence. Canadian bankers considered the ideal clerk to be a young gentleman from a middle-class background, and usually recruited such employees in Britain (Lowe, 1987).

When large numbers of such young men enlisted to fight in the First War, however, women were re-evaluated. For example, in the Bank of Nova Scotia's Ontario region, the proportion of female clerks rose from under 10 per cent in 1911 to over 40 per cent in 1916. 'Simply put,' Lowe concludes, 'bankers preferred to hire a middle class female than an educated working class male . . . The war provided opportunities for women to establish themselves as the most economical labour supply for routine clerical tasks.'

How did clerical work come to be considered feminine?

As long as there were few if any women clerks, most women probably considered the work unfeminine and therefore unsuitable for them. For there to be a change, a few employers had to decide that hiring women as clerks was a reasonable and profitable thing to do. They had to find a few women to take the jobs, which probably was not difficult. Once that happened, the growth of the idea among employers and among women workers that such jobs were suitable for women was only a matter of time. The job of bank teller, which once required a male to signal the bank's financial probity and expertise, has also gone from all male to predominantly female. (Bergmann, 1986: 37)

Service industries continued to expand throughout the 1920s, and women generally held on to their foothold in clerical work. From one point of view, their gains were illusory, since the categories of clerical jobs that had been feminized not only became as dull as assembly-line work, but had also been defined as dead-end jobs: women were expected to leave them upon marriage, and most women eventually married. 'Fast-track' job sequences had been restricted to male recruits. Still, women had made a small step forward, since they were no longer limited to domestic service or factory work before getting married.

Female clerks were well established in the Canadian federal civil service by 1900, and by 1908 made up more than 20 per cent of the inside workers. Such government jobs paid poorly but steadily, and there was no shortage of women to fill them. They took the competitive entrance examinations that had been introduced in 1908, and applied for the jobs. Their large-scale appearance on the scene appears to have threatened higher officials, who were very concerned at the prospect of whole offices' becoming female-only. In addition to seeing women as temporary workers, present just until marriage, they feared that having too many of them at lower levels of the service would limit the pool of men from whom the next generation of officials could be selected (Morgan, 1988).

Accordingly, in 1910 the Civil Service Commission published a report that recommended drastically limiting the role of female clerical workers. First, they were to be completely excluded from the first and second divisions of the service. Even in the third division, they were to be barred from certain job classifications that might conceivably require carrying heavy files or travelling any distance in the company of a male colleague. In 1918, the Civil Service Act allowed the Civil Service Commission to limit job competitions on the basis of sex, and in 1921, married women were prohibited from holding permanent posts unless they were without husbands or no other candidates were available. Such a policy, called a 'marriage bar', was common in the 1920s and 1930s.

As a result of these restrictions, the rapidly rising demand for clerical labour was channelled into a specific and limited range of jobs that paid poorly and required workers to type and take shorthand. The holders of such jobs were not permitted to accompany senior officials on trips, and could not expect to reach any position of authority. In short, they were jobs designed for unmarried women. Men, on the other hand, were hired as general clerks, and could expect promotion up the normal ladder of progressively more responsible jobs.

The profession of law offers another example of feminization, though the changes here have been more recent. In 1951, only 197 women were working as lawyers in Canada, compared to 8,841 men. By 1971, the number of women had more than tripled to 785, while the count of men had almost doubled to 15,585. The legal profession expanded dramatically during the 1970s, so that by 1981, there were 5,175 women lawyers compared to 29,030 men. By then, there was one woman lawyer for every seven male lawyers in Ontario, and one for every four or five in Quebec (Hagan, 1986).

Women have increased their access to this traditionally high-prestige profession. But their growth in opportunity has been part of a structural transformation of the legal career itself. The entire profession has undergone massive expansion since 1971, as part of the growth of very large law firms. Surveying lawyers in Toronto, where most of legal work in anglophone Canada is done, sociologist John Hagan has concluded that the (newly) large law firms organize the work and payment of their (often female) junior associates along distinctly exploitative lines. High salaries can be earned there, but the environment of cut-throat competition demands courage and very long days at work. It is the younger lawyers—men as well as women—who are most likely to be members of this new 'professional proletariat' (Hagan et al., 1988).

Given what is expected of them in modern society, the male lawyers have very little option but to stay and work the 12-hour day. This will be easier if they have a traditional partner to look after the home. By contrast, women lawyers who cannot hope to have a traditional wife at home may end up working the 'double day'. This is why Statistics Canada reports that 47 per cent of women lawyers work part-time and that women lawyers earn, on average, about 58 per cent of the salaries of men lawyers (McKie, 1986). On the positive side, the expectations held of them by their families and friends allow them to have more choices and perhaps more varied lives.

If the First World War established single young women as a good source of clerical as well as factory labour, the Second World War did the same thing for married women, even those with children. Mobilization was more extreme during the Second War than the First, and towards the end of the 1939-45 period, even married women with children were being recruited for war work. Federal-provincial child-care agreements were made that eventually resulted in the funding of day nurseries in Ontario and Quebec in 1942 (Anderson, 1988; Pierson and Cohen, 1986: 49). One comparison alone shows this effect of the war: in 1917, roughly 35,000 women worked in central Canada's munitions factories; by 1943, approximately 261,000 women were producing war materials.

After each war, publicity campaigns pressed women to give up their jobs so that they could be taken up by returning servicemen. As part of this strategy, Susan Prentice (1989) has shown for Toronto, subsidies to day-care were gradually removed after 1945 by federal, provincial, and municipal levels of government, until by 1951 they had been completely phased out. Such policies were based on the idea that a married woman's place was in the home, but they were also motivated by fear of the political consequences of large-scale male unemployment. (For a similar pattern in the US, see Kerr, 1973.) This fear of unemployment was appropriate in 1945, given Canadians' experience of massive unemployment during the 1930s. Even before the Great Depression, however, the economy had begun to shift in important ways. During and after the First World War, domestic service was still the most common occupation for a woman. The proportion of women working as domestics did not fall below 20 per cent until the 1920s, when the clerical and sales sectors were expanding and feminizing. The Depression, which lasted throughout the 1930s, caused women to be laid off before men and to revert to nineteenth-century methods of domestic production, such as taking in lodgers. It also caused marriage and fertility rates to drop to unprecedentedly low levels. After the Second World War ended, many policymakers feared a return to high unemployment levels, and were particularly concerned to make men's employment a higher priority than women's.

There has undoubtedly been a decrease in occupational segregation by sex since 1900, but it has occurred sporadically. The clearest evidence of a marked decline is from the US during the 1940s, when women filled traditionally male jobs during the war (England, 1981). Segregation by sex increased again in the 1950s, but during the 1960s and 1970s it continued its general decreasing trend. Nevertheless, the 1981 census showed that Canadian women were still concentrated in secretarial and clerical work, sales, services, health, and elementary-school teaching.

At the same time, there has been an increase in the availability of part-time and part-year work; kinds of work that are particularly attractive to married women. Between 1971 and 1981, the number of women who had worked for at least part of the preceding year grew from 3.5 million to 5.2 million. As the historians remind us, women have always done a great deal of what amounts to part-time work in household production and in the informal sector of the economy. Since the household and informal sectors have decreased in relation to the massively increasing formal part of the economy, women do many of the same part-time economic activities, but in return for a weekly pay cheque. Women often work in food-preparation industries, in teaching, and child-care, or in the garment industry—activities that used to be carried out on a do-it-yourself basis or as an informal exchange with neighbours.

There can be no doubt that employers used to be prejudiced against hiring women. Part of this prejudice was directed specifically at married women, and was bound up with ideas about the proper place of husbands and wives in marriage. However, it was also linked to beliefs about women's being unsuited for physically demanding tasks and particularly suited for painstaking, detailed work. Such thinking can be seen in the rationalizations offered either for not hiring women at all, or for confining them to very low-level jobs, many of which had been created specifically as female 'job ghettos'. Since the 1960s, such prejudices have not been well received, and they are no longer accepted as excuses for gender segregation.

But bosses are not the only ones to blame for historic patterns of discrimination. Maureen Baker and Mary-Anne Robeson (1981) have shown how male-dominated labour unions exerted their influence to prevent women from being employed in the occupations over which they had control. Their rationalizations were similar to those used by employers. Certainly the 'marriage bar' continued to be enforced in certain British industries, at the insistence of organized labour. Catherine Hakim notes: 'The marriage bar became widespread in the second half of the nineteenth century, and was abolished from the 1940s onwards . . . for example the marriage bar was abolished in the Civil Service in 1946, but the

Union of Post Office Workers ensured its operation until 1963' (Hakim, 1987: 555, citing Lewenhak, 1977 and Walby, 1986). She goes on to mention Walby as noting that 'abolition of the marriage bar constituted a fundamental change in women's position in the labour force and was a key factor in the rise of part-time work after World War II' (1987: 555).

Are women getting the 'good jobs'?

Patterns of employer and union practice have meant that some jobs and clusters of jobs—even careers—are more or less 'sheltered'. One reason why women's paid work exhibits increasing variety, fluidity and idiosyncrasy today is that many of the jobs designed in this century for women, and particularly for married women, are 'unsheltered'.

'Sheltered' jobs and job-clusters are stable, relatively well-paid, and disproportionately occupied by men. Dismissal is possible but unlikely, since continuing employment is protected by custom, collective agreements, or the maintenance of a shortage of workers with the required qualifications. At an extreme, each employing company or government agency can be considered to have its own 'internal' labour market, which defines the jobs in which new entrants usually join the firm, and the customary chain of promotions that is possible from each starting point.

Unsheltered jobs never require more than the minimum training, are relatively low-paid, offer little or nothing in the way of benefits or security of tenure, and typically demand few skills. Recalling the eighteenth and nineteenth centuries, when casual labourers were hired by the day, and unskilled factory work could be and often was done by children, such arrangements provide a flexible work force.

What is new in the prosperous West is that factory systems of production and distribution have de-skilled many jobs that previously demanded expertise; for example, the skills of a trained cook are not required in a fast-food restaurant like McDonald's. Even so, the system of 'putting out' work is still with us, especially in the Toronto garment industry and in word-processing. In their book *The Seam Allowance* (1982) Laura Johnson and Robert Johnson show that piece-work is very widespread in the trim and accessories sectors of the garment industry.

In the past, many writing about the future believed that the relentless march of technology and capitalism would result in a society where the vast majority were either unemployed or restricted to routine jobs. Current thinking about the 'declining middle class' revives this spectre of a society increasingly polarized between people working in sheltered careers and an expanding, perhaps increasingly feminized, sub-middle class working in one unsheltered job after another (Leckie, 1988).

A related theoretical approach uses the industrial classification of jobs to explain why some people have better jobs than others. Margaret Denton (1984) used data from the Royal Commission on Corporate Concentration to divide industries into CORE and PERIPHERY sectors. The CORE, dominated by large and highly concentrated corporations, includes (a) utilities, transportation, communication, (b) finance, insurance, real estate, and (c) mining. By contrast, enterprises in the PERIPHERY are small and not concentrated, including such industries as (a) trade, (b) construction, (c) personal, business, and community services, and (d) agriculture, forestry, fishing. A third sector is the STATE (Public Administration), where people are employed by federal, provincial, municipal, or local governments.

Denton's research revealed that—at least in 1973, when her data were collected—women's income was worst in the PERIPHERY sector, less bad in the CORE, and best of all—though still markedly worse than men's—in the STATE sector. These findings are in line with the common observation that careers in the public service are the most highly sheltered, and those in small 'peripheral' organizations the least.

Part-time work

Part-time work carries costs and benefits for both employers and employees. On the employer's side, part-time work reduces the costs of both wages and non-wage benefits and increases flexibility, since part-time workers usually receive less job protection than full-time workers and are more difficult for unions to organize. However, the work force is accordingly less committed, turnover is higher, and training costs are considerable.

Employees may take part-time work if no other work is available, even though they would prefer full-time. But they may favour part-time over full-time work if they value time spent outside paid work sufficiently highly. Men rarely choose to work part-time in the sense of part-weeks or part-months, though in some regions seasonal (part-year) work is common. On the other hand, women raising children may seek part-time work if it costs them more to pay for child-care and related household services than the family could gain in wages.

Part-time workers are flexible only in the crude numerical sense that they can be easily replaced, and may be appropriate for semi-skilled work at best. Workers who are truly flexible—that is, who can easily do a wide variety of tasks and quickly learn new, complex skills—are scarcer: they are valuable to the firm, and embody investments the firm has made in their training.

Employers offer part-time work for various reasons. Service establishments, for instance, need to stay open in the evenings or on weekends. In other cases, the employer may wish to retain some numerical flexibility, or keep his costs to a minimum: part-timers are often paid a lower hourly rate than full-time workers, and may receive lower levels of non-wage benefits. Among the many other reasons why demand for part-time workers may increase are changes in technology, in production technique, or in need for and availability of capital (Tegle, 1985).

CONCLUDING REMARKS

In the early nineteenth century, most positions in the paid work force—prostitution and domestic service apart—were filled by men. Women carried out a wide variety of economic activities, most of which were family-based and outside the formal economy. In the course of modernization, some occupations expanded rapidly. In some of these cases—elementary-school teaching, clerical and sales-service jobs—a shortage of qualified men allowed women to be hired at a lower wage-rate. A 'marriage bar' was still in effect, and such jobs rapidly became primarily feminine in composition. Their duties were defined in such a limited way as to make them unattractive to men, who wanted career prospects and high wages.

Jobs that were 'feminized' in this way became part of a separate, primarily female labour market. Women usually left the formal economy when they married or started bearing children. Some occupations, like nursing, have never attracted many men. In many others—law, for example—the massive preponderance of men has begun to diminish since 1945.

The period from 1945 to 1968 may have been an aberration in the history of the North American family. With memories of the

1930s Depression still alive, the end of the Second World War was followed by a period of unprecedented and unexpected material prosperity. The prevailing cult of femininity and motherhood— which resurrected the notion that women should leave paid work upon marriage or the birth of the first child—produced a temporary reversal of the long-term decline in fertility. Accordingly, the 1961 census found less than 30 per cent of Canadian women in the labour force. Since the 1960s, however, this pattern has broken down. By 1986, over 55 per cent of adult women participated in the paid work force, compared to 75 per cent of men. In 1988, 57 per cent of married women with children under the age of six had jobs.

Over the first six or seven decades of this century, North Americans tried—though interrupted by two World Wars and the Great Depression—to realize an ideal of the role-differentiated but cohesive family unit working in 'separate spheres', with the man as sole wage-earner and the woman as mother, domestic provider, and emergency wage-earner. This goal was most closely approached during the years between 1951 and 1965.

In the 1970s and 1980s, however, Canadians have returned to the situation in which many families are very much dependent on the economic contributions of both husbands and wives. What may be new is that women now think of themselves as individuals with a moral duty to realize their own potential, rather than gaining meaning from being members of an interdependent family unit. Yet they are obliged by economic reality to stifle their individual ambition or pay the consequences. This contradiction is further irritated by very high material expectations. On this, Hagan (1986: 7) comments: 'The children of the baby boom grew up in a period of prolonged economic growth and attendant rising expectations of social mobility and economic mobility—for women as well as for men.'

It was in the 1960s that post-secondary education started expanding and oral contraception became widely available, and both of these changes enhanced women's freedom to act as individuals. Whatever the exact priority of causes, women began to spend a much greater proportion of their adult lives in the paid work force.

Some did this by continuing to work after marriage, some by re-entering the work force after their children had gone off to school. Others adopted the ideal of the uninterrupted career path traditionally taken by men. Some women 'made it', in the sense of making the same progression as men in their careers. However, the great majority found that they were trapped in clusters of jobs that paid poorly, gave little reward to experience or initiative, and led nowhere.

Women have tended to shift between jobs and labour-market statuses because their jobs have not encouraged commitment. As Graham Lowe has shown, many of their jobs were designed that way, in the 1920s, a period when men were trying to preserve the economic basis of patriarchy.

Our summary statement that women's adult lives have become 'individualized' is in many ways consistent with the proposition that the paid jobs made available to women are largely in unsheltered labour markets and/or in PERIPHERY industries, especially services. The *variety* of jobs open to them is wider than ever before. But because of the way these jobs have been organized—on a part-time and/or limited-contract basis—women are encouraged to be more *fluid*: they move more rapidly from one job to another. The nature of the alternatives available to them also makes women's behaviour more *idiosyncratic*, sometimes appearing random in the sense that it is more and more difficult to predict.

In the last two chapters, we have seen how changes both in their personal lives and in the labour market led more women to enter the paid labour force in Canada. We have hinted that they did so in a way quite different from men: they did not simply adopt male work patterns. Instead, they adapted to paid work by 'individualizing' their life patterns. In the next section, we prove this claim with evidence from Canada and a variety of other industrial nations. We begin that task with a chapter that formally defines and explains precisely what we mean by 'individualization'.

II

PROOF OF INDIVIDUALIZATION

3

The Rise of Individualization

CHANGES IN WOMEN'S WORK LIVES

What does it mean to be aged 35 in our society? What sorts of things happen to you? To answer this question, let's use our imaginations to survey those university students we described in our Introduction. What were they doing, or what will they be doing, at age 35?

When 50-year old MARGARET was 35, she had already reached the height of her teaching career. Off and on, she had been teaching for over a decade. She felt she was doing a good job, and she and her husband had worked out good arrangements for taking care of their daughter and the household chores. She had no way of knowing that when her daughter became old enough to take care of herself, little mystery would remain in her marriage and career, and that by 45, she would be wondering what to do next.

ROSA was 35 only two years ago. That was two years after her husband had left her and the two children for a younger woman with whom he is now living. The split was friendly: his monthly support payments made it possible for Rosa to attend law school. During that time, her husband has also been taking care of one or both of the children, as required by their legal agreement. After she graduates, she and the children will be on their own.

ANNA will be 35 in two years. By that time she will be only half-way through her undergraduate program, if she stays with it. While she is strongly determined to finish, financing the return to school is difficult. Her parents are helping out, at least for now. It seems unlikely that she will be married, let alone a mother, by the time she is 35. In a way, her experience of age 35 will be like SUZY's or BRENDA's experience of age 20: a time of no adult responsibilities and much financial dependence.

GAIL won't be 35 for eight years. Little does she know that, after spending two years in professional study, she will still have trouble finding a job in her preferred line of work, hi-tech librarianship. Her ability to seek good jobs outside Toronto will be limited by her marriage to a young businessman, who won't want to move; and Gail won't want to risk breaking up the marriage. So she will work at a high-level clerical job and consider the possibility of yet another retraining program at the university. By the time she is 35, her marriage will have broken up, without children.

CARLA will be 35 in ten years. The next decade will be a very busy one: She will take a year off to read, garden, and make a bit of money with some part-time tutoring; for a few months, she will waitress; then she will do secretarial work every morning for four months. With her husband, she will move out to the west coast, where she will have a baby. By 32, when her child is 5 years old, she will stop dreaming about a return to full-time studies and will start doing something about it. But by this time she will no longer be interested in getting a Ph.D. Instead she will decide to become a medical doctor, even though that means starting back at the beginning to study the sciences. By age 35, she will have picked up all her undergraduate science credits and be waiting for admittance to McMaster Medical School in Hamilton.

What about SUZY, BRENDA, and DIANA? They are simply too far away from age 35 for us to know the answer. SUZY and BRENDA will have to live almost as long to get there as they have already lived in their entire lives. Still, there are a few things we can predict with reasonable safety. First, all three will work for pay during some of the time between now and then. Second, they are unlikely to have more than three children between them by the time they are 35. Third, at least one of them will divorce or never marry, though each will have cohabited with a man. At least two will have returned to school for more education. By age 35, at least one will be working at something that she never dreamed of doing when she was 18.

And what about FRANK and LES? FRANK was divorced at the age of 35, a very painful and confusing experience for him. Somehow, he had always imagined that he would have a marriage like his parents'—for always. At first he couldn't understand his wife's unhappiness with their marriage and blamed it on the women's movement. He misses having his children with him, although he sees them regularly and remains on good terms with his former wife. While he dates a few women regularly, he does not like this type of life. He wants to remarry and establish a stable household;

however, his experiences make him wary, unsure of his own judgement. In the meantime, his studies are opening up new possibilities in his thinking about his job and his situation in life. He is planning to complete his degree and then bid for a transfer to a more important and interesting administrative job in a smaller community. There he hopes to find a woman who shares his career interests and his desire to live in a small town. By the time he is 45, he hopes that his life will have stabilized.

LES will not be 35 for another 15 years. He sees his career in very straightforward terms. He will finish his undergraduate degree, travel for a year, enter the best law school he can find, and practise corporate law. He has no doubts about these plans, and his financial planning, with his parents, is based on this sequence of events. But he cannot imagine his personal future. He is attracted to women who have career plans of their own, but he finds them very involved in their own work. So for companionship he goes out with a woman from his high-school days. She works as a secretary and wants to marry and have children. He does not want to get involved this way. His male friends are busy with sports, school, and their girlfriends and he is quite lonely. Les will marry a woman he meets in his year of travel, when they are both 23. In order to make it possible for them both to study, both will have to hold down part-time jobs. His grades will slip and he will not get into the law school of his dreams. Although he believes in the equality of women and the need for his wife's education, he will be extremely worried about his own future. When his wife is offered a very good job in Alberta, Les will be totally unwilling to give up his job to move. Because he is not succeeding in his own eyes, the marriage will suffer. And by the time he is 35 Les will be divorced and supporting a child, working in a highly competitive law firm that demands long hours and complete availability, with very little time for himself. Still, he will be looking for a career woman with whom he can share his life.

As we said earlier, no two of these lives are alike in important details. Where education, marriage, work, and parenting are concerned, the combinations and timing of changes are unique. This change to more individualized lives appears even more starkly when we compare women with their mothers.

A simple thought experiment

To better understand the process we are calling the

'individualization' of women's lives, try this simple experiment. Think about a woman currently in young adulthood—say, about 35 years old, born in 1955—and then contrast her life history with that of her mother, born in 1925, up to age 35.

What strikes us first is how hard it is to summarize the lives of a 'typical' young woman. Consider just two or three variables like marital status, the number of children borne, and work activity. You are unlikely to find any two histories that are alike. So, among female acquaintances in their mid-thirties there are women who have been divorced, or are currently divorced, or have never been married, or are married to previously divorced men, or are married to men never married before. There are women with no children, a few children, and many children; women with plans for having no more children and other women with plans for having more. There are women caring for their own children and women caring for the children of their spouses' earlier marriages.

Among women born in the 1950s, life patterns are numerous and complicated. By contrast, their mothers' histories are much simpler and more similar. A woman aged 35 in 1950 was typically married and living with her original spouse and the children of that marriage. She was either a full-time housekeeper or a full-time paid worker. If the latter, she had typically waited to enter the labour force until her children were attending school full-time.

The contrast between generations is even stronger if we compare the marital, parental, and occupational *changes* that women make between the ages 30 and 35, or 35 and 40. The current generation of young women is not just varied, it is also enormously fluid. These young women are much likelier than their mothers to do different things at ages 30, 35, and 40, for example. Women expect change. Says one of Jones's respondents: 'Five years from now I may not be [at home with my children]. Things may change'. Movements in and out of paid work, in and out of part- and full-time work, in and out of full-time education, are much more common today than a generation ago. So too are movements in and out of marriage.

The growth of part-time work both symbolizes and facilitates this new fluidity. Part-time paid work has become much more common in the last few decades. Accordingly, the female movement between part- and full-time work, and between part-time work and housework, has increased dramatically. Another way of saying this is that as part-time work becomes more available, women's work-force fluidity increases. The same is not true of men.

Another common observation is that women are more likely today to hold paid jobs in non-traditional occupations: in those occupations historically dominated by men. These include law, medicine, pharmacy, and various kinds of skilled and semi-skilled manufacturing, construction, and transportation jobs, among others. Female job ghettos remain. But women are less confined to sales, clerical, and semi-professional work (nursing, teaching, social work) than they were in the past.

To summarize, young women today hold a wider variety of positions occupationally than their mothers did at the same age. They also play a wider range of marital and parental roles, for these domains of activity have also become much more diverse. Second, women's lives today are much more fluid than in the past. Third, partly as a result of the first two changes, women's lives are much more idiosyncratic than in the past: less predictable, more 'tailor-made' to suit family circumstances and personal needs.

And what about the future? Will all women be able to move freely between the public and private domains, or will it become less and less acceptable for women to be homemakers? How long will this last, and what will succeed it? These are questions we are far from able to answer; we won't even try. Our concern in this book is individualization and the conditions that led up to it.

During our present period of history, women's work and personal lives are changing in complicated, unique ways. No two women will experience the age of 35 (or any other age) quite the same way. No two women will experience the transition from school to work, or marriage to parenthood, or divorce to remarriage, in quite the same way or even at the same age. Because there are so many changes and combinations of changes, we cannot consider them all. Furthermore, even if we wanted to, data in such detail cannot be derived satisfactorily from existing sources. So for purposes of simplicity we shall confine our attention to movements in and out of the labour force. But what is true of individualization in the realm of work is equally true of individualization in all the areas of personal (or intimate) life. Individualization works the same way in both spheres; moreover, what happens in one sphere inevitably affects what happens in the other.

INDIVIDUALIZATION

What do we mean by individualization? In more precise terms, how are we defining this way of looking at adult women's lives? Three conditions make possible and predict the further individualization of adult female lives. They are the growth of variety, fluidity, and idiosyncrasy.

The growth of *variety* is marked by an opening of all adult statuses to women and, conversely, by the weakening of job ghettos. Women come to occupy more statuses and distribute themselves more equally among these statuses. Our hypothesis predicts that, in future, women will distribute themselves ever more equally between domestic work, full-time and part-time work outside the household, and full-time education.

The growth of *fluidity* is marked by increasing movement between these same statuses. Fifty years ago, child-bearing locked the average woman into domestic activities for life, and housework offered little chance of exit. Since then, higher education and the growth of part-time work have made movement among all adult statuses easier than ever before. One woman told Jones's interviewers: 'I like to work—I may come back to the business after trying retirement. It's really my husband's idea to retire early. He wants to travel but I don't care for it that much.'

In theory, as new opportunities have opened up, employers could have filled them with younger, incoming women, also locked into quite distinct (though different) work statuses. But this has not happened. Both older and younger women have become more fluid. In this way, both have been able to take advantage of new opportunities.

We can measure the growth of female fluidity by looking at the chances that individual women will move between pairs of statuses: for example, between domestic activities and part-time work. This kind of movement has increased in the last fifty years and we believe it will increase further. Under conditions of 'perfect individualization', movements among all major statuses will be frequent and almost equally common.

The growth of *idiosyncrasy* is marked by increasing variation in the predictors of labour-market status. Today we need much more information about a woman to predict her status than we did a generation ago. Traditional predictors (age, marital status, number of children, family income, religion, region of residence, and so on) are losing their importance. The decline in their predictive power demonstrates the growing idiosyncrasy of adult female lives. At the limit of idiosyncrasy, we would need as many unique combinations of predictor variables as there are different women.[1]

But in fact no life is wholly unique. What we mean by 'social structure' is precisely that people do *not* organize their lives by pulling options out of a hat. In reality, people live out many fewer varieties of life than are theoretically possible. That is why we must understand the impact of a changing social structure on women in the twentieth century. In so doing, we find that while women's lives are far from unique, many more kinds of lives are actually being lived than in the past.

What is happening to women these days is new, important, poorly understood and—above all—unique to women generally. But why should that be so? Don't men have an equal stake in the divorce explosion? in the flight from parenthood? in the massive entry of women into paid work? And is there any evidence that they are remaining the same in their work patterns while women are 'individualizing'?

CHANGES IN MEN'S WORK LIVES

Variety

In fact, the changes in women's lives that we discuss in this book are part of a general change in all adult lives. Like women's, men's lives too are rapidly changing and becoming more complex. For simplicity, consider only the changes in male variety and fluidity in the last decade or so.

We can see these changes by comparing men in 1977 and 1985, using labour-force data on men from Statistics Canada's Annual Work Patterns Surveys of 1977 and 1985. In 1977, male labour-force participation was very high at all ages and for all levels of educational attainment. Overall, highly educated men were more likely to be working for pay (or looking for work) than were less educated men. For example, of men aged 35 to 44, only 76 per cent with no formal education or some elementary education were in the labour force, compared with 90 per cent of men with some secondary education, 93 per cent of men with a post-secondary certificate or diploma, and 97 per cent of men with a university degree.

Labour-force participation varies with age in a different way, rising rapidly in the twenties, staying at this plateau through the thirties and forties, then falling to nearly zero only after the sixties. For example, of men with some post-secondary education, labour-force participation rates rose from 32 per cent at ages 17 to 19 to 54 per cent at ages 20 to 24, 94 per cent at ages 35 to 44, 75 per cent at ages 55 to 64 and back down to 22 per cent at ages 65 and over. Thus in 1977 most men worked for pay. As university students, both FRANK and LES fall into this group. Their life plans are still centred around their employment. Any questions in their lives concern their personal relationships, not their work in the labour market.

But by 1985, at every age and education level, men were less likely to be in the labour force than they had been in 1977. At every age, men were more likely than before to be doing something other than working: continuing school, returning to school, or taking early retirement. As one of Jones's male respondents admitted, 'Her income is sufficient so I don't need to work at all. If she didn't [work], my employment would be more important financially.'

By 1985, men were not only less likely to be in the labour force than they had been in the past, but those who remained in the labour force were working a wider variety of hours than they had in 1977. Consider the variation (or standard deviation) of hours worked in the week before the respondent's Annual Work Patterns Survey (AWPS) interview. In 1977, highly educated people had more similar work patterns (that is, a smaller variation in hours of work) than less educated people did. At all education levels, variation was highest in the age groups 20 to 24 and 55 to 64, when many people were in the process of entering or leaving the paid labour force.

By 1985, the same patterns of variation by education and age were evident; but across the board, variation in hours of work had increased. Now, even the relatively homogeneous male university graduates were much more different from each other than they had been in 1977. In eight years, the (median) standard deviation of hours worked by this group had increased by over 10 per cent.

Think of men aged 35 to 44 with some post-secondary education, for example. By 1985, only 89 per cent were in the labour force at all, compared with 94 per cent in 1977. Of those who were working, the standard deviation of hours they worked in a week had risen in the same period from 16.21 to 17.82. In short, men's lives had become more varied.

Women's life patterns also changed over this period. Increasingly, education and age were affecting women's labour-force participation the same way they affected men's; and overall, more women were in the labour force at every level of age and education. As a result, male and female patterns had started to look more similar than before. For example, where labour-force participation by university graduates had fallen from a median of 89 per cent in 1977 to 84 per cent in 1985 for males, it had risen for female university graduates from a median of 70 per cent in 1977 to 78 per cent in 1985.

Where variation in hours worked is concerned, the pattern is slightly different. Between 1977 and 1985, women remained highly varied in their hours worked, while men became almost as varied as women. So, for example, among people aged 35 to 44 with some post-secondary education, the male standard deviation in hours worked rose from 16.21 to 17.82 between 1977 and 1985, while the female standard deviation barely rose at all, from 18.49 to 18.54. Again, from these data one would predict an eventual convergence of male and female work-lives.

Fluidity

However, middle-aged men and women were not becoming equally fluid, or likely to change their work status in a given year. One good way of measuring fluidity is to use the AWPS data from 1977 and 1985, where people were asked how they had spent the preceding year. Those who answered that they had been out of the labour force *and* working or seeking work at various points in the preceding year can be classed as 'fluid'.

In 1977, male fluidity was relatively low. Fluidity tended to decrease with higher education; and after ages 17 to 19, when it peaked, it declined steadily with age. In 1985, the same pattern of variation by age and education was still to be found. However, at every age and educational level, fluidity in 1985 was much higher—generally three or four times greater—than it had been in 1977.

In 1977, overall female fluidity was slightly higher than men's in general, and much higher than men's—about double—at the higher educational levels. That is, highly educated women were much more fluid than highly educated men. Fluidity varied less with education for women than it did for men, perhaps because of the women's ghettoization in marginal work. And, as with men's fluidity, there was a steady decline in women's from ages 17 to 19 on. Indeed, the age-decline in fluidity was about the same for women as it was for men.

By 1985, like men's, women's fluidity had grown considerably, by a factor of two, three, four, or five, depending on educational level. So, for example, in 1977 10 per cent of 30-year-old women with level 4 education (i.e., a post-secondary diploma or certificate) had been fluid in the preceding year; in 1985, 26 per cent of age 30, same-education women had been fluid. In 1977, only 4 per cent of age 30, same-education men had been fluid; by 1985, 15 per cent of age 30, same-education men had been fluid.

In general, education continued in 1985 to have a less regular, linear impact on women's fluidity than it did on men's. Indeed, for women there is a complex interaction between age and education where fluidity is concerned. In general, women under 20 are most fluid, whatever their education. From 20 to 45, less educated women are slightly more fluid than more educated ones. After 45, more educated women are much more fluid than less educated ones. An example is one of Jones's interviewees:

> I'm going to school to study English and French. After 37 years in nursing, I'd rather do something different. You get burnt out after 37 years in nursing. I want something that will be personally satisfying and intellectually stimulating.

It is this pattern of high fluidity among more educated women over age 45—women like MARGARET—that is new. It does not appear in the 1977 data, where education continues to make relatively little difference to fluidity among women past childbearing age. Nor is this pattern found for men: at all ages below 65, less educated men are more fluid than more educated men. Over 65, there is no relationship between education and fluidity for men.

In short, between 1977 and 1985, fluidity increased for both men and women. The difference lies in how higher education affected it. For men, higher education continued to reduce fluidity at all ages. For women, however, higher education, which in 1977 had increased fluidity for very young women and reduced it for older women, had changed its role. By 1985, higher education was increasing fluidity for women both before *and* after child-bearing—that is, in the ages below 25 *and* over 45. This finding supports Picot's conclusions (1986: 27) from the Family History

Survey data that, between 1974 and 1983, women were making approximately twice as many transitions in and out of work as men, on average.

The individualization of men's lives we have observed suggests that a more and more complex division of labour is increasing the variety and fluidity of everyone's life. It also indicates the growing need for greater workplace flexibility (illustrated by the greater use of part-time workers) that is opening up more varied work opportunities. Finally, the increased need for more education and recurrent education has changed the patterning of all adult lives, both male and female.

Attitudes regarding male employment are changing too. Here is what two of Jones's respondents had to say:

> If a husband wants to stay home, that's fine. However [a woman and her husband] work it out is okay.

> What I feel about women should apply to men as well. If a man wants to stay home and the wife go out to work, he should have a right to that chance as well.

What, then, is distinct about women in this context of overall change? It is, first, that women are fighting their way against historic discrimination and towards greater choice and variety, while men are simply giving up some of their traditional work opportunity in favour of more education and/or leisure.

Second, women have to contend with a 'double burden', while men do not. Men are individualizing their lives around one main constraint—paid work—while women are individualizing theirs around two equally compelling constraints—paid work and domestic work. So long as women bear children and take the prime responsibility for them, their lives will be more complex because their personal 'life-equations' will have to find an optimum level in the face of *two* constraints. This greater complexity of women's lives does not show up in labour-force data, but rather in time-budget data, which illustrate the double constraints of domestic and workplace demands.

For both males and females, the rates of fluidity are increasing. But the female pattern of age/education fluidity remains distinct from the male and in future the latter will probably change relatively less than the former. As a result, one expects that a man's life will have more in common with his father's than a woman's with her mother's life. A man's life will also have more in common with his brother's life than a woman's with her sister's. Ten men reaching age 35 will have had more similar experiences, and shared more characteristics with each other, than will ten women at the same age.

To take the very simplest example, men at any given age and level of education are more likely than women of the same age and education to be working for pay, and indeed to be working full-time for pay. For their part, some of the women are working full-time, others part-time; others are in school; still others are doing full-time housework. Among people who are working for pay, men vary less in the hours they work than women do. Though males are becoming more varied over the course of time, they are still less varied than women and show no certain sign of catching up to them. Thus 'individualization' is largely a woman's life experience.

Another thought experiment

To understand why this is so, let's consider how our male university students differ from our female students, and why.

Compared with SUZY: A bright male student would be less uncertain about what he was going to specialize in. Male students are more likely to enter science, commerce, or professional (or pre-professional) courses at university. There is no question in LES's mind about his future in law. Female students are more likely to enter humanities or social-science programs, which have less obvious, immediate, or certain job consequences.

Compared with BRENDA: No male student plans to organize his life around a spouse, or thinks he can eliminate problems of career planning and income security by getting married. LES will not take his high-school girlfriend seriously because that would interfere with his career plans.

Compared with DIANA: Male students do not worry much about gender discrimination, because they do not often suffer it; nor do they worry much about marital breakdown for economic reasons, although they may worry about personal support.

Compared with CARLA: Male students do not have to consider whether to quit school to have babies, nor do they often migrate because their spouses are migrating.

Compared with GAIL: Male students are less likely to pursue unmarketable degrees in the first place, and for this reason they usually experience less immediate need for retraining upon graduation.

Compared with ANNA: Again, men rarely throw caution to the wind and migrate across the continent to be with a lover or spouse; as a result, they are less likely to be picking up the pieces a decade later.

Compared with ROSA: A man who divorces is less likely to keep the children. Because he has never sacrificed his career for marriage and child-bearing, he has little need to re-train in the event of a divorce.

Compared with MARGARET: A man who hits a career peak and profound boredom in his thirties or early forties is less likely to stay with his spouse. Margaret is taking recreational university courses; a male in her position would probably have launched a second marriage by now.

No one-sentence summary can account for all the gender differences we have identified above; nor is it the goal of this book to do so. But women's and men's lives are very different in a great many details. In particular, women's lives are much more fragmented, changeable, dependent, and tied up with other people's lives. For this reason alone, it is not surprising that women's lives are more 'individualized' than men's.

In the late twentieth century, men's lives remain much more uniform than women's.[2] More women than ever before have been exposed to a greater amount of paid work, usually in jobs organized on the assumption that the job-holder can easily be replaced. This has made women's lives more variable—that is, less like one another's—and in most cases, women's lives have not become like men's. Their movements in and out of the labour force have become ever less constrained by lack of opportunity or by child-raising duties. As a result, more women have made these decisions on idiosyncratic, personal grounds. In each instance, the woman's education, human capital, values, and aspirations all have come to count for a great deal more than they did in the past.

Living in a modern capitalist society pulls both sexes towards similar living and working patterns. Unless men's lives change dramatically, however, male and female experiences will grow even more different in the future. We can see no convincing reasons why women will not continue to experience the increasing variety, fluidity, and idiosyncrasy that we are calling the 'individualization' of adult female lives.

Women's lives are becoming more idiosyncratic

Not so long ago, age played a very important part in people's lives, especially women's. Linda Waite wrote in 1981 that if someone wanted to guess whether an individual woman was currently in the labour force, the most useful single piece of information would be her age. Certainly, in 1955, if you knew a woman's age you could probably guess her marital status and how many children she had borne (what demographers call her 'parity'). If you knew her age, marital status, and parity, more often than not you could correctly guess her daily activity: whether she was in school, in full-time paid work, part-time paid work, or fully engaged in housework. As a statistician would say, little of the variation in women's daily activity was due to other factors.

Today a statistician would do poorly predicting marital status and parity from a woman's age, and even worse predicting her daily activity from her age, marital status, and parity. Consider the fictional women we have discussed. They are all becoming educated, yet they range in age from late teens to early fifties. Clearly, age has no important bearing on women's education any more. Similarly, our imaginary women are all becoming educated, yet they include almost every marital status: never married, married, and divorced (we have not included a widow in our group, but one could easily fit the picture). Clearly, marital status has no important bearing on women's education any more.

Parity is somewhat different. If you add or subtract children from any of the scenarios we have presented, you change the picture very dramatically.

Imagine SUZY: bright and 18, with a little baby. She will probably not be able to continue in school unless she gives up the baby for adoption or her parents agree to take care of it. The same is true for BRENDA and CARLA. And if they are without spouses, things will be very tough financially as well.

Imagine CARLA: if she decides to have that baby she and her husband are talking about, she is unlikely to get back to doctoral studies very soon. A baby would likely change the course of her life, at least for five or ten years. The same is true for GAIL: if she has a baby, her chances of returning to school and re-training are also significantly reduced. Even well-intentioned husbands do not help out much with babies and domestic chores.

Imagine ANNA: with four years of college to go, she must

certainly avoid having a baby, especially with no spouse on the horizon. The odds are already against her getting her BA; parenthood would simply make the odds worse. That would put her in the same position as ROSA, but without any financial or other support from an ex-spouse.

Imagine MARGARET: without a daughter to take care of, she might have addressed her own interests and emotional needs a lot sooner than she did. Perhaps this would have meant returning to school earlier, or solving her problems in another way entirely.

What these speculations suggest is that while age and marital status no longer have a great deal of impact on women's lives, parenthood does. Parenthood is uniquely limiting for women, much more than for men. Only if this gender difference disappears—through the elimination of normal child-bearing or the vast extension of public child-care—will women's lives stop being shaped by it more than men's. Nevertheless, it has become somewhat more possible to combine the status of mother with that of student or worker through the spread of commercial child-care services.

Leaving parenthood aside, *much* of the variation in a women's life pattern is due to other factors, and it is in this sense that we mean that idiosyncrasy has increased. These 'other factors' that are more likely to affect women's life patterns today than in the past fall into two main categories: namely, supply- and demand-side variables.

On the supply side, some of the unexplained variation in women's lives will be due to different attitudes, values, tastes, and beliefs. Some of these are traceable, in turn, to different religious, ethnic, class, regional, or other origins—but not all. To some degree, women are living more different lives today because they have more choice. They exercise their choice differently because they value different things. As one woman told our interviewers, 'Every woman is different—some women don't like to work, some do. Women who do work find it difficult to do housework as well.'

Also on the supply side are those characteristics known as 'human capital'. All of these, but especially educational attainments, qualify people to compete in certain job markets. They also predispose them to use their time in certain ways, not others.

The home environment also influences a woman's life history. If married, what is her spouse's income? Can she afford to forego full-time paid work? This is something that many of Jones's respondents commented on. For example: 'In terms of income, if he is earning less, it's more important that I work. If he is earning a lot, there is less pressure on one. It's affected me in terms of how flexible my job can be, because we've moved around because of his work.'

How do her spouse and children feel about her taking a full-time paid job? How willing are they to share domestic duties? How do her employer's requirements fit in with her family's (especially her husband's) demands? These are some of the domestic issues that sociologists are paying more attention to, especially through the study of 'time budgets'.

On the other side of the equation are employers' demands for workers. A higher demand for labour makes it easier for women to get the kind of work they want at the level of pay that would make taking the job worthwhile. Over the past decade, employers have created many part-time jobs in the clerical-sales-service sector. Opinions differ on what has caused this growth of part-time work, and whether the trend will continue. Technological change may account for some of the new part-time jobs: for example, some expensive equipment must be run more than eight hours a day to justify its cost. Other jobs, like nursing, may provide round-the-clock service. Increasingly, sales jobs in the retail sector may take on this character.

In some countries, part-timers are denied important benefits, such as health insurance or pensions, and are not protected by conventional employment legislation. Where part-timers receive these benefits, they become more expensive to hire; but they are also less motivated to transfer to full-time work.

Employers may use part-timers to give themselves the 'numerical flexibility' of being able to call in marginal workers as needed. We must consider not only the general level of unemployment but also the level of unemployment in sectors of the economy where women are likely to look for work. Technological change also influences the demand for workers in traditional 'female' occupations. Consider, for example, the effect of computerization on work opportunities in clerical and sales jobs: jobs will be eliminated, and women—the typical holders of such jobs—will suffer the worst consequences.

No one knows yet how free trade between Canada and the US, or within the European Economic Community after 1992, will affect 'feminized' sectors, or the economy in general. It seems very likely that those most hurt will be people working in the secondary (unprotected) labour market. Especially vulnerable are the kinds of jobs—data entry and semi-skilled manufacturing—that can be easily shifted to lower-paying parts of the world. Since women have been most often employed in such jobs up to now, they stand the greatest chance of being hurt by free trade.

Besides the economy, a second major exogenous factor is the state of legislation bearing on women's lives. We are not likely to see the future society Margaret Atwood has described in her *Handmaid's Tale*: a society that treats women as child-bearing, house-keeping chattels. Equally, we are not likely to see a return to limited choice in contraception, abortion, and child-bearing; nor a return to limited choice in marriage and divorce.

On the other hand, we might very well live to see legislation that (a) effectively limits discrimination against women in hiring, pay, or promotion; (b) prorates (and makes portable) benefits for part-time work; or (c) provides widely available day-care of regulated quality. Anti-discrimination legislation would make full-time work more attractive. Relatively more rewarding part-time work would increase the likelihood of fluid movement in and out of part-time and full-time paid work.

High-quality day-care would increase the likelihood both of child-bearing and of early return to paid work afterwards. Said one woman: 'If I had cheaper day-care I would go out to work. It is not worth it for me to go out to work because my day-care expenses would eat up my salary, and I don't want to go to work for $100 a week.'

Once age, marital status and child-bearing are no longer the prime influences, public-policy variables assume a great deal of influence over women's lives. By combining with other personal characteristics in a multitude of ways, they contribute significantly to the making of idiosyncratic lives.

Is individualization really fragmentation?

What we may be witnessing today is a progressive fragmentation of women's lives. Men's lives are keeping their historic unity or integrity, and women's lives are not. Indeed, women's lives have always been vulnerable to patriarchal control and economic hardship. From this standpoint, the observed growth of variety is really the growth of a marginal female work force: a work force that is badly paid, largely unprotected by unions (hence denied security and benefits), and driven into part-time work by the need for wages 'at any cost'. Part-time work is the employer's way of getting manageable workers at low cost.

The observed growth of fluidity may really be a response to part-time or short-term jobs that are insecure and unattractive, but available when good full-time work is not. By this reasoning, fluidity reflects both the instability of the economic system and discrimination against women; the observed growth of idiosyncrasy is the result of long-term, nearly random fluidity in which women float about on a sea of uncontrolled influences. Whether these influences are seen as constituting a 'free market' or as the deliberately contrived agents of a plan to create a source of cheap and flexible labour, in this view 'idiosyncracy' appears to be a polite term for 'exploitation'.

However, if social vulnerability is really the main factor driving individualization, then the most vulnerable women of all—those with the least choice—should be the most various, fluid, and idiosyncratic. This group would include women with little education or other human capital, older women, women without husbands, and women whose husbands earn little or no income. By this reasoning, poor and working-class women should be increasingly fluid, and women in the middle and upper classes unchanged.

On the other hand, some believe that the growth of individualization reflects not fragmentation, but a growth of choice and opportunity for women. If that is the case, then women with the opposite characteristics—those possessing the most 'human capital'—should be leading the most individualized lives. In practice we see a great deal of support for both interpretations and in this book we shall use survey data to assess them. In particular, in our last chapter we will investigate two main themes.

First, we shall consider the relationship between 'individualization' and 'improvement'. Some might confuse 'individualization' with what developmental psychologists have called 'individuation': the growth and strengthening of a person's sense of self. We do not claim that individualization, as we define it here, necessarily contributes to individuation, nor even that individualization is a good thing in any respect. We simply want to describe and understand what has happened to women's lives, by comparing today's lives with earlier women's lives. Then we can see better what women have gained and lost.

Second, we shall investigate the relationship between 'individualization' and 'equality'. We have already indicated that we see little evidence that male and female lives are converging, so they are not likely to become equal by becoming the same. Will individualization make them different (and separate) but equal? That is a harder question to answer, but we will try to answer it nonetheless.

We do not assume that individualization either ensures or rules out gender equality. In fact, gender inequality seems to be a social or cultural universal: it appears in all societies of any size and complexity beyond the simplest hunter-gatherers. Moreover, we see no simple progress towards gender equalization in our society. If anything, the signs indicate that the Canadian state is retreating on this issue. So long as this gender inequality exists to a marked degree, women will enjoy a wider choice of lives simply because what they give up is worth little—certainly less than what a man would have to give up to get a change of similar magnitude. Women float between the domestic and paid economies because neither option is overwhelmingly attractive. Given an opportunity to choose among equally limited or undesirable alternatives, they move about more frequently to meet more idiosyncratic needs, respond to new opportunities, and solve new problems resulting from large-scale social change.

Our book focusses on changes in the realm of work: specifically, on changes in the pattern of women's work. However, the individualization we are discussing in relation to work is occurring in other domains—marriage, parenthood, recreation—as well. In fact, the individualization of work both influences and is influenced by individualization in the other domains. We often refer to the connection between changing patterns of marriage and child-bearing, and their influence on female work. Ultimately, the history of individualization is the story of an unfolding relationship between family life and the economy.

This story has obvious significance for Canadian public policy. Women's lives—whether as workers, mothers, wives, sisters, or friends—are the locus of enormous changes for a great many Canadians. Their changing marriage and fertility patterns have important economic implications—for education and labour-force participation, to name only two areas. The converse is also true: changes in education and labour-force participation influence marriage and child-bearing plans. These interacting changes affect birth rates and population growth, the age structure and availability of young workers, internal migration, saving and spending, and the future of the environment—issues that are crucial to debates about, say, the need for increased immigration, or for affirmative action for women. Clearly, policy-makers in these areas need to understand what is going on.

CONCLUDING REMARKS

In the first chapter, we showed how dramatically women's personal lives have changed in response to easier divorce, better contraception, and more educational and occupational opportunities. The result was a level of unpredictability that showed up in individual women's lives—the lives of GAIL, ANNA, and ROSA, for example—and also made women's lives quite unlike each other's. But this increase in complexity and unpredictability was necessarily related to changes in the workplace, as both cause and consequence. It is in the workplace, where we have the best data measuring changes in women's adult lives, that we can best see this individualization playing itself out. New demands for female labour, combined with new motives for supplying it, produced a new kind of female life pattern: individualization.

When we read the survey evidence, three major themes seem to recur: the low level of jobs women typically hold; the prevalence of part-time work for women; and the incidence of pauperization, especially among female single parents. The data argue, uniformly, that women pay the price of bringing up the next generation.

To be sure, 'individualization' also means an increase in variety, fluidity, and idiosyncrasy, with which comes the appearance—if not always the reality—of choice. It means less predictable, less similar lives—a growing gap between the lives of women and their female friends. It means a discontinuity between generations of women—between women and their mothers. It means a growing dissimilarity between the lives of women and men—between women and their husbands.

When gaps like these open up, certain consequences are inevitable. One is *confusion*: People will ask: 'Where is this process heading? Is it good or bad? If bad, can we stop it? How? Why am I getting this life, and not the one I had planned?' Another consequence is *anomie*, or normlessness: 'What are the rules of living in this new order? Are there to be new ideas of good and bad, right and wrong? How should I plan my own life, and help my daughter to plan hers?' A third is *disorganization*: 'How can people organize a happy, comfortable family life under these circumstances? How can we balance the demands of work, parenthood and marriage? Is there any possibility of planning for the future?'

Today, ever-married women have more years in which to work for pay. They are better educated than previous generations, and some of them have jobs that offer non-monetary satisfaction. The increasing demand for clerical, sales, and service workers has come at a time when, in many cases, the single household income is no longer sufficient to support the lifestyle we now regard as adequate. In some cases, earning a wage may give women some clout in household decision-making. In others, earning plays another role: women who are divorced or separated are largely responsible for the care of children, and have no alternative but to work for pay. This last group may be duplicating the experience of black American women that Daniel Moynihan (1965) described two decades ago; we do not know if Canadian children will suffer the same consequences that Moynihan found in those families.

In the chapters that follow, we examine in detail the evidence of individualization as we have outlined it above. First, we look at data on women's work lives from a variety of Western industrial capitalist societies. We find there are variations within the general patterns, and these raise some interesting and important questions. Then we look very closely at the evidence of individualization within Canadian society. (We discuss the methods of research and types of data in the appendix.)

In the last section of the book we consider the implications of the individualization process. What impact is it likely to have on women's lives by the year 2025? How will it affect Canada's supply of labour? In the book's final chapter, we ask whether or not the patterns of individualization we have studied reflect any of the many versions of 'equality' that are so extensively discussed in the feminist and public-policy literature.

Notes

[1]To some degree, the growth of idiosyncrasy is merely the product of continued, year-by-year fluidity. Consider the arithmetic of the matter. In any given year—say, when she is 25—a woman may occupy any one of four statuses (domestic work, part-time *or* full-time paid work outside the home, or full-time education). And let us assume that what this woman is doing in a given year does not necessarily preclude her doing something else the following year. If, each year between the ages 25 and 64, this woman randomly chooses among the four statuses anew—if in effect, she picks her year's activity out of a hat—how many different sequences can result? The answer is $.4^{40}$, and runs to 24 zeroes—clearly more possible lives than there are women in the world (let alone Canada).

[2]We say this while recognizing the importance of Hogan's (1981) findings. They show that many American men are deviating from the traditional sequence of completing education, getting married, and entering full-time work. Still, men's lives typically lack fluidity and idiosyncrasy, as we have defined these concepts here. They even lack variety. Men occupy a wide variety of full-time paid work roles, but they are rarely found in unpaid or part-time work. They rarely choose part-time work and choose housework even less often than that. Still, almost exclusively, men are lifelong, full-time paid workers.

4

Cross-National Evidence
of Individualization

In this chapter we will show that there are distinct similarities among Western industrial countries in the changes affecting adult women's lives. In all of these countries, women's lives show more variety in statuses, more fluidity among statuses, and more individual variation, or idiosyncrasy, than in the past.

For example, the 'kiddy-dip' in labour-force participation—the result of child-rearing—is found in all these societies. Rates of divorce and remarriage have increased in all of them. In all cases, women earn about two-thirds of the wages of men, and their adult lives reflect their economic vulnerability. Age at marriage is increasing in all these societies; and, to a large degree, care of the old remains a responsibility of women.

But despite these similarities, there are differences among the countries we have studied. For example, even the shape of the 'kiddy-dip' varies from one country to another. Such variations show the effects of two major differences among countries. These *differences* are the result of (a) the state of the national economy, and the types of jobs available, and (b) the taxation and social-security regime that exists in each country. This chapter illustrates both the similarities and the differences with data from several industrial countries.

Nevertheless, our analysis puts particular emphasis on Sweden and Great Britain, for several reasons. First, both countries have excellent statistical agencies for collecting labour-force and demographic data: we can feel confidence in what these data tell us. Second, both Sweden and Great Britain have a lot in common with Canada: all three are highly industrialized, 'modern' mixed economies in the northern hemisphere. Culturally and climatically, as well as economically, the three countries have a great deal in common.

But there the similarity ends. Sweden has a small, homogeneous population in a country with a strong economy and very progressive social-welfare arrangements. Great Britain, on the other hand, has a large, heterogeneous population and is economically in decline. Since the late 1970s the British government has been systematically dismantling its social-welfare system. Thus comparison of Sweden and Great Britain permits us to see the effects of economic prosperity and progressive social planning on women's lives. The variations represented by the other countries we discuss—France, West Germany, Japan, and the United States—illustrate the effects on women's lives of relatively high levels of prosperity (compared to Britain) and intermediate (and variable) levels of social planning.

After the nation-by-nation survey, we make more explicit cross-national comparisons. The chapter ends with some conclusions about the importance of social planning.

SWEDEN

Changes in the Swedish family

In Sweden, as in Canada, recent generations of women have borne fewer children than earlier ones. In fact, Sweden displays one of the longest fertility declines on record. For example, Swedish women born in 1945-46 bore 1.9 children on average, compared to 2.1 children for women born 1930-31 and 2.5 for women born 1890-91. In addition, the average age of first-time mothers has increased from 24.4 years in 1974 to 26.0 years in 1980, a tendency that compresses the period of child-bearing. Much of the recent fertility decline is caused by a drop in third births since the middle of the 1960s (Hoem and Hoem, 1987: 3).

The Swedish divorce rate has been notoriously high, but it is currently levelling off and may go into a decline. This must be understood in the context of a very high incidence of non-marital consensual unions and dissolutions, which do not enter official statistics of divorce (Hoem and Hoem, 1988). Swedish consensual unions have much higher dissolution risks than formal marriages. Ideational changes are important here: 'More than before, it becomes mainstream behavior to assert one's independence and break up from a relationship when its future seems too bleak' (Hoem and Hoem, 1988).

At the time of writing, over 80 per cent of women with children are counted as being in the Swedish labour force. Even though some of them are on maternity leave, the proportion of mothers who work for pay is certainly above 50 per cent. This reflects

> changes in women's roles and personal values, changes which have had a profound impact on the situation of families and have led to the emergence of a two-child norm . . . while factors like [economic influences and education] may have been largely relegated to determinants of the TIMING of the births in a woman's life. (Hoem and Hoem, 1987: 4; emphasis in original)

As recently as the 1950s, never-married women made up the majority of the female labour force, and it was not until 1965 that the proportion of married women exceeded 50 per cent (Sundstrom, 1987: 20).

The role of social and fiscal policy

Sweden, with high rates of female participation in the work force, is often regarded as one possible model of 'modern' social and economic organization. The 1970s saw the introduction of social policies intended to encourage women to enter the paid work force and stay there (Sundstrom, 1987:23-6). There has been little concern for promotions or occupational segregation by sex; rather, the objective is to produce a flexible labour market for capital and industrial expansion (Ruggie, 1984). Such problems with the Swedish approach have been pointed out by Erneling (1987). Nevertheless, Swedish part-timers receive the same hourly wages as full-time workers, as well as proportional non-wage benefits.

The best-known Swedish policy is the parental leave system, by which one parent may have twelve months' leave at any time before the child is four years old, 90 per cent of the pre-tax income being replaced for nine of the twelve months. (In Canada, since 1971 the Unemployment Insurance system pays 60 per cent of insurable earnings for 15 weeks.) Since entitlement depends on the parent's having been continuously employed for 180 days before taking the leave, the scheme encourages a continuous work history. Furthermore, the person taking the leave is classified as being employed thoughout its duration—a definition that makes cross-national comparisons difficult.

Another example is the size of central government subsidies for day-care: in 1985, 45 per cent of all pre-school children were in public child-care facilities. Another, more subtle factor is the taxation system. In 1971, the system of joint taxation of married couples was replaced by separate taxation. Given the steeply progressive graduation of tax rates, this change so increased the profitability of married women's paid work that an 'unfairness' issue arose. After taxes, part-time workers (chiefly female) were receiving higher hourly rates than full-time workers! (Sundstrom 1987).

Both West Germany and Sweden have child allowances. The German government permits a tax deduction for each dependent child, but the Swedish government does not. Yet, unlike West Germany, Sweden has been able to encourage both child-bearing *and* the labour-force participation of mothers of young children (Gustafsson, 1985)

Movement in and out of the labour force

Swedish women, with traditionally higher rates of labour-force participation than American women, have tended to work slightly fewer hours and are much more likely to work part-time on a continuous basis. American women are more likely to work continuously on a full-time basis, or to interrupt full-time work, than to take part-time work (Sundstrom, 1987: 113).

In Sweden, part-time work increased dramatically after 1970. Fully one-quarter of Swedish women 16 to 64 years old remained outside the labour force in 1970-72, but only one in seven remained so in 1984-85. By contrast, only 12 per cent of women 16 to 64 were continuously in part-time work in 1970-72, and this share had doubled to 24 per cent in 1984-85. The percentage of women continuously in part-time work peaked at 26 per cent in 1982-84 (Sundstrom, 1987).

The subsequent decline in continuous part-time work may have resulted from a 1982 cut in tax rates. The tax cut made it more profitable for women to work longer hours, and this is what they did. The share of employed women who worked full-time increased, and those working part-time worked more hours.

In Sweden the supply of female part-time labour is elastic. But other countries, without Sweden's experience of full employment, have passed through a very difficult period of economic readjustment. Part-time jobs created in times of high unemployment are not the same as part-time jobs created in times of low unemployment, or high labour demand. Likewise, women seeking paid work in a depressed economy are in a very different situation from women seeking work in a period of full employment.

THE FEDERAL REPUBLIC OF GERMANY

West Germany has an even lower fertility rate than Sweden, and it may actually be discouraging female labour-force participation. As noted, the Swedish system taxes all individuals separately. Under the German tax system, however, the same tax rate that applies to a single person will apply to the total income of a married couple. Given a progressive tax structure, this system discourages families from earning two incomes.

On the other hand, maternity protection is compulsory in Germany. A voluntary agreement between employer and employee is also possible, providing maternity leave for four months. The German *employer* pays a significant part of the cost of both schemes. By contrast, in Sweden income provided during a parental leave is financed through health insurance, like any sickness compensation.

Swedish feminists fought to get the latter plan, and legislators in West Germany debated a similar extended maternity leave in 1984-85 under the label of a 'guaranteed job'. However, politicians, both male and female, opposed the plan, fearing that it would discourage employers from hiring women. In the US, the National Organization for Women (NOW) has opposed the same plan for similar reasons.

Though traditionally free, in Germany day-care was only open for a few hours each day. This Kindergarten system has expanded its service and charges fees that are proportional to a parent's income. By contrast, child-care in Sweden expanded earlier—very rapidly after 1965 and through the 1970s. Today one-third of all Swedish pre-schoolers are looked after in child-care centres, or by day-care mothers (Gustafsson, 1985). Child-care is publicly subsidized and effectively free to all. Where older children are concerned, the German mother is expected to be home to serve lunch, whereas in Sweden, all children receive a free school lunch. The Swedish school day finishes at 2:00 for younger children and between 3:00 and 4:00 for older ones.

This extended comparison shows that Sweden and Germany differ in many important ways. One could reasonably debate which differences are most important, or even best, from the point of view of women's employment. Undoubtedly, the method of financing the parental leave is crucial: it poses a significant cost to the employer in Germany, but not in Sweden (Gustaffson, 1985).

It is clear from this comparison that two neighbouring, highly industrialized European countries can deal quite differently with the same problem.

JAPAN

Japan differs culturally in a great many ways from Sweden and Germany, but in one respect it is similar. Like the Swedish and to some degree the West German, the Japanese culture is oriented to collective planning: it restricts women's lives, but also supports them. Social and economic planning is much more a part of everyday life and experience than it is in North America or, increasingly, in England. But, unlike Sweden's, Japan's culture restricts women today almost as it might have done a generation ago.

About one Japanese woman in three receives a post-secondary education, nearly the same as for men. But two-thirds of the female post-secondary students get their education at junior colleges, which men almost never attend. Employers rarely consider these two-year college programs equal to a university education. Women who do go to university tend to enter quite different courses from men. Only 20 per cent, compared with 70 per cent of the men, enrol in courses that lead to good jobs: namely, courses in law, economics, or the applied sciences.

The employment pattern of the Japanese female work-force shows the industrial world's deepest 'kiddy-dip'. Up until marriage, nearly three-quarters of Japanese women aged 20 to 24 are employed, with most of the rest engaged in some form of higher education. Most women marry between the ages of 24 and 27, and fewer than 2 per cent remain unmarried.

Like her sisters in the West, a Japanese mother typically has two children today. Because of reduced fertility, the period between the birth of the first child and full-time school attendance by the last has been compressed to under ten years. Since mothers tend to withdraw from the work-force during those years, only about half of all the Japanese women aged 25 to 35 work for pay. Japan's roughly 20,000 day-care centres look after two million children. They are generally open from nine until five, which does not offer much help to anyone with a serious job.

An Equal Employment Opportunities Law passed in 1985 supports the rights of working women. This law does not force employers to guarantee women equal treatment; it merely commits them to 'strive towards' it. Though it prohibits various forms of discrimination, the law does not penalize violators (*Economist*, May 1988: 22).

Clearly, Japanese women are quite a distance from the kind of adult living pattern observable in Western Europe and North America. But the groundwork for social planning is there, supported by a strong economic base.

FRANCE

In France, the average age at female first marriage rose from its lowest ever in 1975 to 24.5 years by 1985. As in Sweden, rates of cohabitation without marriage have increased among both younger and older age groups. By 1985, more than one woman in seven between 25 and 29 years of age lived in such a union. Cohabitation rates are particularly high in large cities. Divorce legislation was liberalized only in 1975, so it is too soon to know how divorce rates are likely to stabilize. If current trends continue, analysts expect one in five marriages contracted in the 1970s to dissolve (*Données sociales*, 1987: 487, 504, 523).

Many elementary school-age children in France have no compulsory classes on one weekday—usually Wednesday—and make up the lost school time on Saturday mornings. It is accepted that working mothers will often need to take Wednesdays off to tend their children, although local government (the *mairie*) typically provides children with Wednesday activities at a low cost to parents. As a result, many French children gain some experience of organized day-care (LePrince, 1987: 511). There are strong expectations that grandparents will babysit.

In France, the labour-force activity rate among women aged 15 to 74 rose from 38 per cent in 1954 to 44 per cent in 1987. Over this period, women with children were particularly likely to increase their labour-force activity, and by 1987 married women without children were about as likely to work for pay as single women. Much of the increase since 1982 has been due to the rapid growth in number of part-time and limited-contract jobs, and other marginal forms of attachment to the labour force (Belloc, 1987: 112).

Limited contract work for a period of a few months is now common in France. During a period of high general unemployment that started in 1982, people in 'regular' part-time work—15 to 29 hours per week, and not looking for other work—made up the largest of the 'marginal' categories, and between 1982 and 1987 this category grew only slightly (Thélot, 1987). On the other hand, the categories of 'fixed contract' and 'trainee' grew dramatically over the same period.

The first of these growing categories is particularly likely to include women who are increasing their participation in the work force. More and more, French women undertake marginal paid jobs rather than remain entirely in domestic labour or in informal paid labour, as their mothers might have done. Materially speaking, the increased availability of such marginal work may not be good for women: they would do better with permanent jobs. However, the fact that women undertake these marginal paid jobs testifies to an increase in 'variety'.

THE UNITED STATES

A recent study, based on fifteen years of survey data from the National Opinion Research Centre, concludes that marriage in the United States is a declining and weakened institution. The data show that marriage is declining because women feel they are getting less out of the arrangement than they once did (Glenn, 1987: 352).

In its place, recent demographic trends in the US have given women 'new lifestyles'. For various reasons, the proportions of single-person households, one-parent families, and unmarried couples have all increased dramatically. As well, Americans seem to have returned to a late-nineteenth-century age of first marriage. By 1983, the median marriage age for women had risen to 22.8 years from its low point of 20.1 years in 1956—even higher than its previous high of 22.0 years (on average) in 1890 (Bianchi and Spain, 1986: 11). More marked still is the increasing tendency of young women to remain single. For example, 25 per cent of the women 25 to 29 years old were still unmarried in 1983, compared to 20 per cent in 1979, 11 per cent in 1970, and 9 per cent in 1960. The 20 to 24 age group showed a similar pattern—56 per cent of such women had remained single in 1983 compared to 32 per cent in 1953. This shift is mainly due to the delay of marriage. The incidence of 'lifetime singlehood' is still very low, around 9 per cent according to Bianchi and Spain (1986: 14). The US trend towards delayed marriage is also found in Canada, France, and

delayed marriage   C, US, UK

Great Britain, all of which had around 55 per cent of their 20 to 24 year old women in the never-married state in 1980-83.

As in other countries, divorce rates in the US have risen since the 1960s. The US has historically had the highest divorce rate of any industrialized nation, and the percentage of first marriages ending in divorce has increased from 13 per cent for women born in 1900-1904 to 38 per cent for women born in 1945-49. In similar fashion, the percentage of second marriages ending in divorce is 44 per cent for women born in 1945-49 (Kitagawa, 1981: 6). As a result, over half of the American marriages beginning in the 1970s will likely end in divorce (Bianchi and Spain, 1986: 23-4). The risk of divorce drops very slowly with duration of marriage, and remains at 30 per cent or more throughout the first ten years of marriage, according to these analyses. We need not emphasize the 'negative' aspect of changes in these indicators of family disruption and dissolution; percentage increases can seem desceptively large if they arise from low values in earlier years. But the family is changing in a way that allows, even forces, more women to organize their lives in non-traditional ways.

Bianchi and Spain remark that

> working for pay, and working more continuously throughout life . . . seems economically rational in a world in which half of women who marry eventually divorce and the other half tend to outlive their husbands. Greater attachment to work provides women with more independence and marital choice—they can delay marriage or leave an unhappy marriage more easily . . . women's work motivations have become similar to those of men. (1986: 168)

They also point to the slow wage growth of US males over the 1970s and 1980s (1986: 167-8)—a point confirmed by Martin Dooley's analysis of trends in earnings of Canadian families (1989). Simply put, wives' earnings were needed in order to maintain real incomes, or to increase them in line with increasing material expectations. In the US as in Canada, the largest increase in labour-force participation rates has been among married women with children—and especially among the more highly educated women of this kind (Bianchi and Spain: 167, citing Michael, 1985). Delayed marriage and child-bearing are associated with smaller completed family size.

In the United States, as in Canada, this century has seen strong trends to urbanization and to the growth of demand for teachers and office workers. Nevertheless, traditional attitudes towards the family came back in bad economic times. Patricia Huckle (1982) shows how the 1930s Depression in the US led to the passing of legislation requiring school boards to first lay off married women with working husbands. The Second World War brought married women into the paid work-force and involved the federal government in the provision of day-care. The Lanham Act of June 1942 was interpreted to consider child-care centres in war-impacted areas as public works and therefore eligible for federal funding and matching state grants (Kerr, 1973: 163). Federal funding was removed after the war, at the end of February 1946, leaving state and city administrations to deal with the programs. Politicians such as New York's Mayor LaGuardia and Governor Dewey had negative attitudes to working mothers, and placed day-care funds under the administration of the departments of Public Welfare. Those protesting day-care cuts were described as communists (Kerr, 1973: 169). As Kerr notes:

> Central to the return to normalcy was propaganda encouraging mothers to stay home. Magazine articles extolled the virtues of motherhood and popularized research done in the 1940s that described the damage to children such as orphans who had been institutionalized. No attempt was made to distinguish between such experiences and group care for children who stayed with their families. The little federal day-care money that was left was channeled through the welfare system for programmes that served, inadequately the very poor . . . Fear of communism touched all areas of life and . . . the child-care centre was regarded in some parts as a Russian invention. (1973: 166)

Since that time, public funding of day-care in the US has been much studied and debated but has failed to gain the political support necessary for a significant program to be implemented. A typical story is President Nixon's veto of the Comprehensive Child Development Act in 1971, on the grounds of the undesirability of 'communal approaches to child rearing', which work 'against the family-centred approach' (quoted in Powell, 1987: 116).

At the end of the 1980s, American politicians are under pressure to do something about access to day-care. Liberal Democrats argue for subsidy and regulation and propose child-care subsidies tied to federal standards and targeted to poor families and to the Head Start program. Conservatives prefer to give tax credits to the poorest families with children and leave provision of day-care services to a minimally regulated market.

In a comprehensive study of the baby-boom generation in the US, Russell (1987) states bluntly that women work today because they like it. Moreover:

> Women today are creating their own work traditions and they are changing men as they do it. Most baby-boom men are married to working wives, and most working wives work full-time. The lives of baby-boom women and men are increasingly alike. Both go to work in the morning; both return home at the end of the day (Russell, 1987: 60).

There is some truth in these assertions, but Russell's claim of gender convergence is undermined by evidence she presents of greater (and growing) female fluidity:

> Overall, American men today have been working at their current jobs a median of four years, down from 5.7 years in 1963 . . . Women have been at their current jobs a median of only 1.5 years, down from three years in 1963 . . . Men aged 35-44 have been at the same job a median of 6.6 years, down from 7.6 years in 1963 . . . Women aged 35-44 have been at the same job a median of 3.5 years (1987: 65).

It would therefore be unwise to conclude that women's lives are becoming like men's (though this is true for their age at first marriage [Bianchi and Spain, 1986: 11]). Today, women combine paid work and child-bearing more variably than ever before. In what used to be called the 'conventional pattern', a woman leaves the labour force at the time of her marriage or the birth of her first child, and never returns. In the 'interrupted pattern', she returns to the work force after bearing her last child. In the 'double-track pattern', she returns to the labour force before the last child is born. It is this last pattern, 'the double-track', that has become much more common in the US and elsewhere.

Changes in wives' freedom to make decisions are influenced by changing contributions to family income. In 1940, about 84 per cent of white married women and 69 per cent of non-white married women contributed nothing to the average American family's cash income. By 1980, the proportion of non-contributing wives had fallen to 31 per cent among whites and 27 per cent among non-whites (Sorenson and McLanahan, 1985). Moreover, in 1960 only one wife in ten earned as much income as her spouse. By 1980, one in four non-white women and more than one in six white women were doing so—a change that suggests the potential for greater 'economic power sharing' in the American family.

During the 1960s, working wives averaged about 65 hours a week of paid work and domestic labour combined, but their husbands did only 57 hours per week. The 1970s showed more similarity of husbands' and wives' total work time, but husbands still performed only one-sixth the hours of housework that their wives did. It is the highly educated working wives who are most likely to have husbands who participate in housework. However, husbands with high incomes do hardly any of the household chores. In one researcher's graphic phrase, husbands can 'take work home', while wives can only 'take their home to work' (Bianchi and Spain, 1986: 233).

Once again, a woman's educational level is the key to her independence. Not only can a women with educational qualifications command a higher salary and a job with career prospects; she brings these benefits to her partner as a modern equivalent of the old-fashioned dowry—one whose expected value over her working lifetime is the equivalent of a small fortune. Furthermore, her wage-rate may very well be close to that of her partner, in which case she will have more bargaining power over major purchases and who does the housework and child-care. If the relationship must be dissolved, she can support herself financially. Her education will also give her the sophistication to pursue the ex-partner through the courts for any child-support payments due.

Most recent data point in the same direction: American wives are less economically dependent on their husbands than they were forty or even twenty years ago. What has typically determined the spousal difference in economic contributions to the household is a combination of hours worked and hourly rate of pay. Historically, wives have worked fewer hours than husbands outside the home, at lower rates of pay. To the extent that women approach pay equity with men and work longer hours outside the home, their power in the household will continue to rise.

GREAT BRITAIN

[In Britain] marriage and childbearing are being increasingly postponed and perhaps foregone. The proportion of births born outside marriage has increased dramatically . . . to over 20 per cent in 1986. Childlessness is expected to become more common. Cohabitation has emerged as a widespread form of pre-marital living arrangement and is virtually the norm between marriages. Consensual unions with children may be on the increase. First marriage rates have declined dramatically, and divorce rates have increased. (Kiernan, 1988: 307)

Everything in this description recalls the Swedish pattern examined above. Even so, Britain has not only the highest divorce rate, but also the highest marriage rate in the EEC (*Social Trends*, 1989: 41).

British figures show that if 1979-80 fertility and divorce rates persisted, one child in five would witness his or her parents' divorce before the age of 16. By 1984, 13 per cent of British families with dependent children were one-parent families, most of them female-headed and the result of separation or divorce.

More than half of all the one-parent families rely on state benefits ('welfare') as their major source of income. In this respect, however, British women are somewhat different from their counterparts in other industrial countries. Only half of lone mothers in Britain worked for pay in 1979, compared to 86 per cent in Sweden, 68 per cent in the US, 59 per cent in West Germany, and 78 per cent in France (Kiernan, 1988).

These national differences probably reflect differences in the availability of day-care services. Good day-care at a reasonable price is particularly rare in Britain. Perhaps for this reason, British women heading one-parent families soon enter one form or another of consensual union.

One British study showed that 40 per cent of women who divorced during 1979-80 had remarried within two years. 'Living with a partner, especially an employed partner is the major route out of poverty for lone mothers' (Kiernan, 1988: 307). Even so, the shortage of day-care means that most British women will wait until their youngest child is five years old before re-entering the paid work force.

In Britain, children's exposure to day-care has been declining. The proportion of children under three years old who are cared for in public day nurseries has dropped from 17 per cent in 1948 (a reflection of war mobilization) to less than one per cent in 1986. Local authorities have no statutory duty to provide day-care places, so day-care is a convenient target for spending cuts. Only about 100 companies in Britain provide nursery care. The British system treats child-care as a private responsibility, and an expense that is not even tax deductible.

Despite these difficulties, nearly half of all British mothers with children under five are employed at least part of the time outside the home. They manage this by working evening shifts and relying on husbands, relatives, and paid babysitters for child-care. This may explain why part-time work attracts British women far more than it does French women.

British women tend to *seek* part-time work. Working mothers take it regardless of their social class. French women, by contrast, tend to accept it only if no full-time work is offered (Gregory, 1987). Working part-time in France is mostly involuntary; it is more often offered by employers than sought by employees; and the lower down the class ladder a French woman is, the more likely she is to accept the offer.

The British case offers a lesson in women's responses to adversity. The labour-force participation of women in their thirties and forties has risen steeply since 1960. Moreover, successive generations of women aged 30 and over have shown higher participation rates at a given age than preceding ones. The largest increase in female participation rates has occurred among older women, largely in part-time work (Martin and Roberts, 1984).

Even among women whose youngest child was between 5 and 10 years old, the percentage working for pay rose from 40 to 63 per cent between 1954 and 1979. This increase was composed of a large growth in part-time and a small decline in full-time employment.

British women are also re-entering the labour force earlier after child-bearing. Only 13 per cent of the women who bore a child in 1950-54 returned to the work force within one year; by 1975-79, this percentage had doubled. Moreover, with each passing generation the number of years elapsing before a first return to work after childbirth has steadily declined, from a median of 9.7 years for women bearing a child in 1950-54 to 3.7 years for women bearing a child in 1975-79 (Martin and Roberts, 1984).

Comparatively speaking, older generations of British and US women spent averages of 8.5 years and 7.7 years, respectively, between first birth and first return to work. Younger generations have spent considerably less time out of the labour force, 4.3 years and 1.6 years for the British and American women respectively. Within these groups, strong statistical trends confirm that in both countries women have been returning to work earlier after bearing children (Dex and Shaw, 1986).

As a result, younger generations of women spend a larger part of their adult lives working for pay. For example, assuming that 1980 employment rates prevail, by age 60 British women who were 20 to 24 in 1980 can expect to spend 67 per cent of their adult lives working for pay. Their mothers' generation, on average aged 55 to 59 in 1980, will have spent only 59 per cent of their lives from 20 to 60 working for pay (Martin and Roberts, 1984: 122).

Comparison of British evidence with data from the United States shows that part-time work is much more common in Britain than in the US. As they aged, British women changed from 58 per cent full-time and 6 per cent part-time in 1968 to 25 per cent full-time and 33 per cent part-time in 1980. Over the same period comparable US women changed from 22 per cent full-time and 17 per cent part-time to 50 per cent full-time and 15 per cent part-time (Dex and Shaw, 1986: 142). In the British case, part-time work grew much more common between 1968 and 1980, while in the US it went unchanged.

There are good reasons for employers to provide part-time work in Britain. Many British part-timers work less than the 16 hours per week that would entitle them to significant job-protection and fringe benefits. British employers enjoy tax advantages if they hire part-timers. As well, low-paying part-time jobs abound in the public sector, particularly in connection with the National Health Service. In the US, comparable workers tend to be provided by companies under contract. These companies hire full-time workers who provide part-time services to a variety of client organizations.

A number of factors that were important in the older generation have apparently become less so for younger women. Older women may have spent time 'saving up' to have children after they were married. Women's attitudes and husband's earnings appear to have less influence on younger than on older women, especially in the US. Maternity leave has also reduced the time spent out of employment before the first return in Britain. Maternity leave take-up in Britain is linked to occupation; for example, semi-skilled factory work appears to offer fewer opportunities for leave. Nonetheless, where women do take maternity leave, it has a major effect on their work experience.

Relatives, particularly husbands, are crucial to the child-care patterns of British women, providing the largest portion of such care. In contrast, American women rely more on formal and paid child-care. This also overlaps with their greater propensity to work full-time, often at higher paid jobs (Dex and Shaw, 1986: 70-1). These trends to a shorter work interruption for child-bearing support our fluidity hypothesis. But one cannot ignore large national differences in the incidence of part-time working and patterns of child-care.

The British Census Longitudinal Study followed up the same people between 1971 and 1981. Our analysis shows that the major change for women was a net shift out of full-time and into part-time employment. By 1981, women in the age range 26 to 59 were distributed nearly equally among work statuses: 30 per cent in full-time employment, 28 per cent in part-time employment, and 37 per cent in domestic labour, as 'housewives', with 5 per cent students or not seeking work.

Of women in full-time employment in 1971, a minority—44 per cent—occupied the same status ten years later. Of the remaining 56 per cent, 18 per cent had moved to part-time work and 32 per cent to the 'housewife' status. Of those employed part-time in 1971, 44 per cent were still (or again) in part-time jobs, while 29 per cent had moved to full-time work and 23 per cent had become 'housewives'. Of those who were housewives in 1971, half were in the same status ten years later, while 15 per cent had moved to full-time employment and 32 per cent to part-time employment. Status retention over a ten-year period is remarkably strong for this group of women.

These status shifts are not necessarily 'one-step' moves. For example, a woman who was employed full-time in both 1971 and 1981 might have occupied one or more other statuses between those years. Nevertheless, these data point in the direction predicted by our theory of individualization: they show both growing variety and considerable fluidity.

Part-time work plays an increasing role in the lives of women, and movement between the statuses of full-time employment, part-time employment, and 'housewife' are considerable. Division of the sample into three age groups, each observed in 1971 and 1981, shows that by 1981, fewer women 35 to 39 were housewives and more held part-time jobs. A similar pattern holds when we compare women aged 45 to 49 in 1971 and 1981. The observed change may be a cohort effect, or reflect the slump in the

British economy that occurred towards the end of the 1970s. In either event, these data show that variety is increasing dramatically among British women.

What are the causes or sources of this growing variety and fluidity? How much is simple job-changing and how much is movement among labour-force statuses? And what causes greater or lesser fluidity in this respect?

Influences on in and out movement

Robert Wright and Andrew Hinde (1989) used British data to examine women's movements between full-time work, part-time work, and being out of the paid labour force. They report that, net of other factors, more recent generations of women have higher rates of leaving full-time employment and lower rates of leaving part-time jobs. Similarly, older women are more likely to leave full-time jobs and less likely to leave part-time ones. On the other hand, women with academic qualifications ('some A-levels') have lower rates of leaving full-time work, but higher rates of leaving part-time jobs. This suggests that older and less educated women are more fluid—or vulnerable?—than younger and more educated ones; and that all women are more fluid than same-aged women were a decade or two ago.

More recent generations also have higher rates of *entering* the labour force on a part-time basis, although membership in a given generation does not seem to influence the rate of transition from non-employment to a full-time job. Similarly, the older a woman is at the time of her transition out of non-employment, the higher her chance of entering part-time work and the lower her chance of entering full-time work. By contrast, highly educated women have lower rates of entering the labour force on a part-time basis, and higher rates of entering it full-time than less educated women.

In general, direct shifts between full-and part-time work are less frequent than direct shifts between paid employment and non-employment. However, more recent generations have lower rates of moving directly from part-time to full-time work, and higher rates of moving from full-time to part-time work, than earlier generations do. Further, the older a woman is at the time of her transition, the lower her likelihood of moving from part-time to full-time and the higher her likelihood of moving from full-time to part-time work. Finally, highly educated women again show the opposite pattern: namely, higher than average rates of moving from part-time to full-time work and lower than average rates of moving from full-time to part-time work.

Other factors also influence the pattern of movement. For example, a higher national unemployment rate generally increases the chance of transitions out of paid employment into non-employment, and decreases that of transitions from non-employment to full-time work. To conclude, the sharp upward trend in part-time labour-force participation in Britain seems due to the actions of older married women and more recent generations of women with lower levels of educational attainment. After leaving the labour force, these women have higher than average rates of re-entering on a part-time basis and lower than average rates of leaving part-time employment. To a smaller degree, they also have higher rates of moving into part-time directly from full-time work and lower rates of moving directly from part-time to full-time (Wright and Hinde, 1989).

Thus, at least in Britain, mature women from more recent generations are behaving in newer and more 'fluid' ways. Part-time work is an important part of this new pattern of fluidity, but it seems to reflect vulnerability to market forces more than it does free choice.

COMPARATIVE DATA ON FEMALE LABOUR-FORCE PARTICIPATION: EVIDENCE FROM THE EUROPEAN COMMUNITY

Throughout Western societies, economic studies 'have consistently underestimated the strength of women's increasing labour force participation' (Townson, 1987). In 1975, one in every two married Canadian women aged 20 to 44 worked for pay, and some observers doubted the figure could go higher. Yet by 1986, the participation rate for this age-group had risen to 70 per cent. Townson remarks that econometric studies seem to ignore the importance of changing attitudes among women, especially their rapidly growing desire for financial independence.

Currently, the participation rate over all age groups for British married women is very similar to the rate for married women in Canada: just over 50 per cent. In the early 1980s, Danish married women showed the highest rate of economic activity in the EEC (64 per cent overall) and Irish married women the lowest rate (17 per cent). France, Great Britain, and Germany were above the European Economic Community (EEC) average, with activity rates for married women of 48 per cent, 47 per cent and 41 per cent respectively. These data show that we cannot ignore the extent and meaning of national variation. But we would be equally wrong to ignore strong cross-national similarities.

For example, labour-force activity rates usually peak among married women in their early twenties and gradually decline thereafter. Profiles of female labour-force participation by age group also typically show a 'kiddy-dip' or 'M'-shaped pattern because most mothers interrupt their working careers in order to care for their children and act as 'housewives'. Our understanding of these patterns remains incomplete, because they reflect the mixed effects of age, period, and cohort on work behaviour. However, profiles for different countries at the same time point, and for the same country at various time points will typically show some variation of the standard 'kiddy-dip'.

British women, for example, offer an interesting variation. During their child-rearing years, their labour-force participation falls into a 'trough' that is deeper and longer lasting than one finds in any other OECD country except Japan (Delacourt and Zighera, 1988). The extremity of this change in behaviour with the onset of parenthood must reflect insufficient day-care facilities; but this cannot be the whole explanation.

Another pattern that seems to hold up across nations is the difference in activity rates of married, widowed, and divorced women. EEC countries' national labour-force surveys are combined and harmonized at the Statistical Office of the European Community (EUROSTAT) to show labour-force activity rates by marital status, sex, age, and country. Once again, cross-national differences are large. Take the 1985 activity rates of married women between 25 and 49 years old: over ten EEC countries, the average activity rate is 54 per cent. The range of variation around this mean is quite wide. Denmark is highest with an activity rate of 86 per cent, followed by France, then the United Kingdom, Belgium, Germany, Italy, Greece, the Netherlands, and Luxembourg. Ireland has the lowest rate, at 29 per cent.

In comparison, widowed or divorced women aged 25 to 49 have consistently higher economic-activity rates, averaging 75 per cent in the ten EEC nations. Here the ten countries vary much as they did when we considered married women, only the rates are about 20 per cent higher than those for married women in the same country and age-group. Exceptions are Denmark (where participation rates could hardly go much higher than current married women's rates) and the United Kingdom (where they could go higher, but don't).

More varied labour-force statuses

British censuses give us some historical perspective on the growth of variety in labour-force statuses. They show that whereas 36 per cent of British married women were economically active in 1951, in 1981, that was true of 61 per cent; however, the percentage of women in full-time work went practically unchanged. Almost all of the increase was due to a growth of part-time employment, primarily among women who were taking shorter average absences from work after bearing children (Joshi, 1989: 158).

We have already noted that, in many ways, Britain is unique where the employment of married women is concerned. But it turns out that similar patterns underlie the growth of variety in other industrial countries. For this reason we need to explore the dynamics of part-time work, in order to understand recent changes in adult women's lives.

PART-TIME WORK

Definitions of part-time work vary greatly between countries, a fact that in itself suggests the individualization of work patterns. Further, the number of hours per week that counts as 'full-time' work has been decreasing in most OECD countries. Perhaps the only thing one can say with certainty about part-time work is that it comprises less than the customary number of hours (per week or per month) in the employment unit.

Statistics Canada now defines part-time work as paid employment of less than 30 hours a week. Part-time work tends to be part-year work.[1]

The proportion of women working part-time has been rising in many European countries, but not in the United States, according to the OECD Employment Outlook of 1988. Gower (1988a) agrees with the conclusion that American part-time rates are low. He shows that in 1980, one-half of Canadian women 16 to 19 years old (who were heads of households or spouses thereof) worked less than 35 hours a week (the US part-time cut-off), compared to 60 per cent of comparable US women; by 1987, the Canadian rate had climbed to 70 per cent, compared to 67 per cent south of the border. Overall, part-time employment was more common among employed Canadian women than among their American sisters—in 1987, about one Canadian woman in three compared to one American woman in four in part-time work.

Because definitions vary, it may be desirable to subdivide the concept of part-time work into 'regular part-time work' and 'irregular part-time work'. In a German study, nearly one-third of employees who were not working full-time described their jobs as 'marginal' or 'irregular' part-time jobs (Büchtemann, 1987). The remaining two-thirds had 'regular' part-time jobs, usually involving more than 20 hours of paid work a week. Some of the 'marginal' part-timers also worked more than 20 hours a week, but more than half worked less than 15, and some had no normal working hours at all. These numbers suggest a very substantial involvement of German women in marginal work.

Moreover, 'fluidity' is also increasing. 'Marginal' workers, who tend to work less than 20 hours a week, are an increasing portion of the German female work force. Data from Büchtemann's study show that 8 per cent of women in regular part-time employment in 1985 had been in full-time employment in 1984; 69 per cent had previously been in the same kind of employment status; 14 per cent had been in marginal part-time employment; and 9 per cent had not been employed at all. To summarize, between 1984 and 1985 one woman in three had changed her employment status—a high degree of fluidity, in our estimation.

Many industrial countries have seen part-time employment increase as a percentage of total employment. Over the 1970s, part-time work increased dramatically in Sweden, from under 20 to 25 per cent, and substantially in Canada, Japan, France, Germany, and Belgium. Great Britain and the United States kept the part-time share roughly constant, at about 15 per cent (to 1981).

These trends continued during the 1980s. The recession of 1981-83 taught many managers the financial benefits of having a work force that was easy to lay off in bad times. Many jobs that had been full-time were contracted out, redefined as short-term contracts, or made part-time work. By 1987 the share of part-time jobs had increased to around 20 per cent in Japan, the United States, Belgium, and France.

In Europe at least, governments saw some of their economic problems as being due to an inflexibility of labour that they called

'Eurosclerosis'. Too many workers had rights in their jobs—effectively, they had job tenure, like civil servants and university professors. To change this, governments made it legally possible for employers to hire workers on limited contracts that would carry no obligations for continuing employment—an Americanization of the labour market and of workers' rights (Vogelheim, 1982: 115). The intention of this may have been to loosen up the labour market and, indirectly, to reduce the incidence of youth employment. However, the actual result was to encourage the hiring of women in low-wage jobs (Büchtemann, 1987).

Generally, countries with high levels of female labour-force participation also have a high incidence of part-time work, but there are exceptions. One is Finland, where women occupy 48.3 per cent of all jobs, but the incidence of part-time work is comparatively low. On the other hand, the Netherlands, with very high unemployment, has a comparatively low female labour-force participation rate, but a high rate of part-time work (OECD, 1985). This confusing complexity tells us that, within each country, social, economic, political, and cultural factors are mixing in often quite distinct ways. We can never safely ignore the national context within which global trends like individualization are played out.

Countries as contexts

Data from the Statistical Office of the European Community (EUROSTAT) show the full extent of part-time work in six of the larger EEC countries. In the mid-1980s, fewer than one in seven workers (male and female, of all ages) worked part-time. However, more than one in every three married women aged 25 to 49 did so. The incidence of part-time work increases in the 50-64 age-group, when 42 per cent of married women, 23 per cent of single women, and even 3 per cent of men are working part-time.

Analyses by Delacourt and Zighera (1988) show particularly low rates of part-time work in Italy, Ireland, Luxembourg, and Greece, and much higher rates in the other six countries. Some interesting anomalies emerge from such comparisons across nations. For example, the United Kingdom and the Netherlands have very different overall participation rates by women, the United Kingdom's rate being higher. But in both cases, even one child is enough to make the mother likely to drop out of full-time and into part-time paid work. Generally, the presence of children has different effects on female work patterning in different European countries (Delacourt and Zighera, 1988: 17).

CONCLUDING REMARKS

Analyses of recent data from a variety of industrial countries are made more complex by the uniqueness of each country. Persistent high unemployment rates in the 1980s also injected complexity: we run the risk of mistaking correlates of an economic slump for a lasting trend.

Nevertheless, the European and American data tend to support our individualization hypothesis. More recent generations of women are exhibiting more variety, more fluidity, and more idiosyncracy than earlier ones. This seems true of all the countries we examined, and the process is apparently unfolding rapidly. However, whereas in Europe and especially in Great Britain individualization is occurring at lower end of the labour market, in Canada, as we shall see, it is occurring at the higher end, among the most educated women.

The Swedish pattern is a prototype that many Canadians want to follow, and in time all advanced industrial societies may indeed follow it. The Swedish pattern combines high rates of female labour-force participation with a high level of child-care provision. This implies a strong sensitivity to Sweden's interest in present and *future* prosperity. The next generation is not, as in the United States, Great Britain, and (to some degree) Canada, being sacrificed because of high day-care charges, insufficient spaces, and overburdened mothers (Humphreys and Rubery, 1988).

In Sweden we find the usual high divorce rate following liberalization of the divorce laws. Here the state plays a strong role (some would say 'too strong') in people's work lives, combining high taxation, a plan to retrain the able-bodied unemployed, and a pro-natalist policy with inducements for women to have continuous part-time employment. Much day-care is provided and regulated by the state.

In the United States, intermediate between Sweden and Britain in a number of respects, whites show a relatively low incidence of part-time work. Low taxation is combined with a limited role for the state in enforcing anti-discrimination laws (the Civil Rights Act and various Executive Orders) that put gender discrimination into the same category as racial discrimination (Freeman, 1976).

The marketplace provides pay-as-you-go day-care. The American black experience is similar, except for a very high incidence of female-headed households and the double handicap of both racial and gender discrimination against women.

Britain illustrates an extreme version of a social problem: a large proportion of women working part-time to meet their needs for additional income. Apart from legislation on pay equality, the state's role is largely limited to that of employer of low-paid part-time women. There is no state-provided day-care. It will take another decade or two to see the full consequences—social, economic, and cultural—of this neglect of the next generation's needs. But it is already plain that the system does not work in the interest of mothers.

In Britain, as in most of the other countries we have examined, the flight from parenthood continues. The flight should be most extreme in countries, like Britain, that make parenthood (and especially motherhood) most costly. But it is also to be observed in France, Germany, and the rest of the Western world. Everywhere family sizes are falling, facilitating women's labour-force participation and the economic survival of the poor and middle classes.

The next chapter will examine the individualization of women's lives in the Canadian context.

Note

[1] According to Veevers (1986), '42 per cent of women who were working entirely part-time worked the entire year. Nevertheless, the majority of women working entirely part-time were also employed part-year'.

5

Canadian Evidence
of Individualization

In this chapter we look at evidence that in Canada, as elsewhere, variety, fluidity, and idiosyncrasy are increasing in the lives of average women.

These changes must be viewed against the international backdrop sketched in the preceding chapter. As elsewhere, the divorce rate in Canada reached high levels after liberalization of the divorce laws. By comparison with other industrial countries, Canada combines a weak federal government and a highly regionalized economy; this makes consistent social planning more difficult. Despite a high level of taxation and some state-subsidized day-care, child-care expenses are only partly tax-deductible, and this tends to benefit the rich more than the poor. The part-time work force is proportionately higher in Canada than in the United States, but lower than in European countries. Canada, unlike Sweden and like the US, has always recruited any additional labour power it needs by increasing immigration quotas. In these respects, Canadian women find themselves midway between their Swedish and British counterparts.

Demographer Pam Smith (1988) has recently published estimates of working-life tables for Canadian men and women. These cover the period 1921 to 1981 and show how changes in life expectancy combine with increased participation rates. Women's life expectancy at age 15 has increased from 53.4 in 1921 to 65.0 in 1981 and the overall participation rate has risen from 18 to 52 per cent over the same period. Twenty-year-old Canadian women can now expect to have 37 years of working life—only five years less than comparable men. Smith's analysis also shows that by 1981, the working-life expectancy of married women was only three years less than that of single women. As we have said repeatedly, marital status is becoming irrelevant to female work-patterning. Gender, however, remains an issue.

It used to seem 'natural' that some jobs, even whole industries, were almost entirely male or female. Secretaries and nurses were almost always women; truck drivers and mechanics, hardly ever. The sexes differ physically, to be sure; but differences in occupation arose for other reasons.

To some degree, they were the product of traditional gender attitudes and stereotyping of the kind expressed by one of Jones's respondents:

> A woman can't do everything a man does. In the Bible, a man is the one who should be providing for the woman. A woman shouldn't try to do the work a man does, like construction. Rather she should work in something she can do.

But for the most part, the problem was—and is—discrimination pure and simple. As Jones's respondents observed even in 1988:

> Middle-aged women are discriminated against. Employers want nice-looking young women. The middle-aged women have a difficult time competing in the work market;

> There is no equality. Men still have the upper hand in the business world;

> We still have a long way to go, it's a man's world still;

> There is a lot of hidden discrimination. Certain jobs are usually filled by women but they are usually lower-paying;

> The economy is not set up for full employment so that women's needs are often in conflict with men's needs. The support is not there for families to allow women to use their abilities to the fullest;

> Jobs are still stereotyped either consciously or subconsciously, and jobs that women have are generally lower-paid;

> Younger men are given opportunities over the experienced women in my office . . . Somehow the men keep control. Any social activities are arranged with the men in mind.

Until the 1950s, the majority of women working for pay were employed in only a handful of job classes: they were segregated by sex. But since 1951, *all* major industrial job classes in Canada have opened up to female workers. The proportion of women working in four white-collar industries—trade, finance and insurance, services, and public administration and defence— has increased dramatically (Armstrong and Armstrong, 1984). Of course, so has the proportion of male workers in these same industries (cf. Fox and Fox, 1987): both changes reflect a major shift in the organization of the economy. However, sex segregation has — also diminished, with the result that women are doing a wider variety of jobs than ever before.

EMERGING VARIETY

Census data show that since 1941, the proportion of paid female workers in leading female occupations—teaching, nursing, clerical work, sales, and light manufacturing, among others—has dropped progressively from 62 per cent (in 1941) to 54 (in 1951), 53 (in 1961), 46 (in 1971) and 40 (in 1981) (Armstrong and Armstrong, 1984: 34, 36-7; cf. Fox and Fox, 1987; also, Porter in Boyd et al., 1985: 59-61). Some differences in definition make these data less than completely comparable, but they point in the direction of 'individualization'.

Female entries into traditionally male-dominated occupations show the same trend. Especially among younger women, many entries into these occupations have been due to 'additional effort', not 'natural evolution' (Boulet and Lavallée, 1984: 16). They reflect a change in occupational choices and opportunities, not merely an overall increase in the number of female workers. Between 1971 and 1981, the entry of women added 29 per cent to the growth in size of male-dominated occupations. In 1971, women had made up only 11 per cent of all members of these occupations, but by 1981, they were nearly 19 per cent: an increase of over 50 per cent in ten years (Marshall, 1989: 9).

The patterns of recent occupational change vary a great deal and are not easily summarized. Some occupations not only increased their female numbers significantly over the 1970s, but grew generally. They include 'supervisors in sales' and 'accountants, auditors and other financial officers'. Some occupations that were traditionally female-dominated grew without adding any more men: for example, 'bookkeepers and accounting clerks', 'tellers and cashiers' (Fox and Fox, 1987).

Jones's respondents explained the continuing gender segregation of these jobs in a number of ways:

The men don't want the pressure there is in the accounting department;

Most men would find this job too boring and repetitive—they

wouldn't last too long doing this—they go for the jobs that have more variety and prestige;

Typing and office work is traditionally done by women;

Women can handle the boredom and monotony better than men can. Men would go crazy doing what I do;

[My work's] not macho enough for a man. There's not many men who type;

Men are more interested in problem-solving. If a man is not going to find a problem-solving job, he'd find something more physical.

Still other occupations—for example, 'sales clerk (commodities)'—grew in size but declined in the proportion female. Yet again, some traditionally female-dominated occupations did not grow at all (e.g., 'elementary school teachers') or actually lost numbers ('office machine operators'). Finally, Fox and Fox show that some traditionally male occupations grew substantially without adding many more women. These include 'sales and advertising managers', 'production managers', and 'mechanics and repairmen'. As one respondent in the Jones survey said, 'Women just don't seem to get into this career area [i.e., business] as frequently as men do'.

Differences in type of change derive in part from the fact that different occupations show different age patterns. Where no growth is occurring, the age pattern may limit the speed at which an occupation can change its membership. Gender balancing is slower in a stationary occupational category, just as it is in a stationary (or declining) population. For this reason and others, gender segregation remains high in absolute terms.

Where segregation has declined at all since 1971, large numbers of women have entered occupations that were almost wholly male in the past: 'Twenty per cent of the growth in the female labour force between 1971 and 1981 took place in occupations less than ten per cent female in 1971' (Fox and Fox, 1987). Gender segregation continues to limit the variety of jobs women can and do enter. However, the data leave little doubt that women's labour-force statuses are becoming more varied.

More varied labour-force statuses

We can measure these changes in female labour-force status by comparing successive generations of women, using the 1984 Family History Survey (FHS). These data show that only about one in three women born in the 1920s and one in six women born before that were still in the work force by 1984. Women born before 1920 faced social norms that opposed women working for pay and offered fewer opportunities for working. They are much less likely than younger women to have *ever* worked for pay.

By contrast, about two-thirds of the women born in the 1940s, 1950s, and 1960s (aged in their twenties, thirties, and forties at the time of the survey) were in the labour force in 1984. About nine women in ten born in the 1940s or 1950s have worked for pay at some point in their lives; and nearly as many women born in the 1930s have also done so. From the histories of women aged 30 and over at the time of the Family History Survey, one can estimate that close to 100 per cent of all Canadian women will eventually work for pay at some time in their lives.

More varied industrial distribution

Women aged 25 to 64 make up the bulk of the adult working female population. These women show a wide variety of work patterns. Even the numbers of hours they work each week vary widely by industry, region, and the woman's personal characteristics. By examining these variations, we can determine the source of recent changes in the variety of women's work. Some industries are offering women more opportunity than they did in the past, and certain regions are changing more dramatically than others. In other cases, it is not the opportunities that have changed, but individual women's use of them.

For example, data from the Annual Work Pattern Surveys (AWPS) show relatively little change in the numbers of women in specific industries in 1977 and 1985. True, in this period the public administration and financial sectors began to hire more women, while retail sales hired fewer. In general, though, in 1985 the same industries in a given region were hiring the same numbers of women aged 25 to 64 as they were in 1977.

By 1985, three industries remained the largest employers of working women aged 25 to 64. These were community services, retail trade, and personal services, together employing between 51 per cent (in Ontario) and 61 per cent (in the Eastern, or Maritime, region) of the paid female labour force. Since the mid-1970s, the average number of hours that women aged 25 to 64 worked in these industries had increased greatly. Increases occured in all regions, but were largest in Ontario and smallest in Quebec. By industry, increases were larger in retail trade and smaller in personal services and community services.

If work experiences were growing more varied in every respect, women would be working more varied hours within every industry and region. However, the AWPS data show that no such change is taking place. The standard deviations (i.e., variations among women) within each regional and industrial job class scarcely changed between 1977 and 1985. This suggests that the overall organization of work is changing very slowly. Employers do not seem to want some women working one hour a week and others working 59 hours for a steady average of 30 hours. Administrative rigidity sets limits to how varied women can become in the hours they work for a given employer.

Some women solve this problem by changing jobs. Those who are willing and able to move from one work arrangement to another can live more varied lives even within a structure that is changing very slowly. Other women combine part-time jobs to secure the timetable and total income they require. In this way women produce varied combinations out of relatively unvarying work opportunities. This fact—the infinite complexity that one can create by combining simple elements—is a central, historic fact of women's lives. It is more important today than ever.

EMERGING FLUIDITY

Today women are changing their labour-force statuses more frequently and rapidly than in the past. Movements between pairs of labour-market statuses are more frequent and varied than ever before.

Le Bourdais and Desrosiers (1988) carried out a number of analyses with the Family History Survey data. They focussed on the dynamics of marriage, divorce, and employment, through the following transitions: (a) entries to common-law unions, (b) entries to the first marriage, (c) dissolution of marriage and common-law unions, (d) transformation of common-law unions to legal marriages, (e) entries to employment, (f) exits from employment, and (g) re-entries to employment.

The Le Bourdais-Desrosiers report (1988) emphasizes the discontinuity of women's employment in Canada, the low level of the jobs, the prevalence of part-time employment, and the pauperization of women in female-headed households.

More movement in and out of the labour force

A much higher proportion of women surveyed by the Annual Work Patterns Survey were in the labour force in 1985 than in 1977. Of these, somewhat more in 1985 (27 per cent versus 24 per cent) had spent the previous year doing only part-time work than had done so in 1977. Twice as many (14 per cent versus 6 per cent) had spent the year doing some full-time and some part-time work. These changes show a growth of fluidity in only eight years.

In 1977, women were much less likely to be mobile than in 1985, and much more likely to remain outside the labour force altogether. AWPS data from 1985 show that nearly one woman in four was in and out of the labour force during the previous year. Such fluidity had increased nearly three-fold in eight years.

Influences on in-and-out movement

The AWPS data show that highly educated women are particularly likely to remain in the labour force throughout an entire year. If they are in the labour force at all, they are the most likely of all women to be employed. (If a university-educated woman is not working, she is likely to be outside the labour force, not unemployed.) Yet women with university degrees are also more fluid than most women with less education. We have already noted the considerable fluidity of our university graduates CARLA and GAIL. ROSA too might have echoed the sentiments of one of Jones's respondents: 'It's very difficult to move from one industry to another or be seen as a possible employee in another. It's difficult to get training; I still have to support myself, so that conflict is still there'. Women with some (incomplete) post-secondary education are the most fluid of all Canadian women, outdoing even university graduates in this respect.

Compared to education, marital status has a relatively weak impact on women's status and fluidity. Married women are slightly more likely than average to remain in the labour force throughout the year; single women, to be in and out of the labour force; and divorced, separated, or widowed women, to remain outside the labour force entirely.

Age, on the other hand, still has a very strong impact on labour-force status. Annual Work Patterns Survey data show that older women are much less likely than younger women to be in the labour force. If they are in it at all, they are just about as likely as younger women to be fluid—that is, in and out of the labour force—over the course of a year.

To summarize, younger, more highly educated, and single women participate in the labour force more than older, less educated, and married women. They are also more likely to move in and out of the work force in a given year. This fluidity of highly educated young women is almost directly opposite to what researchers have found in Britain, as we noted in the previous chapter.

Picot's (1986: 18) analysis of the Family History Survey also finds educated young women to be particularly fluid. Holding marital status constant, post-secondary graduation doubles the likelihood a woman will ever enter employment, compared with high-school drop-outs. Holding age constant, a post-secondary graduate is less likely to leave employment in which she has engaged for two or more years. She is also more likely to re-enter employment if she has been out of the work force for two or more years. Indeed, a highly educated woman with one or more children under age six is nearly twice as likely to enter employment for the first time as a woman who did not graduate from secondary school.

In Canada, therefore, highly educated young women—even those with children—are a peculiar group. They are more likely than other women to be in the labour force at a given moment. When they are in the labour force, they are most likely to work full-time, as we shall see. They are also very fluid, moving in and out of the labour force easily and often.

Spells and survival times

A useful index of fluidity is the average number of employment or non-employment 'spells' per year a woman has had in her life up to the date of the interview. By this measure, a woman interviewed ten years after leaving school and who had always been in full-time employment would have had one spell in ten years, or 0.10 spells per year.

Among women in southern Ontario younger generations average many more spells per year than older ones. For young women, the most common transitions are between full-time work and being out of the paid work force. As these women age, part-time work becomes an important intermediary status between periods of full-time employment and periods spent outside the paid work force.

Are more recent generations of women spending less time in each labour-market status they enter than earlier generations did at the same age? If so, women are becoming more fluid. The southern Ontario data show that an average woman stays in full-time work for just under eight years before changing to one of the three other labour-market statuses. She averages just under four years in a 'spell' spent outside of the paid work force. Spells of part-time work are shorter than that, averaging just over two years.

The data show that earlier generations of women take a longer time to change statuses than younger ones do. This is particularly true of transitions from full-time and part-time employment to non-employment, and from non-employment to part-time employment. Broadly speaking, Jones's data support the hypothesis of increasing fluidity. At any given age, recent generations are more fluid than earlier ones.

In these data, higher education also proves to have an important effect. The more education a woman has, the less time she will spend (on average) before changing from full-time to part-time employment, non-employment to full-time or part-time employment, or full-time to part-time employment. This supports our hypothesis that more education increases fluidity.

Fluidity and family responsibilities

Valerie Oppenheimer (1982) argues that a woman's decision to work for pay is one of many possible 'adaptive strategies' in the face of familial economic difficulties or 'life cycle squeezes'. Other strategies include non-marriage, delayed marriage, reduced total child-bearing, economic contributions by the children, and increased contributions by the husband.

According to Oppenheimer, we cannot predict a woman's movement into and out of the labour force from her marital status, age, or spouse's income alone, or even added together. It is the interaction of these influences, given other choices she has contemplated or already made, that determines a woman's labour-force participation. So, for example:

For [men] going into higher level occupations, the first squeeze seems to be the most intrinsically stressful, given their steep age-earnings profiles. Marriage postponement and the employment of the wife early in marriage appear to represent important types of coping mechanisms developed to deal with these problems. However, the historically flat age-earnings profile of men in manual occupations suggests that delayed marriage and child-bearing would just increase the severity of the second squeeze. Hence early marriage and child-bearing appear to be the more adaptive strategy (Oppenheimer, 1982; 355)

Although they are becoming less significant, family responsibilities are still an important factor in a woman's decision to go to work or not. Many of Jones's respondents spoke out on this issue:

When I was home I was happy with the children. I wasn't interested in working until the first four were in school;

My domestic situation is too demanding for me to work right now but I would like to work in the future;

I'm retired—at my age I don't see the point of holding down a regular job if I don't need to. My husband is also retired and if I had a [regular] job it might interfere with his plans for vacations and so on;

Children come first, therefore I wouldn't consider working full-time until they are in school full-time;

I don't know if my family is ready for me to go out to work. There's a lot to do here. The amount [I earned] would not be worth paying a babysitter for three kids, and I might exhaust myself and can't afford a burnout.

Nevertheless, our theory of individualization predicts that women's lives will be ever less influenced by such responsibilities. Confirming this view, the AWPS data show that in 1985 women cite personal and family responsibilities less often as a factor in taking part-time work or leaving a job than they did in 1977. In 1985 they are much more likely to mention involuntary economic factors ('could only find a part-time job'; 'lost job or laid off') than they did in 1977. In both 1977 and 1985, marital status remains a weak predictor of whether a women works part-time and whether she leaves a job: far weaker in this respect than age or education.

Women aged 20 to 44 are particularly reluctant to say they take part-time work for personal or familial reasons, or because they 'did not want full-time work'. By 1985 they are more likely than before to say they take (involuntary) part-time work because that was all they could find. Also, they are less likely than in 1977 to say that they left their last job for reasons of personal and familial responsibility, and more likely to say that they were laid off.

Work interruptions

Work interruptions are another form of fluidity that shows growing individualization. Of female Family History Survey respondents who had ever worked for pay, by 1984 just under 45 per cent had interrupted their work once, 12 per cent twice, and nearly 4 per cent three or four times. If fluidity is increasing, we can expect to find (a) more interruptions among younger generations of women, but (b) ever shorter interruptions, (c) more post-interruption changes in work status (for example, from part-time to full-time status, or vice versa) over time, and as a result, (d) more post-interruption status changes per person over a specified period of time.

Interruptions are associated with certain key life events: specifically, marriage and child-bearing. Thus women who have ever married and borne children should display the highest rates of interruption. As expected, the FHS data show an average of 0.810 interruptions for all women who ever worked for pay, 0.938 interruptions for ever-married women among them, and 0.997 interruptions for women among them who have borne one or more children.

Of all women who interrupt their work for the first time in a given decade, later generations are more likely than earlier ones to interrupt their work many times. This suggests more fluidity among the younger women, more willingness of young mothers to use day-care, and, in younger couples, more support for the idea that women should work for pay.

Our second hypothesis is that interruptions will grow ever shorter. On this score, the FHS data show that among women who first interrupt their work in a given decade, the interruptions become briefer, the later the generation. For example, women first interrupting their work in the 1950s interrupted it for 22.6 years, on average, if they were born before 1920 (and in their thirties at the time). They interrupted it for only 14.3 years if they were born in the 1940s (and in their teens at the time).

Durations of interruption vary much less after 1960 than before that. A woman's decade of birth also matters less as time passes; progressively, first interrupters allow themselves less and less time off work, whatever their age at first interruption. Women in southern Ontario show ever earlier returns to paid work after child-bearing. Only 18 per cent of women born in the 1920s returned to work within one year of bearing a child; but 70 per cent of mothers born in the 1960s did so. These findings also support the 'increasing fluidity' hypothesis.

A third hypothesis is that, progressively, women will make ever more status changes (for example, from part-time to full- time, or vice versa) during their lives. The FHS data show that, among women first interrupting their work in a given decade, younger women are more likely than older ones to change statuses upon a return to work. Also, women in their teens, twenties, or thirties at the time of their first work interruption are more likely to change their status upon returning to work than are older women, whatever their generation.

Status changes are particularly common among women born in the 1930s and 1940s who first interrupted their work in the 1960s. These are women born a decade before the baby boom, for whom work opportunities were fewer and child-bearing norms higher than they are today. Rather than take an unbroken period off work to raise their children, these women alternated between full- and part-time work.

In conclusion, both the Family History Survey and the Jones survey data have supported the hypothesis that interruptions are increasing in number and decreasing in duration. As well, status changes are becoming more common and (for the average woman) more frequent with the passage of time.

More fluid movement in every industry

By 1985, a large proportion of female respondents in the Annual Work Patterns Survey—in some cases nearly 50 per cent (in personal services)—who identified a particular industry as their own locus of work were reporting a combination of employment, unemployment, and absence from the labour force in the preceding year.

However, the variations by industry are quite large. For example, in personal services year-long employment is much less likely for women aged 25 to 64 than it is in community services, public administration, or transportation. (This difference among industries probably has to do with the degree of unionized job security that each of these industries affords.) On the other hand, women aged 25 to 64 who work in retail sales and community services are much more fluid than other working women. In these industries, movement between the statuses 'employed' and 'not in the labour force' is very common. In fact, it is two or three times as likely as movement between 'employed' and 'unemployed' statuses.

Some fluidity is voluntary and some is not. Movement out of employment into unemployment is probably not voluntary, while movement out of the labour force may well be. AWPS data show that industries vary noticeably with respect to these two axes of fluidity. For example, women in finance and public administration are less likely than other working women either to leave employment for unemployment or to exit from the labour force. That is, both voluntary and involuntary movement are rare in the course of a year. At the other extreme, women in personal services, business services, construction, and the manufacture of non-durables are much more likely than average to leave their jobs both voluntarily and involuntarily.

Women in heavy industry show high rates of (involuntary) movement into unemployment and low rates of (voluntary) movement out of the labour force. Finally, women in retail sales, community services, and agriculture enjoy the best scenario: higher-than-average voluntary movement (out of the labour force) and lower-than-average involuntary movement (that is, unemployment) during a given year.

For women aged 25 to 64, fluidity of all kinds increased between 1977 and 1985. Voluntary or 'chosen' fluidity—movement in and out of the labour force—increased more than a median amount in precisely those industries where easy movement between employment and housework was already relatively high and unemployment was relatively low in 1977. It increased less than the median amount in heavy manufacturing, where unemployment was already relatively high. Most important, chosen fluidity is increasing in two of the industries that employ very large numbers of women: retail sales and community services. (The other large employer, personal services, shows a leap in both voluntary and involuntary fluidity between 1977 and 1985, so losses offset gains here.)

Similar findings emerge from the US National Longitudinal Survey of Labour Market Experience, which studied women aged 30 to 55 over the period 1966-77. Researcher Lois Shaw (1983: 56) reports: 'The reasons for noncontinuous employment vary among middle-aged married women. Our major purpose has been to determine the extent to which such work patterns are responses to family and personal constraints and preferences and to what extent they reflect poor job opportunities for middle-aged women in recent years.'

She concludes that both personal and structural factors influence what we call 'fluidity' and she calls 'irregular' or 'noncontinuous' employment. Attaching relative importance to these factors is no easy matter:

> Family responsibilities remained an important reason for irregular work patterns for women in their mid-thirties to mid-fifties. Health was an important cause of intermittent employment and of long periods out of the work force, especially among black women. High family income allowed some women to work intermittently or to leave the labor force entirely. However, women who had worked steadily for at least five years were not likely to decrease their attachment in response to high family income. A family's migration to another area often resulted in interruption of employment for white women (Shaw, 1983: 56).

Many factors besides the state of the labour market influence middle-aged female participation. Yet changes in the labour market also exert an effect, especially on women who are already vulnerable:

> High unemployment rates in some areas affected the work behavior of women who had not previously become well established in the labor market. Unemployment and job leaving were also common among women who had not worked steadily in the preceding five years. Among women who had worked most of the time in the recent past, a small minority, generally the less educated, also experienced job loss due to business conditions and considerations . . . Women who were new labor-market reentrants left the labor force again in areas of high unemployment (Shaw, 1983: 57).

This concludes our discussion of fluidity among Canadian women. The next section investigates whether idiosyncrasy is increasing, as our theory of individualization predicts.

EMERGING IDIOSYNCRASY

The theory of the individualization of women's lives argues that traditional predictors of labour-force status are losing their ability to predict effectively. As a result, we need more information today than we did in the past to predict a woman's labour force behaviour. As 'idiosyncrasy' increases, the number of predictors needed expands and the average contribution to explained variation of each predictor declines.

Predictors of current labour-force participation

Special tabulations of data from the Canadian Labour Force Survey measured labour-force status (that is, whether a woman was in the labour force or out) for all women who were heads of households or the spouses of household heads. Multiple classification analysis for each one of the years from 1976 to 1987 reveals a predicted decrease in the proportion of variance explained by traditional predictors: namely, age, marital status, and presence and age of children. By 1987 these variables were much poorer predictors of labour-force participation than they had been in 1976.

Different surveys with smaller samples but a richer selection of measured predictor variables show some of the other factors influencing women's work decisions. Using data from the Family History Survey, we predicted current labour-force status from age, presence of a spouse, number of children living at home, and also educational attainment and province of residence.

All of these variables contribute significantly to the prediction of labour-force status. Current participation in the labour force is likelier the more highly educated the woman is, the more recently she was born, the longer ago her first child was born (that is, the older her first child is today), and the fewer the children she has borne to date. On the other hand, these variables account for just under 12 per cent of the variation in labour-force status—a weak basis for predicting behaviour.

To determine whether we are leaving out important predictor variables, we may examine another body of data, which includes fewer cases but even more predictor variables: the Quality of Life 1981 survey. Here the predictor variables are age, marital status (that is, single or not), number of children, educational attainment, region of residence (Maritimes, Quebec, Ontario, or other), language group (English, French, or other), religion (Catholic, Protestant, or other), and husband's income.

Once again, number of children, years of education, and

residence in Ontario are statistically significant predictors of labour-force participation. None of the other variables significantly influences labour-force participation. The proportion of variance explained by all of these predictors is still under 14 per cent. We have not increased our explanatory power very much by adding to our list of predictor variables. The only newly discovered influences are region and educational attainment.

To determine whether we are missing important combination effects between these predictor variables, we may try analysis of variance (ANOVA) and multiple classification analysis (MCA) on the Family History Survey data. However, these results merely repeat what the regression analysis has already shown. Once again, we find that younger, more highly educated women with fewer children are most likely to be in the labour force.

Our theory of individualization claims that, over time, traditional predictor variables will have a diminishing influence on labour-force participation. As predicted, ANOVA reveals significant interaction effects for all variables paired with the woman's decade of birth. For example, the effect of education (or number of children borne) on labour-force status depends on when the woman was born.

Our theory argues that, with each succeeding generation, the variance explained by traditional variables will diminish; and the Family History Survey data support this theory. For example, education has less and less influence on current labour-force participation with each successive generation of women. This supports a point made earlier: namely, that less-educated women will increasingly engage in the labour force in the ways highly educated women have done for decades. Likewise, the influence on labour-force status of marital status (or the presence of a spouse) also declines with each generation, though somewhat less regularly than for education. Younger married women are less discouraged from labour-force participation than older married women.

Yet even taking variables three at a time, using ANOVA, explains little more variance than when we used regression analysis and simply added them, one at a time. In other words, we gain little by examining the interactions among variables. Any large improvement in the prediction of current labour-force status will have to come from studying more (and better) predictors.

Predictors of cumulative labour-force participation

A similar examination of the Family History Survey data to find predictors of lifetime work experience (that is, whether a woman ever worked for pay) produces similar results. As before, the predictors account for a small proportion of variance: in fact, just under 10 per cent. Once again, the main predictors are educational attainment, number of children borne, age, and decade when married. The women most likely to have ever worked for pay have received the most education, borne the fewest children, married most recently, and, holding these constant, are oldest (since they have had the longest opportunity to work.)

As before, analyses using ANOVA and MCA show that the interactions among these variables, though statistically significant, are not very large. The same variables that predict current labour-force participation also predict lifetime labour-force participation. This is not surprising, because a lifetime is only a sequence of current experiences.

Analysis of variance weakly confirms our individualization theory: confirms, because the effects of education and parity change with time and generation, as we expect; but weakly, because the levels of statistical significance attained are low. Over the long haul, whether a woman will ever work for pay is better predicted by her education than her marital status or child-bearing record. Among younger women, however, education has less predictive power. For them, cumulative labour-force status is also very similar to current labour-force status, and in this case the best predictors of both are marital status and, secondarily, child-bearing.

Predictors of hours worked

Data from the Annual Work Pattern Surveys also permit us to examine the growth of idiosyncrasy between 1977 and 1985. In what follows, we determine whether the predictive power of age, education, and marital status changed between 1977 and 1985 within each of the thirteen industries, especially in Ontario and Quebec, where women participate most in the labour force.

The data show that within those industries in both provinces, our predictive power declined between 1977 and 1985 in 16 cases out of 26 (2 provinces x 13 industries). This result is little better than a coin toss. It leans in the right direction, but is very weak evidence of increasing idiosyncrasy.

Other findings are more compelling. When we control for marital status and education, age significantly influences the hours that women aged 25 to 64 worked in *only* 2 of 52 (that is, 4 regions x 13 industries) regressions. This is what our theory has predicted. It means that age is no longer a significant predictor of hours worked.

Marital status continues to have a significant influence on hours worked, though larger in some industries than others. But as our theory would predict, its impact was weaker in 1985 than it was in 1977 in both Quebec and Ontario, and by 1985 it had fallen dramatically. Of the three major industries employing women aged 25 to 64, only in community services did marital status continue (in 1985) to influence hours worked. Both in Ontario and in Quebec, married women in community-service occupations work fewer hours a week for pay than women who are not married (holding age and education constant).

By 1985, marital status had no significant effect on hours worked within either of the other industries employing large numbers of women: retail sales and personal services. Indeed, the influence of marital status on hours worked in *most* industries was weaker—both smaller and less significant—in 1985 than it was in 1977. The idiosyncrasy hypothesis predicted this decline in the influence of marital status on work behaviour.

On the other hand, educational attainment gained importance, also as we would have predicted. Coefficients measuring the predictive power of education were larger in 1985 than in 1977. This increase was slightly larger among Ontario women than among Quebec women. In Ontario (1985), education had a stronger influence on the hours that women worked in all three of the industries employing the most women. In Quebec in the same year, the influence of education was significant only in retail sales and community services.

Let us now shift our attention from hours worked per week to weeks worked per year. Data from the Annual Work Patterns Survey show that in 1977, unmarried, highly educated women under age 55 worked the most weeks during the year. By 1985 all kinds of women averaged more working weeks than in 1977, but unmarried women were still working more weeks (on average) than married women.

Highly educated, young married women were numerically a new force in the workplace by 1985. Perhaps because they were fewer to start with, married women contributed the most dramatic (percentage) increases in labour power between 1977 and 1985. Even in absolute terms, however, in the 1980s highly educated married women were giving the largest number of 'new weeks' to the labour supply.

The data on hours worked per week tell a similar story. Age, education, and marital status are all important determinants of hours worked. In every industrial and regional job class, the average hours worked changed between 1977 and 1985. A gap between married and unmarried women remained; but in absolute terms, highly educated, married women under the age of 55 were the largest *per capita* contributors of 'additional hours' between 1977 and 1985.

The data clearly support our theory. Within the main female-employing industries of Canada's most urbanized, highly developed labour markets—Ontario and Quebec—age has lost all of its importance as a predictor of hours worked; marital status has lost some of its importance; and education—a non-familial variable—has gained importance as a predictor. Yet overall, these three variables are less able to predict the hours that women worked in 1985 than they were in 1977. The weakness of our predictive power attests to the strength of our theory of individualization!

Predictors of work interruptions

Work interruptions are the flip side of labour-force participation. Therefore the same predictor variables should influence them as influence labour-force participation and hours worked.

Analysis of the Family History Survey data shows that the total number of work interruptions increases with a woman's age (since more years have been at risk). Holding age constant, work interruptions are most common for women with a spouse and children at home, especially if there are many children and they are young. Another strong influence is the decade in which a woman's first child was born. This finding demonstrates the effect of the short-term maternity leaves that have become more widely available, especially after 1971, and younger women's increasing tendency to return to the labour force after childbirth.

The oldest women will have lost the most years through work interruptions, since they have had the most years to lose. Holding age constant, the women who have lost the most time from paid work because of work interruptions are those who have borne the most children, received the least education, married a long time ago—when different family norms prevailed—and currently live with a spouse.

The data suggest that young well-educated women, who have borne relatively few children, are likely to stop and then restart working after each birth. They bear their children within a short time span, and a high proportion of all their children are at home while they participate in the labour force, despite many interruptions.

More interruptions as time goes on

Findings by Picot (1986: 16), using the same Family History Survey data but a different analytic technique, are similar. They show that, whatever the reason for the interruption, and however long it lasts, women interrupting work at some moment between 1973 and 1983 were more likely to re-enter the work force, and after a shorter time, than women interrupting work at some moment between 1960 and 1969. This shows a rise in the willingness of women to move in and out of the work force, and a rise in employers' willingness to have them do so.

The women Jones interviewed had a lot to say about the 'individualization' of their own lives and those of other women:

They should let women do whatever they want; make their own choice. It's their life, they know what's best for them;

I think women should be able to get more education and be more independent and get out in the work force to get more jobs . . . Women work hard and try to do their best while they work. They feel better themselves when they have a job and feel more independent;

It should be a personal decision. Women should work if they want to, whatever their situation;

Women have a right to choose their own destiny—just like all other people;

I think women should have freedom of choice of whether they go to work or not.

CONCLUDING REMARKS

This chapter and the one preceding it have presented strong support for the individualization theory, using a variety of data sources and analytic techniques. Where related analyses have been available, they have typically obtained similar results.

If women's lives are individualizing, as we say, what are the implications for government policy? For women planning their lives? For adjustment to change in the areas of personal life, family and work? These are the kinds of questions we shall address in the concluding section of this book. We begin with a chapter that projects the individualization process to the year 2025, in order to evaluate its consequences for labour supply.

III

RESULTS OF
INDIVIDUALIZATION

6

Future Trends in
Women's Labour-Force Behaviour

We approach long-term forecasting in a spirit of creative discovery. The purpose of modelling is not to make a specific prediction. Rather, it is to trace as logically as possible—sometimes using numbers—the likely consequences of changes in specified conditions. In this chapter, we shall examine current trends in work, and then construct a simple model of female movements through the labour force that will agree with the observed data, enable us to project future trends, and be sensitive to variations in our assumptions. This kind of modelling allows us to estimate some parameters of the female adult life cycle that are otherwise hard to measure, such as mean number of moves in and out of the labour force and expected length of time in the labour force.

Discussions of modelling assumptions can become technical. Some readers will prefer to skip this chapter, and others will skim it for its conclusions, but committed readers will think through with us, part by part, what it takes to make reasonable guesses about women's work patterns 35 years from now. In doing this, you may want to remember that if you are in your teens or twenties now, this model will help you think about your daughter's future life. In 2025, you will be able to watch your daughter check our conclusions.

A SIMPLE (BUT BAD) APPROACH

Forecasts of the size and nature of the labour force are based on demographic projections of the age/sex composition of the population combined with estimates of the 'activity rate' of each segment of the future adult population. To supplement this, economists and sociologists often make up multiple regression-based 'labour supply' models, which interact with the demand for labour to produce specific rates of labour-force activity.

The very simplest approach to forecasting is to project forward existing trends in labour-force participation. This assumes that present trends will continue, more or less unchanged, into the distant future. We can make such a projection with a method called logistic regression, using special tabulations from the Labour Force Survey, 1976 to 1987. Participation in the labour force is then predicted from age, marital status, family composition, and year.[1]

The core of the projection is provided by regression coefficients for calendar year, and there are three of these, one for each type of family composition. Using this method, we find that the rate of increase of labour-force participation is greatest among women with children under six years of age, and smallest among women with no children under 16. This analysis, which assumes that the 1976-87 trends will continue, ends up predicting that the participation rates of mothers with pre-schoolers will overtake those of the other two groups—even of women with no children at all!

In effect, the model is saying that what is increasing fastest now will always be increasing fastest. This is like predicting that your three-year-old kid brother will grow six feet taller than you because right now he is growing so much faster than you are. This implausible result illustrates the danger of relying on simple regression-based models that may, as in this case, assume that a temporary increase will continue forever.

The alternative is a scenario approach: What if women of the future were to live perfectly individualized lives? Given what we have learned about individualization, what would their work-lives look like?

PROJECTING FUTURE WORK-LIVES

Our data have tended to validate the theory of individualization. Let us take this theory to its limit and try to imagine what results the condition of complete or 'perfect' individualization would provide.

Perfect individualization

Under conditions of perfect individualization, women's lives will be 'perfectly' varied, fluid, and idiosyncratic. 'Perfect' *variety* will mean lives varied as the distribution of labour-force statuses itself. That is, there will be no difference in the variety of occupational statuses that men and women hold. Gender will no longer affect the allocation of jobs.

What 'perfect' *fluidity* might look like, on the other hand, is impossible to say. The comparison with a male standard may not be appropriate here. Women's lives have always been more fluid than men's, and our model argues that this difference will not only continue, but even increase. However, we cannot identify all the forces that may influence women's fluidity—among them, the availability of child-care, labour demand, and the ratio of part-time to full-time work. For this reason, we must treat fluidity as the outcome of other processes we understand better.

Finally, women's 'perfect' *idiosyncrasy* can be specified in relation to an absolute standard, not in relation to men's behaviour. At its limit, idiosyncrasy will be marked by the ability of a great many personal characteristics each to contribute a very small amount to the prediction of labour-force participation. For the purposes of modelling, then, no particular trait will affect labour-force participation very much: we can ignore the influence of any individual variable.

One modelling strategy that we shall use acknowledges the continued but changing importance of variables like age, marital status, parental status, and education. We start by asking questions. Will a woman living in the year 2025 be like the average Canadian woman today with respect to her entry and exit from the labour force? Or will she be most like a woman who today is (a) young, (b) highly educated, and (c) with no or few children—that is, a woman with the (current) maximum rates of labour-force participation and retention? And what are the consequences of her being like the latter 'high performer'?

Then we need to estimate the proportion of Canadian women who will fall into each category of interest in the future. For example, if we hold that educational attainment will continue to influence women's work behaviour in the future, we shall have to estimate how many women will attain each level of education—unless we assume that, by 2025, virtually all women will have attained what is today considered 'higher education': that is, post-secondary education. Data on rapidly rising female participation in higher education might justify such an assumption.

Similar assumptions can also be made about marriage and child-bearing. In these cases too, more and more women are moving in the direction of work-promoting behaviour (c.f., Vlassof, 1987: 6, 7): continued low fertility, later ages at first birth, lower rates of first marriage, higher marital instability, more widespread (and effective) contraception, higher opportunity costs of child-bearing, and relative economic hardship. We can safely ignore currently important predictor or control variables, because they are losing their original predictive importance and/or women are becoming more homogeneous in these respects.

But we shall begin by ignoring even these influences. Specifically, we begin by ignoring all variables but current and cumulative labour-force participation. This approach allows us to use a common model that is justifiable, effective, and intuitively sensible.

The Markov chain model

This model assumes that by 2025, individualization will be 'perfect', and no predictor variable will stand above the others in its predictive power. As a consequence, we will not need to take any particular predictor variable into account (or hold it constant) while projecting labour-force behaviour. If ignoring so many other variables sounds implausible, let us recall a common model that does the very same thing. The demographer's 'life table' distinguishes people only by their age and gender and treats all other social (e.g., social class), economic (e.g., frequency of unemployment) or psychological (e.g., stress level) traits as irrelevant to predicting the risk of death. Of course, these factors all do influence the risk of death, but individually their effects are very much smaller and less agreed upon than the effects of gender and age. For most purposes, those traits are insignificant, and demographers (like the actuaries who work for insurance companies) ignore them.

Now imagine that improvements in medicine, genetic engineering, or other technology vastly reduce the effects of gender on risk of death. Death risks will now be predictable from a large number of variables taken altogether, but no single variable will be very important. Under this condition, we can ignore tiny variations due to gender (and other particular variables) or we can try to identify and gather together the many small effects of a great many variables, including gender.

However, at least two objections can be raised to the Markov models we are proposing: (a) they are 'ahistorical'; and (b) marginals in the models (that is, the proportions of women working at any given time) are a result of labour-supply, not labour-demand, characteristics. Let us examine each of these concerns briefly.

Ahistoricity. A Markov model assumes that the probability of leaving a given state is dependent only on the state itself, not on the personal history of the individual. Thus if the Markov model is valid, we should not care whether a person has been unemployed 1 year, 2 years, or 5 years: his/her likelihood of returning to work within the next year should be the same.

However, some research has already called the Markov model into question where various kinds of movement are concerned. It may be that 'movers' and 'stayers' are different kinds of people, with different probabilities of leaving a given state within a given period of time. So, for example, geographers and demographers sometimes speak of 'hypermobile' people as being particularly likely to move many times in a short period (e.g., Stone, 1978). A technical solution to this problem is to add the relevant states with their correspondingly different transition probabilities to the model. But this approach sacrifices the simplicity that is the whole appeal of the Markov chain.

In his paper examining data from the Family History Survey, Picot (1986: Table 5 *et passim*) shows that people's chances of leaving and entering employment *do* vary according to the number of years they have spent in the opposite state. This variation occurs even when Picot controls for gender, age, marital status, parity, marriage history, and educational attainment. Three or more interpretations of his finding are possible.

The most obvious is that a Markov chain does not adequately describe entries to and exits from the labour force. To take a strong example, a person's chance of entering or leaving employment may diminish with the time she has spent in the opposite state, because she has made a large investment (of time and psychic energy) in that state. The opportunity cost of leaving one state for another will increase with the length of time spent in the first state. If so, a Markov model would have doubtful validity.

A second interpretation is that entering and leaving probabilities are influenced by characteristics that Picot has failed to identify and control for. If he *had* identified and controlled for these, one might argue, he would have arrived at different results, in which case a Markov model might still be appropriate. Such unmeasured variables might include family income, labour-market experience, local labour-market characteristics (measured directly, or indirectly by size or affluence of community, province or region of Canada), personal tastes/values (measured directly, or indirectly by ethnicity, religion, region of the country, language group); and so on. If this were the case, when using the Markov model we would be obliged to control for whichever variables influenced entries and exits.

Finally, Picot's choice of hypothetical model—married, no children, no failed marriage, and completed secondary school— may describe some Canadian women some of the time while failing to describe most Canadian women most of the time. And even if it does characterize many women today, it may not characterize many of them by 2025. For example, a great many women already have a failed marriage and some post-secondary education, and these proportions are likely to continue increasing over the next forty years. Conceivably, the probability that these women will change their state is less dependent on the time they have spent in it, and Markov modelling is appropriate for them; but Picot does not provide us with data on this group.

In the absence of information on the validity of Picot's objections, we shall proceed as though the Markov model were still appropriate, and turn to the second potential objection.

Labour supply versus labour demand. Economists sometimes accuse sociologists of paying too much attention to the characteristics of individual job choosers (the labour suppliers) and not enough to the quantity and character of labour demand. Of course, the labour market is nothing less than what is both supplied *and* demanded: that reciprocity is what makes it a market. However, the inference we take is that economists accuse sociologists of attending too much to personal choice and not enough to structural constraint (an odd criticism, for the most part, as the roles are usually reversed).

In the present instance, we analyze patterns of labour-force participation as measured by both current and cumulative rates of participation (that is, by women who *ever* worked for pay). These parameters are understandable on both the individual and aggregate levels. They measure both the past and present choices of individual women and the constraints they experience(d) in the labour market. In this sense, our model measures both supply and demand in the labour market. Thus it satisfies the inclinations of both sociologists and economists.

The general model

Accordingly, the model by which we propose to understand and project the rising labour-force participation rate of women is a discrete two-state Markov chain model. The two states are 'in labour force' and 'out of labour force'. Hypothetically, women make the transition once a year, if at all; they are at risk of making it forty times (that is, for forty years).

The model will ultimately estimate the following dependent variables: (a) mean years spent in the labour force; (b) mean number of exits from labour force (per woman); (c) mean number of entries into the labour force (per woman); and (d) proportion of women who never left the labour force. The key independent variables in the model are n, the proportion of adult women in the labour force at a given time; and k, the proportion of women changing their status in a given year. These will be measured directly or, where necessary, estimated from other available data. Like the life table we spoke of earlier, this model ignores labour *supply* variables (that is, such characteristics as education, parity, marital status, and age) while varying current and cumulative rates of participation, which reflect both labour demand and supply.

Model marginals

We begin by comparing the experiences of groups of women born at different times. Except for the first group, each generation comprises a decade; thus we have six generations to compare: (born) before 1920; 1920-29; 1930-39; 1940-49; 1950-59; and 1960-69. Retrospective data are from the Family History Survey (1984).

Currently in the labour force

About two-thirds of all women born in the 1940s, 1950s, or 1960s (aged in their twenties, thirties and forties at the time of the survey) are currently in the labour force—whether employed or unemployed. By contrast, only about one-third of women born in the 1920s and one-sixth of women born before that (aged in their sixties and over at the time of the survey) are currently in the labour force. Overall, in 1984, about 58 per cent of respondents were in the labour force.

But this information on current labour-force participation has only limited usefulness. First, it confuses age, period, and cohort influences on work behaviour (and norms). Second, it tells us little about the ways in which women's organization of their lives has

Figure 6.1 CURPAR: Proportion of Women in the Labour Force in the Year Specified

CURPAR   % of women in labour force at year

Censal Year

changed over time, for it ignores the extent of movement in and out of the labour force.

Ever in the labour force

If we look at the lifetime (retrospective) evidence on labour-force participation, we get a slightly different picture. The data show that about nine women in ten born in the 1940s or 1950s have worked for pay at some point in their lives; nearly as many women born in the 1930s have done so too. The percentages are much lower for women born before 1920, when women were much more strongly discouraged from working for pay. They are also lower for women born in the 1960s, who have not been exposed to as many years of opportunity for paid work as the older women.

These figures show that middle-aged women are the most likely to have done some paid work during their lives. We can assume that the percentage will continue to rise between now and 2025. The percentage for the youngest generation, born in the 1960s, is an apparent oddity. Perhaps that is because some of them are still in full-time education, or have not yet obtained their first job.

As we said in Chapter 2, these data show that in the early part of the twentieth century, the cumulative rate rose very rapidly and

Figure 6.2 CUMPAR: Proportion Ever in the Labour Force by Mid-Year of Birth Decade

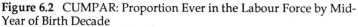

Midpoint of birth decade

had begun to rise less rapidly by the time that rates of current participation started to grow rapidly, in the late 1960s. As a result, rates of movement through a relatively limited number of jobs began to increase before the number of jobs increased substantially. In other words, women used to spend only a short time in jobs outside the home, but in the twentieth century they have been spending more and more of their potential working lives in paid employment.

Consequently, cumulative participation rates began to rise sooner (and faster) than current participation rates. Instead of 10 to 20 per cent ever working for pay, and doing so more or less continuously, in this century closer to 80 or 90 per cent of women have worked for pay at some time in their lives, though they have been doing so only sporadically and briefly.

This shift has had several consequences. First, it has blurred the dividing line between 'working woman' and 'housewife'. Increasingly, women are both at the same time, whereas before 1970 few women ever were. In the second half of the twentieth century, every woman is familiar with the advantages and disadvantages of each status. This growing similarity tends to increase the feelings of solidarity among women, whether they are currently working at home without pay or in paid jobs outside.

Second, this shift has meant that a woman's typical life-course has become even less like a man's. A man would undertake a single activity—typically, paid work of a particular kind—after finishing his schooling, and would continue in that activity until retirement or death. In one respect, the female employment transition made women's lives less like men's and more like one another's, by universalizing their exposure (however temporary) to the work world. But in another respect it made women's lives less like one another's. Decisions to move in and out of the labour force, ever less constrained by lack of opportunity or child-raising obligations, became ever more determined by idiosyncratic, personal factors: by family financial need, the woman's education (or other human capital), her values and aspirations, and so on.

Fluidity in the future

If fluidity continues to increase as it is doing now, how will women organize their work lives in the future? To answer this question, we set up the model as though the pattern of movement observed in 1984 (at the time of the Family History Survey) were static and unchanging. Then we summarize the results and compare them with extrapolations for 1944 and 2024 obtained in a similar way.

The model in 1984

As we noted earlier, 58 per cent of women in the 1984 Family History Survey study were currently in the labour force. Moreover, 84 per cent of the sample had worked for pay at some time in their lives, while 16 per cent had never done so.

Imagine, then, the following conditions. Of every 100 women, 58 are in the labour force in 1984 and 42 are not. By 1985, two women have entered the labour force and two have departed, leaving the distribution unchanged. (Remember, the system is in static equilibrium.) Each year, strictly by chance, two women are 'selected' out of the labour force and two women are 'selected' into it. This random process goes on for forty years, until 2024.

Under these conditions, the pure chance that a women will *never* move into the labour force is approximately 0.14 or $(40/42)^{40}$. Given this model and forty years of chance movement, we estimate the following outcomes for an average woman:

(1) mean years in labour force (i.e., mean years to leave labour force): $1/2/58$, or $58/2 = 29$ years.

(2) mean number of exits from labour force, per person (per 40 years): $(2/58) \times 40 = 1.38$

(3) mean number of entrances into labour force, per person (per 40 years): $(2/42) \times 40 = 1.90$

(4) probability of never exiting/never interrupting work (in 40 years): $(56/58)^{40} = 0.246$

These results compare favourably with results that Picot (1986: 26) has generated with a random 'Monte Carlo simulation', using the Family History Survey data, even though Picot has confined his attention to the period 1974-83, for women aged 18 to 55 only. (In turn, his simulated results compare favourably with the observed data.) Let us examine a few of Picot's estimates.

Average years employed. Picot expects women aged 18 to 36 to spend 5.4 years (of every 10) employed, and women aged 37 to 55 to spend 5.7 years (of every 10) employed. By implication, during the 40 years between ages 18 and 58, Picot would expect average women to spend just under 23 years in paid employment.

The six-year difference between this estimate and our own arises from several differences between our estimation procedures. We are looking at women aged 25 to 64; Picot, at women aged 18 to 58. We start the clock running in 1984; he starts it in 1973. Our procedure rests on (relatively high) 1984 current and cumulative rates of employment, projected into an unending future; his estimates incorporate large recent changes in female participation. As a result, Picot's estimate of years employed is lower than ours, falling about midway between our own 1984 and 1944 estimates (see the section immediately following for our own estimates for 1944).

Picot's rates of entrance and exit are similar to our own, again allowing for some differences in assumptions. Picot estimates 42 entrances per 33 exits (per 10-year period), for women aged 18 to 36, though only 14 entrances per 24 exits (per 10-year period), for women aged 37 to 55. Our overall estimate of 190 entrances per 138 exits (per 40-year period) is far higher than Picot's (which we could estimate from his figures as roughly 109 entrances per 114 exits). But recall that his figures are based on lower-than-today's levels of labour-force stability. Ours reflect the high stability observed in 1984. Once again, for this reason his estimate of entrances and exits falls midway between our own estimates for 1984 and 1944, as we shall now see.

The model parameters in 1944 and 2024

This modelling will be most useful if it allows us to compare women's current work lives with those of women past and future. To accomplish this means estimating some parameters: specifically, the level of labour-force participation and the proportion who would have ever worked for pay, if surveys identical to the FHS were conducted in 1944 and 2024.

Estimating current (or cross-sectional) labour-force participation is easy, given published statistics for 1901-81. The historical data show a rapidly accelerating ascent after 1951. But where will the acceleration level off? Several assumptions could be defended. One is that the ascent will approach 100 per cent labour-force participation by the year 2024. A simple extrapolation of the current trend would justify this view.

Another assumption is that the trend will level off at much less than 100 per cent, say around 80 or 85 per cent. This view is justified by evidence that male labour-force participation rates are falling, and male and female rates are likely to converge by the century's end around the 80 to 85 per cent mark. In general, one can imagine that fewer people—male or female—will be needed to work for pay in future, given automation. The economy will simply require fewer person-years of work per lifetime than it has in the past. What is uncertain is how labour demands will be distributed across the population by gender (not to mention age, educational attainment, region, and so on). This second assumption is the more attractive. So, with historical statistics in hand, we estimate that the labour-force participation of women was 0.24 in 1944 and will have risen to 0.80 in 2024.

Estimating the proportions of women who have ever worked for pay is a little more complicated and involves two steps: (a) estimating the proportions in a generation of women who have ever worked for pay, and (b) combining these estimates with a 'standard population' distribution, which for simplicity will be the Family History Survey sample as presently constituted.

First, we extrapolate forward. Four successive generations in our sample—women born before 1920, and in the 1920s, 1930s and 1940s—have been increasingly likely to have ever worked for pay. (Women born in the 1950s depart very slightly from the value we would predict from earlier cohorts, but women born in the 1960s depart substantially—by about 28 per cent—reflecting the fact that younger women have had fewer years to enter the work force and have been occupied with child-bearing.) In general, the evidence suggests a continuing increase in the probability of women's ever working for pay. If so, the proportions of women ever working for pay will continue to approach 100 per cent, perhaps even reaching 100 per cent for women born in the 1980s and thereafter.

Now, we extrapolate backwards linearly, using the Family History Survey data on generational experiences. They lead us to conclude that women born in the 1880s, 1890s, and 1900s will have had probabilities of ever working for pay of 0.20, 0.38, and 0.56 respectively. There never was a time in Canada when *no* women worked for pay; a small proportion have always done so at some time in their lives. For this reason, we estimate the (minimum) proportion ever working for pay in the 1870s cohort as 0.10, not zero.

We now weight these estimated generational probabilities of ever-working by the numbers of women belonging to each generation in our current sample. Summing across generations, we estimate the proportions ever having worked in 1944 and 2024 at 54 per cent and 99 per cent respectively.

The model in 1944

Using the estimates just developed, we can derive our dependent-variable values for 1944 just as we did for 1984.

In the 1944 we have just extrapolated, 24 per cent of all adult women are in the labour force and 54 per cent of adult women have ever worked for pay. Under equilibrium conditions—that is, with no change in the size of the groups—1.5 women will leave the labour force each year and the same number will enter it. This number of movers yields the required number of women never working for pay in a 40-year period, since $(74.5/76)^{40}$ is roughly the required 46 per cent. From this we can also estimate

(1) mean years in labour force (i.e. mean years to leave) = $24/1.5$ = 16.

(2) mean number of exits per person = $(1.5/24) \times 40 = 2.50$

(3) mean number of entries per person = $(1.5/76) \times 40 = 0.79$

(4) proportion never leaving the labour force = $(22.5/24)^{40} = .076$.

The model shows us 1944 (and lifetimes built on 1944 norms) as involving few women in paid work, a relatively brief average work life, and little likelihood of continuous paid work over a woman's lifetime.

The model in 2024

In the same way, we can project likely changes in the next forty years. For 2024, we have estimated an 80 per cent level of current labour-force participation by women and over 99 per cent of women's ever working for pay. At equilibrium, 2.5 women leave the work force and 2.5 enter it every year. This means that 17.5/20 are *not* entering the labour force in a given year. The probability of *never* entering it for forty years—still assuming a random draw—is $(17.5/20)^{40}$, roughly the 0.5 per cent we estimate will have never worked for pay by 2024. Given these values, we can estimate the following:

(1) mean years in labour force (i.e., mean years to leave) = 80/2.5 = 32.

(2) mean number of exits per person = (2.5/80) x 40 = 1.25

(3) mean number of entries per person = (2.5/20) x 40 = 5.0

(4) proportion never stopping working = $(77.5/80)^{40}$ = 0.281

These extrapolations show that forty years from now, the average woman will spend twice as long in the labour force as an average woman did forty years ago: namely, 32 years out of 40 possible, versus only 16 years in the past. Note also that the 1984 figures are already quite close to what we project for 2024. This suggests that, at least quantitatively, changes in women's work lives in the *next* forty years will be far less dramatic than the changes we have already witnessed in the *last* forty years.

On average, working women will be even more fluid than they are today, as we see if we add together the projected (average) numbers of labour-force exits and entries. At the same time, a large proportion of women will enter and remain in the labour force for an entire forty years. Such continuity will be about four times as common around 2024 as it was around 1944.

Fluidity of highly educated women

Paradoxically, changes in the next forty years will be the least dramatic for highly educated women. That is because educated women have already made a large part of the big leap into paid employment. They have been more heavily involved in the labour force than any other women, at least since the Second World War, and maybe long before that.

Even highly educated women born before 1920 (surveyed in the Family History Survey study) were nearly all in the paid work force at one time or another. Higher education made them 50 per cent more likely ever to participate than the average woman born in the same period. Even in 1984, when these women would have been aged 65 and over, they were still more than twice as likely as the average woman their age to be working for pay.

Highly educated women are going to change the least because they are already closest to the 'individualized lives'—the variety, fluidity, and idiosyncrasy—we are projecting for all future women. As well, highly educated women are already near to the levels of current and cumulative (lifetime) labour-force participation we have projected for 2024. In the next forty years, less educated women will become less numerous, and those that remain will have work lives (and perhaps family lives) more like those of today's highly educated women.

Such a change seems to imply a reduction in fluidity. After all, if all women are working for pay for some part of their adult lives; and if that working-for-pay part of their lives is becoming longer, on average; and if the proportion of women working for pay at a given moment is also increasing; then a very high proportion of all adult female person-years are being spent working for pay. Any movements out of the labour force will have to be rare or—if common among women or repeated (i.e., frequent for a given woman)—merely brief interruptions.

And in fact they are brief interruptions. Remember, we showed that work interruptions *are* becoming briefer and more frequent; and that, in Canada, educated younger women are the most fluid of all women. So younger, highly educated women today are already showing a pattern that we can expect will become increasingly common among women: a lifetime of paid work, punctuated by frequent brief interruptions for housework, child-bearing, education, and perhaps other reasons.

An alternative interpretation is always possible. Perhaps, because of discrimination, highly educated women today are seriously underemployed. The attractiveness of another paid workday is low, both financially and psychologically. A woman whose spouse earns a high income has little incentive to continue in an unsatisfying job, so she drops out for a while. But when another, more promising job presents itself, she drops back into the labour force; and so on over time.

This 'fluid' pattern is consistent with (a) female under-employment and lack of work satisfaction, (b) reliable financial support from a spouse, and (c) work that demands little consistent investment of time (e.g., few skills to be learned, little time needed to build a clientele or a reputation). But in the foreseeable future, discrimination and underemployment may become a smaller problem—or none at all—for educated women. Spousal support may also disappear as a factor: less may be available to an average wife, fewer wives may have it, and all wives will be less certain it will be provided permanently, if at all. Finally, an increasing number of 'good' jobs open to women may demand a continuous application of effort. That is, good jobs may not become more flexible in order to accommodate interruption; women will have to become more rigid to hold the jobs.

If this alternative interpretation is correct, women's fluidity will not continue to increase as it has over this century. On the contrary, highly educated women's lives will simply become like current men's lives. Perhaps even men's lives will become more fluid than they are today. Moreover, other kinds of transitions than the simple kind we have been discussing—in and out of the labour force—may also keep women's lives fluid.

OTHER FORMS OF FLUIDITY

Movement between part-and full-time work

Both in Canada and abroad, part-time work is increasing. In large part, it is increasing at the expense of full-time work. In the future, full-time jobs may become less common; or full-time work status may be limited to specific jobs that require a lot of responsibility or skill (for example, senior decision-makers in business and public administration, or specialists in the professions). In future, the average worker may spend his or her life moving from one part-time job to another; from one set of simultaneous part-time jobs to another; or from part-time work to full-time work and back again. Whether these part-time jobs will be good ones or bad ones by our present standards will depend mainly upon changes in the state regulation of part-time work.

Movement between work and education

To a large degree, easy movement between jobs will depend on the availability of retraining opportunities. Especially where it is a response to technological and economic change, easy movement assumes that some people are willing to learn, and others are willing to teach them. There is already increasing evidence that higher education, continuing education, and occupational retraining are becoming normal parts of adult life. Schooling is no longer confined to childhood and the adolescent years, as it once was. More employers are offering educational leave time, and more institutions of higher education are showing sensitivity to students with adult responsibilities and experiences, than ever in the past.

Job ownership and work leaves

Since people need to continue to 'grow' if they are to maintain an interest in their work—indeed, in their lives—it is in the interest of employers to make this growth process as easy as possible. Such an understanding of the need for retooling underlies the provision of research leaves in universities. It makes sense wherever one can assume a fairly permanent employment bond, high motivation on the part of the worker to produce, and a need for regular upgrading and reskilling. These work (and worker) characteristics may become ever more common in the 'information economy', making work leaves for personal and professional renewal commonplace.

We are far from seeing a wide recognition of the need for and potential benefit of these kinds of flexibility and fluidity. Moreover, the extent to which women (in particular) will take advantage of them will depend on how attractive and available these opportunities are made. To some degree, real availability depends on the availability of good, inexpensive child-care. However, there is already a growing over-representation of women in voluntary part-time work, work retraining, and part-time higher education, and little chance this trend will reverse in future.

For these reasons, the total amount of female fluidity is likely to increase—as we have hypothesized—but the form of the fluidity may shift. Where possible, women will remain within the labour force but shift between part-and full-time jobs, taking leaves for educational upgrading. For the most part, they will remain full participants in the labour force. In future, only women who refuse job changes and retraining will hold the status of 'homemaker' for any length of time.

Projecting female labour supply to 2025

According to the Annual Work Pattern Survey (AWPS), in 1985 the average woman aged 25 to 64 contributed 17.4 hours per week to Canada's supply of paid labour, for a total of 113,184,000 hours per week. How would this supply of labour change between now and the year 2025, under assumed conditions of population growth, aging, educational upgrading, marriage delay, and increases in average participation per week?

Population growth

Between now and 2025, the population of Canada as a whole is likely to grow. How much it grows will depend on changes in fertility, mortality, and immigration. Different assumptions produce at least three quite different estimates of population for the year 2025.

The total female population of Canada is sure to increase to some degree. Even if the proportion of women aged 25 to 64 is the same in 2025 as it was in 1985—50.7 per cent of the total female population—the absolute number of women in this age group will still increase between 1985 and 2025, and so will the total hours of paid labour they produce each week, other things being equal. Depending on which model of total population growth we use, this increase in labour supply will range from 10 to 44 per cent.

Population aging

The Canadian population is aging even as it grows, because of declining fertility. To simplify, we shall adopt Statistics Canada's moderate growth (and moderate aging) scenario as our basis of calculation. 'Moderate aging' will result if fertility holds constant at roughly the early 1980s level (a total fertility rate of 1.66 children per woman; i.e., slightly below replacement) and international migration adds a net 100,000 people to the population each year.

Under these conditions, we can anticipate a total supply of female labour hours 20 per cent higher than it was in 1985, which is 8 per cent lower than it would be if the current age structure were preserved. That is, according to the moderate estimate, population growth will add 28 per cent to the female labour supply (at ages 25 to 64) but population aging will take 8 per cent away, leaving a net gain (between 1985 and 2025) of 20 per cent, all other things being equal.

Educational upgrading

Women have tended to supply more of their labour as they have increased their educational attainments. What, then, will be the labour consequences of educational upgrading in the female population by 2025? To answer this question, we consider two scenarios, one yielding a realistic lower estimate and the other an upper limit. In other respects, the assumptions of the model remain as they were before: namely, moderate population growth and aging between 1985 and 2025.

In the first scenario we assume that by 2025, all women aged 25 to 64 will have an educational distribution that is identical to the distribution of women aged 25 to 34 today. In other words, in future women will receive no less education than the generation of women who are currently aged 25 to 34. In the second, bolder estimate, we assume that all women aged 25 to 64 will have attained some post-secondary education by 2025. As before, the population has grown moderately and aged. All other conditions remain unchanged: namely, women supply the same hours of work—given their age, marital status, and educational level— they would have in 1985.

Our projections show that this educational upgrading will produce an increase in labour supply of no less than 9 and perhaps as much as 16 per cent. The increase in labour supply that is possible through (maximum) educational upgrading—16 per cent—is nearly as large as the increase that results from moderate growth-and-aging of the entire population (20 per cent). Education is a very powerful force for change.

Marriage delay

The Annual Work Patterns Survey data confirm that not-married women—whether never married, divorced, separated, or widowed—supply much more labour power per capita than married or cohabiting women do. Therefore we must consider the future of marriage, and the effect of likely changes in marriage on labour supply.

Recent generations of women, especially more highly educated women, have generally been delaying marriage. It is this trend that we must model. This could be done in a number of different ways, but to simplify the task, we shall make the simplest realistic assumptions and examine their outcome.

In general, we can assume that the patterns of marriage delay observed among women aged 25 to 34 in 1985 will continue. Our high-and low-estimate models build marriage patterns onto the preceding 'educational upgrading' models. In the low-estimate model, we build on the marital pattern that prevails among young women of all educational attainments; in the second instance, the marital pattern prevailing among young, highly educated women.

Specifically, our low-delay model estimates the supply of labour under the condition that by 2025, all women aged 25 to 64 will have the educational-and-marital distribution of all women who are aged 25 to 34 in 1985. In the high-delay model, we consider the supply of labour under the condition that, by 2025, all women aged 25 to 64 will have the educational-and-marital distribution of women aged 25 to 34 in 1985 who have some post-secondary education.

The calculations show that low-level marriage delay has little effect on the labour supply, increasing it by only about one per cent. Increased marital delay—an extension to all women of the marriage pattern of highly educated women aged 25 to 34 in 1985—adds 19 per cent to the labour supply. This effect is larger than the effect of universalizing post-secondary education (16 per cent) and nearly as large as the effect of population growth and aging (20 per cent).

Given current social norms, higher education and later marriage tend to go together; in practice, then, we are likely to get the two together if we get either one. Taken together, these two factors have an enormous effect on the supply of labour—much greater than overall population growth, with or without aging.

Participation increase

Between 1977 and 1985, women dramatically increased their supply of labour, whether we count it in weeks per year or hours per week. To estimate future increases, consider two scenarios. Both build on the assumptions of universal post-secondary education and marriage that is delayed the way it was among post-secondarily educated women aged 25 to 34 in 1985.

In the first model, assume that differences in labour supply due to marital condition disappear by 2025. That is, assume that by then marital status will make no difference to labour supply, and even married women will supply labour at the same rates as unmarried women did in 1985. In the second scenario, imagine the elimination of differences in labour supply due to age (as well as marital condition). That is, assume that by 2025, all women will supply labour at the maximum rate current in 1985—namely, at the rate that highly educated, unmarried women aged 35 to 44 did in 1985.

This last vision of 2025 is as close as we can get to the state of 'perfect individualization', when age, educational attainment, and marital status no longer influence labour-force participation. Under these conditions we can expect the most dramatic increases of all. The first scenario, where married/unmarried distinctions between women disappear, raises labour supply another 42 per cent. The second, 'perfect individualization' scenario raises labour supply 78 per cent above the level where we have merely delayed marriage and upgraded education.

However, one further refinement of the model is needed, and that is to take regional variation into account. Current work opportunities for women vary significantly between regions. For example, residence in Ontario predicts a higher than average participation rate and more working hours per week, presumably because of the greater availability of work for women in Ontario. So perfect individualization would increase labour supply more in some regions than others, given current rates of demand. (Indeed, some urban centres like Toronto may already be well along the road to perfect individualization.)

Regional variations

For simplicity, we include four provinces east of Quebec in the Eastern region and four provinces west of Ontario in the Western region. The Annual Work Patterns Survey data show considerable variations in the mean hours that women worked in each of these regions in 1985, holding constant age, education, and marital status.

In general, Ontario women worked longer hours than women in any other region. Similarities across regions were greatest for highly educated, unmarried women. On the other hand, Ontario seemed to offer more work opportunities for less educated women than the other regions did. Ontario women with primary-school education worked nearly twice as many hours per week than equally educated women in the Eastern and Quebec regions, for example.

The effects of educational attainment and marital status on hours worked also varied significantly among regions, and they interacted differently with each other too. So, for example, educational attainment had a much greater effect on the hours that married women worked in Ontario than in Quebec or the East. The effect of educational attainment on the hours that unmarried women worked was almost twice as high as it was for married women, across the board. But it was a stronger influence on women in the East and Quebec than in Ontario and the Western region. This suggests that educational upgrading between now and 2025 will have a much more profound effect on female labour supply in Quebec and the Maritimes than in Ontario and the West, and the effect on unmarried women will be greatest. Of course, this also assumes that a larger demand for educated women will develop at the same rate as women become available for work.

We saw earlier that unmarried women tend to work longer hours per week than married women, other things being equal. This tendency also varies both regionally and educationally. Across the board, the variation due to marital status was least for women with only a primary-school education and most for women with a post-secondary education. In general, marital status influenced the labour supply of women most in Ontario and least in Quebec.

This argues that, as marriage is further delayed between now and 2025, and participation in higher education increases, the impact of these changes will be felt most in Ontario (and, nearly identically, in the West) and least in Quebec. This kind of change tends to offset the regional variation discussed above in connection with educational upgrading. Still, the regional variation in the influence of education on working hours is far greater than the (opposite) regional variation in the influence of marriage delay. Overall, then, these data suggest that educational upgrading and marriage delay will have higher than average (i.e., national) effects on labour supply in Quebec and the East and roughly average effects in the West.

Our projections of the future show, first, large regional variations in the projected growth of person-hours worked, with the

Eastern region gaining most and Quebec gaining least. Second, they show that all regions together will yield 269,035,000 hours of paid work per week by women aged 25 to 64—and this by 2005. That is, the benefits of change anticipated for 2025 may actually be more than realized by 2005, and then start to decline slightly as population-growth gains are offset by population-aging losses.

Thus major gains in labour participation could be seen within twenty years, under conditions of moderate population growth and aging, universal post-secondary education, and all women's working at the maximum rates currently observed in their region. (In all cases but one, these maximum rates were those worked by unmarried women with a post-secondary education and aged 35 to 44 in 1985. The exception is found in the Eastern region, where unmarried women who were aged 25 to 34 and had taken some post-secondary education participated most in the labour force.)

Regions differ in the relative significance of influences on hours worked by women. In the East, West, and Ontario, the chief percentage gains in labour supply are due to increases in female participation that blur the differences between young and old, or between married and unmarried women. To get the large growth in labour supply implied by these changes would require enactment and enforcement of legislation barring discrimination on the basis of age or marital status, and the funding of improved opportunities for training and infant day-care.

Our projections indicate that educational upgrading will play only a small part in the growth of female labour supply in Ontario and the West, but a quite an important role in Quebec and the Eastern region. It follows that in order to increase female labour supply in these regions, opportunities for post-secondary education will have to improve.

Finally, population growth and aging will play a major part in Eastern Canada, where the population is growing and aging slowly, because of somewhat higher than average fertility; and in Ontario, which is the chief recipient of younger international migrants. Presumably, major shifts in fertility and immigration will have the largest impact on these regions.

These results suggest that there will be enormous increases in labour supply coming from within the Canadian female population. The process of individualization is already advancing smoothly and rapidly, and certain policies will help this process along, making the increases even greater. We will discuss these further in the next chapter.

CONCLUDING REMARKS

Within the main female-employing industries of Canada's most urbanized, 'post-industrial' labour markets—Ontario and Quebec—age has lost all of its importance as a predictor of hours worked and marital status has lost some, while education has gained importance as a predictor. Yet overall, these three variables are less able to predict hours worked in 1985 than they were in 1977.

Under conditions of population growth and 'perfect individualization' as we have defined it here, the labour supplied by women aged 25 to 64 will more than double by 2025, to an average of 40 hours per week. This means that by 2025, population increase, educational upgrading, delayed marriage, and individualization will have produced the equivalent of another 1985 female labour force.

The implication of this finding for labour supply is obvious. If the Canadian economy needs significantly more worker hours, they can be found by increasing opportunities for female post-secondary education and reducing the barriers (in particular, insufficient day-care) that currently limit labour-force participation by the mothers of young children.

To unleash this prodigious growth in labour supply—to unchain this working giant—means educating women more, and making age, marital status, and parenthood less burdensome to working women than they are today. In a word, individualization of the female life-course can do the job, if we want it to.

Our projections argue that the individualization of adult women's lives is the answer to any labour shortage that Canada may experience now or in the near future, if we are willing to pay the price: more spending on education, more spending on day-care, and more spending to counter discrimination against women, especially aged women and mothers. What we cannot tell from these projections is whether individualization will improve women's lives. That question is the topic of the next, and final, chapter of this book.

Note

[1] As we noted earlier, our 'individualization' hypothesis strictly implies that models of female labour supply based on such correlations between labour-force behaviour and personal characteristics of women and their families will be less useful than in the past. Instead, our models will have to include more indicators of demand, but we ignore this for the present. The projection is made separately for women with three kinds of family composition.

Does 'Individualization' Mean 'Improvement'?

The data we have presented make it clear that the situation of women has changed. In this chapter we will show that the situation has not necessarily improved, but that, since the changes for women are far greater than for men, and of a different nature, researchers must now ask different questions about equality, changes in women's status and role, social policy, and the values held about women's lives. In our hypothetical case studies we have talked about some women's lives, and here we will speculate upon their future possibilities. Finally, we will pose some of the theoretical questions for feminist studies in the light of our findings.

WHAT ABOUT THE NEXT THREE DECADES?

The women whose lives we have been describing in this book range in age from their late teens to their fifties. In different ways, all of these women's lives are more varied, fluid, and idiosyncratic than those of women in earlier generations. What will happen to them in the next few decades? How can they plan their lives to minimize distress and maximize satisfaction?

Let us start by looking at the variety in their lives. Each of these women now occupies a greater variety of social statuses than she would have in the past. She may be a paid worker as well as a housewife; a member of public organizations as well as a wife and mother. She manages her own economic life (banking, investments, pensions, and benefits) as well as the household budget. She shares duties and responsibilities at home as well as in the workplace. Finally, she has the chance to be a judge, a politician, a chief executive officer of a corporation, a minister of a church, a principal of a school, a miner, a telephone line 'man', or to work in many other occupations and positions that in the past were open almost exclusively to men as a matter of custom and often as a matter of law.

In short, the segregation between the *public* and the *private* spheres has changed. We are not saying that work is the same for women and for men—far from it. We are saying that the women we have described in this book will move back and forth across the public-private line in ways that are more similar to the ways in which men have always operated. The reduction of *segregation* between the public and private does *not* mean that the *content* of the roles occupied in either sphere has changed. For example, while men have always been fathers as well as workers, the amount of time and energy required of them in the father role has been much less than that required of women, then or now, in the mother role.

In legal terms, too, the variety in women's lives has increased—in this case, the variety of their responsibilities. Women today hold public offices, bank accounts, property, and positions that through most of Canadian history they have not been able to hold. When marriages break up, no fault has to be shown, and in most provinces property is divided equally between the partners in the marriage. (Unfortunately, division of property means little in economic terms to most women, who, despite this 'progressive' law, end up much less well off after divorce, at least in material terms.) The legal fact is that adult women are now responsible for their own economic well-being throughout their adult lives.

This means that women in their fifties, like MARGARET, must look carefully at their legal rights and obligations. Old women are still among the poorest people in Canada. Many live only on the very small pension provided by the government to everyone over 65 years of age, and the Guaranteed Income Supplement, a means-tested income given to older Canadians who have no private pension or savings. Unless women like MARGARET plan very carefully, they will become another generation of poor old women. They need to know that they are legally responsible for their own support and affairs, and because of divorce, may not even be able to rely on the money that women in the past inherited from their husbands.

Younger women, like ROSA, CARLA, GAIL, and the others we have discussed, also have to look at their legal obligations. Who is (or will be) responsible for their children? What happens if they become single parents? We have seen from the data above that young women stand a good chance of being single parents at some point in their lives. While fathers have an obligation in most cases to pay support, collecting it is so difficult that the federal and provincial governments have worked out a scheme to make the payments collectible. For self-defence, young women have to learn about bank accounts and mortgages, about how the tax system works for them both alone and as members of a family.

Women, then, must now hold a wide variety of statuses simultaneously as workers, mothers, and so on, all of which have important legal and economic consequences. And in this respect, gender is more important to women than social class. Whether a woman is rich or poor, well or poorly equipped for the labour market, she is legally responsible for many aspects of her life that in the past were taken care of by her father, her husband, or a male guardian. Changes in marital status or changes in jobs can bring major consequences for any woman.

For men, in a sense we can say that the variety of psychological conditions in their lives is increasing. These are the problems that both FRANK and LES find. They always expected to be husbands, fathers, and workers, but FRANK, at least, never thought that he might have to put a great deal of time and energy into his family roles. He assumed that his work would be his wife's major concern as well as his own. He is coming to grips with a new definition of the role of husband and father, and is unsure how his son should prepare for adulthood. Men can no longer control women; they can no longer count on women's psychological support regardless of their behaviour; they may have to be deeply involved in bringing up their own children. Nevertheless, those changes affect only the conditions inside the statuses they have always held as workers, fathers, husbands, and property-owners. Women, on the other hand, have expanded the variety of statuses they hold, and can no longer count on men for economic support.

Second, let us look at *fluidity*, or the way in which the women we have talked about move in and out of statuses. Why do women have this fluidity? In this case, social class may be more important than gender. One major reason why women move in and out of paid work is their responsibility for the care of their children. Canadians live in a society in which access to child-care is very difficult, especially if you have a low or middle income. There are too few good-quality spaces in most towns and cities, and infant care is especially hard to find. In provinces with low tax bases, like the Atlantic provinces, publicly supported child-care is particularly rare. Even in the richer provinces like Quebec and Ontario, spaces are scarce, and many of them are expensive (Cooke, 1986).

If you are earning a high income and can afford to hire a nanny, you still have problems (nannies leave, get sick, go on holidays) but you are better off than most parents. If you are like the vast majority of Canadian women, you are earning about two-thirds of the wages of a man with the same skills. This means two things. One is that if you are married, you are likely to either leave the paid labour force or work part-time to care for your children because your husband's higher salary means that it makes economic sense for the family. The other is that you cannot afford good-quality child-care and are likely to use unlicensed services that will require you to travel considerable distances to drop off and pick up your child. In the recent past, grandparents often provided child-care, but now most women are in the paid labour force until an advanced age, and this trend will continue. While some extended-family arrangements solve child-care problems for working parents, this is increasingly unusual. Furthermore, Canadians are geographically quite mobile, and grandparents and other relatives often live hundreds or thousands of miles away.

A system of good-quality child-care either in family settings or in schools and public settings has been discussed for years. OECD countries like France, Germany, and Sweden offer the child-care options we described in Chapter 4. Until Canada develops similar support for parents, a much higher proportion of women will appear 'fluid' in the paid labour market than really wish to be.

And child-care is only one obligation that makes women move in and out of the labour market. Another is the care of older parents. As families become smaller, there are fewer children to help—in particular, as most women now are in the paid labour force, fewer of the traditional daughters. Canada has a very high rate of institutionalization of older people: that is, putting aged parents in special homes. Some parents like this arrangement; others do not, and suffer depression, anxiety and sickness as a result. As people live longer, caring for older parents will become a more important problem for the children.

It is still daughters who care for the family (Land, 1978) and here, once again, social class makes a difference. Those with high in-comes can afford to have a companion live with their parents, either in the latter's home or in their children's. Well-off people are also likely to have healthier parents, since income level and health status are highly correlated. In terms of public policy, Canadians are still finding the way forward to proper and equitable care for older people. The role that their children, both men and women, will play in this is unclear at present.

The third major reason why women are 'fluid' is the increase in part-time jobs. Especially in traditionally female job ghettos such as banks, retail stores, and service jobs in many sectors, middle- and low-level positions are being converted to part-time to achieve flexibility in hours, costs, and labour supply. (The data on these changes have been described in detail in Chapters 2, 4, and 5). This is possible for employers because in many jobs, the quality of the work hardly depends at all on training full-time workers. While, as we have shown above, involuntary part-time work is increasing generally, it is *not* increasing in jobs for the very well educated, whose high-status positions require long and demanding hours. Once again, social class and fluidity are strongly related.

The women we have described may experience many types of fluidity in their lives. ROSA has to cope with child-care. She and other women like her all have to think of the care of their parents. BRENDA and GAIL may hold jobs that are converted to part-time work, but CARLA and ANNA are likely to 'choose' fluidity rather than have it thrust upon them. Although gender is important in fluidity, since women still bear the major responsibility for children, social class still dominates. That is, the higher a woman's socio-economic status, the less likely she is to *have* to be fluid in the labour market.

Third and finally, what will happen to the women we have discussed in terms of *idiosyncracy*—that is, the predictability of their lives? In this instance, age is often as important a factor as gender, social class, and other variables. Generally, speaking, it is likely that the younger women we have studied—the SUZYs, ANNAs, and BRENDAs—will marry, remarry, or otherwise form a stable relationship with someone; we can predict this in the aggregate even if we cannot do so for any individual woman. Much of what makes women's lives idiosyncratic, however, occurs because of events that are beyond their control: for example, divorce, widowhood, the state of their health, even changes in the law. We might say that it arises because of women's vulnerability. And to the extent that age increases the risk of such changes in their situation, older women may find their lives becoming increasingly idiosyncratic.

Take the case of MARGARET, who surprised everyone by divorcing her husband of twenty-eight years and now, at 50, is back at school full-time. In due course, she will finish her degree and get a job counselling students at a community college. But she has only about fifteen years left to earn enough money to retire on. Even a highly paid job will mean that she must save a lot for a twenty-year retirement. If she succeeds in buying her own home over that period of time, she will be better off than if she must rent throughout her retirement years. If the law requiring mandatory retirement is abolished, she may have to work as long as she is physically able in order to live decently. But that, in turn, will depend a lot on her health. Over ten per cent of adult women develop breast cancer, for example, usually after the age of fifty, and this requires a fairly long period of treatment and recovery. Will MARGARET have long-term sickness benefits in her job? If her health remains good, what else might make her future life unpredictable? What if she remarries? Her economic situation might improve, but she might also become more 'fluid' in the labour market, changing to a different pattern of labour-force participation to accomodate a husband who moves or retires.

Is MARGARET likely to remarry? Are BRENDA and ANNA likely to marry once, twice, three times or not at all? Part of the answer to these questions can be found in the Canadian research on life satisfaction (Tepperman, 1989). It shows that love and marriage are the chief sources of life satisfaction for Canadians, when spouses offer affection, interest in one's work, companionship, and a good understanding of feelings, as well as sexual fulfilment. All kinds of romantic intimacy bring women somewhat more life satisfaction than they bring men. The corollary is that women experience more unhappiness at being alone, because of widowhood or divorce, than men do.

Will MARGARET find job satisfaction? The data we have tell us that the closer her job requirements match with her education, the more satisfied she will be with her work. This match between education and job is more important than salary for Canadians generally in finding job satisfaction (Tepperman, 1988). But we know that Canadians generally find greater satisfaction in their personal lives than in their work, although both are important. Women, more than men, are 'unwilling to give up leisure and family time for the sake of their careers' (Tepperman, 1988: 107) We know also from survey data that job satisfaction has dropped recently among Canadians, more so among the highly educated than among those with high-school education, and more sharply among women than men. So we can conclude that some of the idiosyncracy in the lives of women is attributable to the search for satisfaction with life, both at work and at home.

In this sense, then, some of the idiosyncracy in a woman's life is a matter of choice. Women have more liberty but less equality than men in this regard. For example, many women take retirement before the age of 65, whether simply because they can afford to or because they wish to retire at the same time as their husbands. The liberty here arises from the different expectations that society has of women and of men; men have less freedom to be idiosyncratic in this way because of the rigid demands that the labour market makes on their lives. Nevertheless, women are more limited than men in the ways in which they can exercise their choice. For example, women's investment in their education shows lower returns than men's (Denton, 1984; Harvey, Marsden, and Charner, 1975); women have fewer opportunities to enter high-prestige, well-paying jobs; and in any jobs they have fewer chances for advancement and influence on decision-making (Peitchinis, 1989). Given that women's jobs are likely to provide them with even less satisfaction than their marriages, early retirement is hardly surprising.

Finally, though, it is worth noting that while some of the idiosyncracy in women's lives is chosen because it promises more satisfaction, that same idiosyncracy may, paradoxically, reduce overall life satisfaction. For, as Tepperman points out, people tend to feel satisfied when their lives approximate their expectations, and those expectations arise to a large extent from looking at what their peers, or reference groups, are doing. Whatever the reasons, when our women—MARGARET, ROSA, ANNA, GAIL—look around, they do not see a pattern they recognize. Unlike their mothers, contemporary women lead widely different lives and, as the data in preceding chapters have shown, their marriages and their work lives are likely to keep on changing. We would expect to find lower levels of life satisfaction, then, because it is difficult to recognize a peer group in their idiosyncratic world.

Before moving on to discuss the more formal and theoretical questions of interest to feminist scholars, let us review the main points of this section. We have outlined some of the reasons why variety, fluidity and idiosyncracy have changed, but not necessarily improved, women's lives; we have also shown why these changes may not increase women's life satisfaction. In addition, we have suggested some of the pressures that contemporary women experience because of their inequality in the labour market (for instance, part-time work) and the inadequacy of government support (for instance, in the form of child-care). When these pressures from the larger society combine with a sense of personal dissatisfaction, a woman may want to change her life; some of the factors that any woman will have eventually to consider have been illustrated by the case of MARGARET.

SOME QUESTIONS FOR FEMINIST THEORETICIANS

What are we to make of the patterns that women have developed over the past generation? We see that they are different from those of contemporary men and different from those of women in the past. Can we say that there is more or less equality for women? Can we say that the status of women has improved? Can we even say that these patterns will be permanent features of the lives of adult women? These questions are asked of anyone studying the situation of women. The problem is how to compare the equality of women now and in the past. There can be no satisfactory theoretical answer to this. Social inequality takes many forms, and it concerns far more than inequality between women and men. For example, social class differences, age differences, ethnic and cultural differences pervade all the modern industrial capitalist societies that we have been comparing in this study.

Let's ask a simpler question. Given all other conditions in these societies, and assuming that our thesis about individualization holds true, are women better off today than in the past?

On the question of equality

It is almost impossible for us to imagine a situation of equality between the sexes in a real society because, as far as we know, it has never occurred in human history. Perhaps there really never has been such a society; perhaps the records were lost; or perhaps it's just that history has always been written by people who failed to perceive or to document that equality: we cannot tell. We must take as a given the fact of male dominance to a greater or lesser degree, and in a wide variety of forms and intensities, throughout human history. Furthermore, this dominance prevails in all documented forms of economic life. Although some believe that capitalism reinforces patriarchy (or the social dominance of men), it can also be argued that pre-capitalist and non-capitalist economies and societies too are dominated by men (Fox, 1988). In any case, since Canadian women have lived within a capitalist system throughout the period we are discussing, and all the societies we have looked at are to some extent capitalist as well, we have no basis for the comparisons that would allow us to judge the relationship between capitalism and patriarchy. What we can say is that economic activity is central to the situation of women in any society, whatever form it takes. Male dominance, or patriarchy, is to be found in the patterns of behaviour in economic life and social life. Those patterns of behaviour in everyday life are expressions of our values, and those values are dominated by the values of men. Over time, even in the short history of Canada, the forms of economic activity have changed, the values have changed, and the patterns of behaviour of women, and toward women, have changed. But for all those changes, which continue to occur, male dominance remains.

For this reason, as well as documenting and analyzing changes in the economic structure of the society and the economic situation of women, we must look at the extent to which the dominant values of the society are changing where women are concerned. Within a capitalist system, have women become more equal as participating members of the society in law, in the economy, or in power? To what extent are women perceived to be more equal than they were in comparison to women in the past and to men today?

Political philosophers sometimes claim that people in modern democratic societies are more concerned with individual liberty than with equality (see, for example, Gutmann, 1980). In the feminist literature, these two concepts are intertwined and difficult to separate because traditionally, in our culture, women have lacked both. For example, the Canadian Charter of Human Rights and Freedoms entrenches in the constitution a series of rights, or liberties, that exist regardless of one's sex (Section 28). At the same time, Section 15 guarantees equality rights and allows affirmative-action programs to exist constitutionally to ameliorate the conditions of inequality. The resulting changes in our laws and customs based on the Charter may allow us to develop a more sophisticated understanding of the differences between liberty and equality in the lives of women. For example, one of the most important steps for women in Canada has been the success of women lawyers in persuading the Supreme Court to use a broader definition of equality than one based on a comparison with men. In situations such as child-bearing, there can be no valid comparison between women and men and so equality rights must be conceived separately (LEAF, 1989).

For our purposes, the concept of equality between the sexes refers to a hypothetical situation in which being born of one sex or the other would imply no intrinsic inequality; if it existed, there would be no important differences in life chances associated with sex. This may sound fairly straightforward, but in fact it is probably impossible to comprehend, let alone measure, all the elements that would be required in order to say that such equality had been attained. With our data we can only make relatively coarse measurements of the distribution of goods, services, and opportunities between men and women. These can, however, tell us something about the degree to which some kind of egalitarianism is being achieved in our society. Some may argue that we are not even going that far—that all we are showing are changes in the patterns of women's behaviour, or the organization of their time. But these changes do tell us some important things about how women mobilize the resources available to them to participate in the society. In that sense they offer a picture of how equality and liberty are used—how choices are made—within the constraints of the society.

The constraints of our society have all been causes of change in the situation of women. For example, it is without question that the demand for female labour drew women, especially married women, into the paid labour force and continues to do so (cf., Oppenheimer, 1976 and Nakamura, Nakamura, and Cullen, 1979). It is also clear that the changing wage distribution in Canada has made two incomes necessary in many families. Structural changes in the Canadian economy—that is, female labour wanted and a second income needed—have had different impacts on men and women. This difference has been documented in Chapter 3 above.

Whether legal changes preceded or followed these structural economic changes is a matter of debate. Certainly the vanguard politics of the feminist movement preceded the changes (cf., Mac-Gill, 1981; Strong-Boag, 1976). The constant work of the women's movement for legal changes in marital and property law, in employment standards, wage laws, and access to forms of training and post-secondary education eventually had their effect on the laws of Canada and the provinces (Baines, 1988; Marsden, 1979; Marsden and Busby, 1990; Peitchinis, 1989). But legal changes often also have consequences no one intended. For example, until the 1970s there were laws setting out special protective conditions intended to help women who worked the night shift. But the unintended consequence was that employers avoided hiring women for this shift because they had to provide transportation for women and not for men. Since the night shift often paid higher wages, the result was the exclusion of women from the highest-paying jobs in their occupation. This example shows how difficult it is to predict whether winning new liberties will necessarily produce greater egalitarianism. And even if we can show greater egalitarianism—for example, that the wage gap between women and men has declined—there is no clear link between that finding and the existence of greater equality between the sexes.

Still, the data we have presented do give us a picture of how the women of Canada, and their comparison groups in other societies, have used the resources available to them—in law, in economic changes, in scientific and technical improvements such as the birth-control pill—and this picture in turn tells us something about their values. One example is the way women have used their legal access (after 1968) to reliable contraceptives to control their family size and spacing and thus to enter the labour force in unprecedented numbers. Women today spend less time on mothering than in the past, and yet they do not typically hold jobs the way men do: they do not simply continue in full-time work until retirement. Rather, as we have seen, they use a variety of strategies in order to be both mothers and workers.

As the labour-force participation rate of women, especially married women, rises, it becomes increasingly clear that women are adopting a different model from men. Whether this model is forced upon them by a lack of options , such as the availability of child-care, or whether women would move in and out of the paid labour force even with those options, we cannot yet determine.

It is impossible to say, therefore, whether the equality of men and women has increased or decreased. All we can say with certainty is that we live in a more egalitarian society in terms of access to both the paid labour force and domestic life, to both the 'public' and 'private' spheres.

On the question of status: men and women compared

The 'status' of women is another angle from which to look at change, one that is somewhat easier to deal with than the question of equality. Sociologically, the term refers to a position in the social structure (who you are), while the term 'role' refers to what you do and the rights you enjoy while occupying that status. Earlier in this chapter, we showed that women now occupy more social statuses than in the past (e.g., as mothers *and* workers). Apparently, then, because women have a greater variety of statuses available to them, they can do more and different things than in the past. Or can they?

A useful related concept is that of status set. In the world of the traditional Canadian woman (pre-1968) the status set was more narrowly confined (i.e., woman, wife, mother, volunteer, sister, etc.) and the most salient of those statuses (the one that determined people's responses) was likely to be mother or wife. In the world we are now describing, the status set has expanded to include occupation, employment, and citizen; the salient status is employment/occupation. But even now, for women, two important statuses held coincidentally may both condition people's responses: i.e., occupation and mother (Mackie, 1983: 280). A man's most salient status is unlikely to be split between his status as father and as worker.

As Mackie points out, salient statuses may have an impact on other statuses. For example, people may omit their age from resumés because it might affect their job chances. Age is a status that conditions responses toward both sexes. Among women, listing marital and family status may limit occupational chances. Failing to hold the status of mother, or worker, may affect other people's idea of the social value of the women concerned. This is not the case for men, whose value is still most closely linked to occupational status. Women's status as mother, actual or potential, seems unavoidable, even among childless women, and defines a different social situation for women than for men.

We have been speaking of women as individuals. By contrast, in public policy the term 'status' refers to the situation of one group in relation to another. Thus the Canadian Royal Commission on the Status of Women (1970), while it fails to discuss the meaning of the term 'status', makes the liberal democratic assumption that there should be 'no distinction in rights and freedoms between women and men rather than a separate status for each sex' (p. xi) and goes on to base its work on four principles: freedom for women to choose whether to take employment outside their homes; shared responsibility for child-care between mothers, fathers, and society; the continuing necessity of special social responsibility for women because of pregnancy and childbirth; and recognition that 'in certain areas women will for an interim period require special treatment to overcome the adverse effects of discriminatory practices' (p. xii). In effect, these principles show us what the Commissioners saw as the desirable status of women.

Another example is a book prepared by Statistics Canada and the C.D. Howe Institute as a project for International Women's Year in 1975. It also addresses the question of status in public-policy terms:

> many of the problems, as well as many of the opportunities, for women in Canada are associated with the mixed capitalistic-governmental nature of our economy—an economy in which, for the most part, only paid productive activity is recognized in measures of economic output, in which success tends to be rewarded by income, and in which status tends to be measured by income. (Cook, 1976: 2)

In this study, the objective of public policy is to create 'opportunity for choice' so that 'the whole range of advantages and disadvantages or costs and benefits of particular choices might be unrelated to one's sex' (Cook, 1976: 2).

In light of the discussion of the sociological meaning of status above, this public-policy use of the term becomes important. For public-policy purposes, status inequality refers to the relationships between groups of one kind or another. For a sociologist studying interpersonal relations or family life, the comparison is between the socially defined positions of one person and another.

When we argued, above, that inequality takes many other social forms apart from gender inequality, we pointed to differences of ethnicity, social class, and culture. What the empirical evidence shows is that whatever categories we use to define inequalities, women are less well off than men in the same social groups. For example, Reitz (1980) has shown that when major categories of ethnic groups in Canada are ranked in terms of economic opportunities, within each of those groups women are less well placed than men, while in the variety of ethnic groups studied by Breton et al. (1989) in Canada, women in each group occupied lower-status occupations than their male counterparts. If social class is measured in terms of the socio-economic status variables of education, income, and occupational status, women receive lower returns on their investment in education than men (e.g., Marsden and Harvey, 1972), and their incomes are lower in every occupational group, even when the occupation is a female-dominated one such as nursing, teaching, or clerical work. Moreover, as women enter male-dominated occupations, the income levels in those occupations decline (Fox and Fox, 1987).

It is more difficult to assess occupational status in terms of gender. Generally, female-dominated occupations have lower status than men's within the same industrial groups (e.g., nursing in comparison to medicine) and, within occupations, women are more often found in the lower-status specializations or subgroups (Boyd et al., 1985; Eichler, 1976)

One aspect of the relationship between status and egalitarianism outside the labour market can be seen in what is known as 'secondary poverty': the situation wherein people lack the knowledge or the education to use their income or assets effectively and, as a result, may live in poverty even when the family's income should be sufficient (Gutmann, 1980: 90ff.). Within families where husbands are the main or only wage earners, women (wives/mothers) may not get enough money from their husbands, may not get it on a predictable basis, or may not know the family's financial situation well enough to 'plan' spending effectively. In addition, since women have both unequal education and unequal opportunity for earnings, they may not have the skills to manage resources. It is these factors that account for secondary poverty.

In our society, where the largest group in poverty is single mothers with dependent children, poverty may be both primary or secondary, often both. Typically, women who find themselves in primary poverty have been in a state of secondary poverty for years. They were housewives or daughters without experience of the labour market. They did not know or learn about the family budget. They are not in the paid labour market and have no marketable skills. In the event of divorce, or for teenagers, pregnancy, under current law regarding marital property or public support women find themselves having to make rapid adjustments to the labour market, single life, and family relations without a spouse and *without skills*. They then enter a state of primary poverty.

The women whose lives we have been discussing here are all in the process of acquiring post-secondary education. This minimizes their risk of living in secondary poverty. The very fact that they have been admitted to university means that they have some skills and education, and the more they complete, the more secure they will be. But at the present time one million Canadian children are living in poverty, the majority in single-parent families, mostly with their mothers. In order to prevent many of these children from growing up into poverty, a great deal depends upon public policy in their lives and in the lives of their mothers and fathers (Ross and Shillington, 1989). In public-policy terms, the status of women differs from that of men, and among groups of women defined by such factors as income, but those differences are 'caused' and reduced by different means. Education still offers the best hope of access to better opportunities (Peitchinis, 1989: 160)

On the question of change: past and future

We have documented a change in the pattern of adult women's lives that, by some measures, may indicate an 'improvement' in the status of women and may, by some measures, reflect a more egalitarian society for women. However, we have argued that this by no means reflects 'gender equality' in society.

We have cast the concepts of variety, fluidity, and idiosyncracy in contemporary terms and measured them with current data. Using statistical indicators of marriage, child-bearing, and labour-force participation rates, we have argued that, in comparison to the past, women today experience more variety in their roles (householder, paid worker, citizen), more fluidity in moving among their adult roles, and more idiosyncracy in the sense that their lives show considerable individual variation, far more than is the case for men. Perhaps this is just a brief period in women's history, and the individualization of women's lives will disappear as new social patterns form. Perhaps, also, we have misunderstood the extent to which the lives of women in the past were individualized.

Before asking whether the changes towards individualization will be permanent, therefore, it is worth asking whether we have given a fair representation of the variety, fluidity, and idiosyncracy of women's lives in the 'traditional period', a period we define as the years from about 1850 to 1968. The key to under-standing this problem lies in the definition of what constituted the 'public' and 'private' spheres in the past. It was in the middle to late nineteenth century that the distinction between the 'public' and 'private' spheres in the lives of women was reinforced among Canadians:

> The proper sphere of women was an obsession of Victorian and Edwardian Canadians, and they delighted in writing about it. Women were told what it meant to be a woman and the proper way to behave. (Prentice et al., 1988: 111)

While the range of paid occupations that women entered be-tween 1850 and 1914 expanded somewhat from mainly domestic service to manufacturing and a variety of service-sector jobs in-cluding office work, teaching, and nursing, nevertheless the domestic, or private sphere, dominated their lives.

To begin, let's look at the ways in which women brought in family income in the 'private' domestic sphere. When the family farm was the source of family income, women's contribution was very clear (cf., Tivy, 1972; Cohen, 1988; Kohl, 1976; Morissette, 1987). Even non-farm women generated income at home in cash and kind that was important to their livelihood and provided variety, fluidity, and idiosyncracy within the 'housewife' role that have never been captured by official data.

For example, several studies have shown that taking in boarders has been—and is still—one of the most common ways of sup-plementing the family's income (Bradbury, 1984; Luxton, 1980; Hollingsworth and Tyyska, 1989). By keeping boarders women acquired the economic status of 'landlady', but since this was never measured in economic data, we have tended to ignore it. In addition, many women worked at home as seamstresses in this period. They took care of other women's children for pay, as many still do. They gardened and then canned the produce; they kept chickens, rabbits and other small animals to supply their own tables (Bradbury, 1984) and to exchange as gifts. Until the 1960s, in fact, in most working- and middle-class households these forms of food production were important substitutions for cash, even in urban and suburban areas.

Besides being important economic roles, these activities added considerable variety to these women's lives. And there were many other ways in which the time of women whose status is described by us as 'homemaker' or 'at home' was filled with variety and diversity. Women with enough income might spend a great deal of time on charitable and voluntary work, most of which took place at home. That this work was important is documented by the National Council of Women in its report of 1900 to the Paris exhibition (National Council of Women, 1900) and in every history of women's rights in Canada. Meetings held in drawing rooms involved sewing and craftwork to raise funds for a variety of causes. This was real work with real economic consequences for the community.

Women of all social classes were responsible for the extensive work involved in maintaining kinship links, whether by visiting in person, by writing, or by telephoning other family members or through the organization of ritual occasions such as weddings, birthdays, and funerals. Often women were the nurses for sick and dying relatives, leaving their own households for weeks at a time to help parents and other members of the family. For many urban Canadians, a summer holiday visit changed the pace of life and provided a variety of activities and a fluidity to their lives similar to those we have described for contemporary women. The major difference is that in our times paid work predominates in these changes and is recorded in official data.

So the question becomes one of what is measured. We are saying that, by official counts, women now occupy a wider variety of statuses among which they move with great fluidity. But we have just shown that the traditional 'housewife' might also have a variety of statuses including landlady, food producer, babysitter, social-welfare worker, and so on. It was only in the late nineteenth century, when the public/private dimension became so emphatic, that we put them all together under one status. In our age, domestic work for the majority of women has become much less various and much more determined.

Consider that now women work for a fixed number of hours in the paid labour force each day or week and have much less time for housework. Holidays have been reduced to those allowed by the employer rather than those dictated by the season, opportunity, or the school term. Most women can now make more money by working outside the home than by taking in boarders or sewing; preserved food bought for cash lasts longer and is generally preferred over home-canned produce. The only 'domestic' work that remains an important source of income today is caring for other women's children.

Because the 'private sphere' was never the subject of official study or measurement, we cannot make a true comparison between the roles of women now and in the past. We can only say that for many women at least, the role of housewife or mother has become less varied, more rigid, more narrow and more constrained than in the past.

As for idiosyncracy, that too is impossible to document. Before the advent of reliable means of birth control, women were always at risk of pregnancy. Older women often had a late child, creating a 'second family' and making their lives more comparable to those of younger women. Circumstances of many sorts—the death of a husband, the inheritance or loss of property, migration—changed the lives of women more then than now when life insurance and a variety of protective measures cushion the dramatic changes faced by previous generations. By contrast, the legalization of the birth-control pill and other reliable methods in Canada in 1968 had the immediate effect of reducing the number of pregnancies among older women. This has led to women becoming more 'predictable' as a source of labour supply, and in that respect less idiosyncratic.

In any event, those aspects of women's lives belonged to the 'private sphere' where, as the law suggested, a man and wife were one person and that person was the man. So aside from what we can learn from biographies and other personal or anecdotal accounts, the richness and variation in the lives of women of those earlier times is lost to us today.

What happened outside the 'private sphere' was in some senses the reverse. The variety of jobs open to women was far more restricted—in contemporary terms, the occupational segregation was much greater—than it is now. In addition, paid labour aside, the positions that women held in the community were much more restricted. Women as members of local councils and school boards, for example, were rare largely because of property qualifications and other barriers (cf., Cleverdon, 1974; Brodie, 1985). Although women gained the provincial vote between 1916 and 1921 except in Quebec, where the vote was not won until 1945, with some notable exceptions this did not lead to women's holding public office. Women were not constitutionally 'persons' until 1929, when they could start to sit as members of the Senate of

Canada, practise law in all jurisdictions, and enter all professions. Financial responsibility was limited. Married women's rights to hold bank accounts were restricted; and even after a series of reforms, divorce was very difficult to obtain until l968.

For women, then, the early and middle industrial periods can be said to have been dominated by the private sphere in which considerable variation was possible, depending upon financial circumstances and family size. This contrasts with the last twenty years, when the private sphere has become increasingly restricted and the public sphere far more various. The status of women is more equal now: many laws have been changed, making it easier for women to compete in the economy, stand equally in the courts, and claim equality under the Constitution. Even though it cannot measure them, therefore, our historical comparison provides a useful picture of these significant social, legal, and economic changes. There is another way of making the comparison, however, which is to recognize that despite these changes the public-private distinction—an inherently unequal one—has not disappeared, and to examine the extent to which it is still in force.

Can women now occupy all adult roles? The data presented in earlier chapters show that while women occupy a much greater variety of occupational roles than in the past, those roles are still different from men's. For example, women are still highly occupationally segregated (Peitchinis, 1989, Chap. 3). As the legal barriers are removed—for example, the barrier preventing women from occupying combat roles in the armed forces—the probability increases that a woman may occupy any available role in the society.

As in the economy, in political life too the possibilities for women have expanded. Women now occupy seats on the Supreme Court of Canada and all the lower courts, though not in the same proportions as men; they occupy seats in the cabinets of both the federal and the provincial governments, although not yet the most powerful positions of finance minister and premier or prime minister. So what we are seeing, by this measure, are the legal and social possibilities for women's greater equality in the public sphere without seeing a changed pattern of participation for women as a whole.

In short, the most powerful positions in the society *might* now be occupied by either sex; yet, for reasons that remain unexplained, so far they have not been. It may be that men and women have different ideas about the desirability of occupying the roles defined as most powerful in industrial society—in other words, different values. Furthermore, as the nature of the society changes toward the 'post-industrial' model, it may be that we are seeing in the pattern of individualization in women's lives the symptoms of a major shift in social organization and social conciousness that is affecting both men and women. The value of our data base is that we are able to show a change.

Is the change permanent for women generally, or for segments of that group, such as age categories? Or is individualization merely a symptom of upheaval, a period of transition, a deviation from some other pattern? In short, will the fluidity, variety, and idiosyncracy we have examined here become institutionalized? Obviously we cannot answer that question. But whether the answer is yes or no, the question itself raises sociological prospects that are quite interesting.

For example, if the answer is no, will the public and private spheres become differentiated again so that adult women are consigned to the private sphere and men to the public? Or will *some* women be consigned to one sphere and the rest to the other? Will mothers be confined to the private sphere by the lack of child-care and proper income support, as some Canadians advocate, while women permanently in the paid labour force simply do not have children? If these outcomes were to occur, what combination of economic and social events would combine with what public policies or legal changes to bring them about? On the other hand, what are the chances of men's changing their social, economic and parenting behaviour to share the 'double burden' and economic opportunities so that women's and men's lives would become more similar and predictable, less variable and fluid for women and more so for men? One leading factor in individualization is clearly the poverty of many women and the relative poverty of all women in the sense that they earn, on average, about two-thirds what men do, own less property, and have less adequate pensions and benefits. Such poverty is inherently unstable because it results in demands for greater redistribution. If these demands are successful, income will become more equal between women and men and perhaps change women's attitudes towards the paid labour force/or the household. If they are not, poverty will drive women to change their behaviour—for instance, to move to more permanent jobs with benefits and therefore to make child-bearing/rearing arrangements that will allow such permanent attachment to their jobs.

As far as the care of children is concerned, there are societies in which some rich or highly educated women have incomes that allow them to support extended family households. There are also communal groupings such as kibbutzim and some utopian communities where children are a common responsibility and all adults share in the productive as well as reproductive activities. Are these likely to be models for Canadian society? Nothing suggests that such models would have widespread support, but much depends upon the reasons why they would be contemplated—whether because of economic demand, state policies regarding the care of children, religious ideologies, or some major cultural shift.

If, on the other hand, the changes we have called individualization were to become permanent, how would these patterns be played out in the labour force, in the family, and in the community? And what sort of state policies would accompany them?

In the labour force, the fluidity and variety of women workers would continue to benefit capital by enabling it to make the most convenient use of labour for the maximum productivity. Modern industrial societies have two basic choices in this respect. Either private companies themselves can absorb, replace and support surplus labour, or the state can do the job through unemployment insurance, retraining, and welfare (as in Sweden, Canada, and the US). Some combination of both already occurs in most places and is likely to continue. Given Canadian history, the state is much more likely to accommodate the employers than the other way around. If employers would rather pay taxes and have the state look after surplus labour—maintaining a 'reserve army of labour' for capital—they will also put pressure on governments to 'reduce the debt' by cutting social costs, thus creating an even more dependent labour force in areas where work exists and supporting a marginally productive population where there is no demand for labour.

In the family, women's status and role have already undergone tremendous modifications. Perhaps the trend towards serial monogamy reflects the institutionalization of these changes. What is certain is that, already, one woman in four will be a single parent at some time in her life (Moore, 1989).

If employers want labour to be easily available, then, a system of child-care facilities will need to be created. Just as publicly funded health care and education (i.e., a flow-through of funds in the tax system from those who create wealth as individuals and corporations) reduce the direct costs of labour to employers, so publicly funded child-care would spread the costs among all citizens and benefit employers seeking a flexible labour force.

It is possible as well, of course, to see the individualization of women's lives as a temporary phenomenon. The trends we have documented are both widespread and long-term, but that does not mean that they will continue. Some entirely new pattern may emerge in the next decade that will make this pattern of female lives as much an aberration in the history of our society as the baby-boom was. Nevertheless, there are some predictions that we can be fairly confident in making.

Since the 1960s, it has become increasingly apparent that all women—not just those in certain social classes, or some individuals—must be prepared to support themselves. Now girls must learn at an early age that they cannot assume the support of husbands through their child-bearing years. Both state support and women's arrangements with their employers will be much more important than they have been in the past. In this context, the economic rights of women—to hold property and divide property upon divorce, to secure loans and make investments, to have the benefits of tax changes in their favour, to have access to secure pensions—have also become more important, and have been leading elements in the legal struggles of women.

For men, the changed pattern of women's lives represents a major challenge to their established ways of doing things. Men have had no such 'revolution' as has transformed the lives of women. Increasingly, however, men find themselves rearing children on their own or on an intermittent basis. Employers can no longer assume that men will always have domestic arrangements such that they can devote all their time to their jobs.

Indeed, this new pattern of domestic life is beginning to put pressure on employers and unions alike to offer employees better working arrangements. More and more contracts now include workplace child-care arrangements and parental leave, as well as better dental plans and other benefits. It is possible to explain these shifts as the product of structural change both in the economy and in family life.

It is also possible to see these developments as representing no major change at all in the nature of industrial capitalism. Rather, they can be regarded as a means of pulling women into the capitalist system in such a way that employers no longer have to be concerned with any concept of the 'family wage' (that is, paying men sufficiently high wages to provide an income for all members of the family, not only the individual employee). In this explanation, women are forced into paid employment because the family requires a second wage. And in entering into this arrangement with capital, women lose the last vestiges of freedom that they had in bearing and rearing their children; they too are put into the cash nexus and subjected to the usual processes of the extraction of surplus labour.

No single theory, however, can account for all the changes we have documented in this book. If we understood the entire complex of causes, we would be in a much better position to predict the future. Certainly all the evidence we have points in the direction of further individualization in women's lives and further change for men. Yet there is a great deal both in the theory and in the data that we don't understand. Of course we hope that students like our SUZY, BRENDA, DIANA, and LES will pursue the questions we have raised. But even if they do not, their lives will still be profoundly affected by the changes that are now underway. We also hope, therefore, that this book will help them prepare to meet the challenges to come.

Appendix

Our Method of Research

Our study tests a number of related hypotheses about the process of individualization in women's lives. This appendix gives more information about the data we analyzed and the techniques of analysis we employed.

In order to demonstrate the individualization process, we have used a mixture of official statistics, historical evidence and survey data. Because we consider that process to be a general one, we have used data from Europe and the US as well as Canada, even though we focus most attention on Canadian sources.

The comparative focus

We have made extensive use of historical and cross-national materials because the process we are studying is slow and universal: a kind of social evolution. Western industrial countries show distinct similarities in the changes in adult women's lives, and we understand Canada's history better against this international backdrop. At the same time, the international pattern is unfolding at different rates in different countries, and with national peculiarities. These peculiarities are almost as informative as the general case.

Cross-national data from EEC countries are used to examine the effects of marital status and age on labour-market status. Such cross-national comparisons allow us to determine whether such characteristics as national history, culture, and unemployment level significantly influence women's labour-force participation or the interaction of labour-force participation with age, marital status, and other personal traits.

Historical data impress on us how much Canadian society has changed in the last fifty years. However, census data from the 1930s and earlier are likely to understate the extent of paid work by a wife. A husband who, as head of the household, was the census enumerator's informant may not have considered such work to be part of his wife's appropriate role; he may even have felt that it reflected badly on his ability to support the household. Fortunately, most of our evidence is taken from the post-1950 period.

There are some advantages in giving particular attention to the period after 1968. First, the 1971 census marks the beginning of an adequate system of occupational classification in Canadian government statistics. For this reason, various survey results can be more readily compared with official figures. Second, this period has seen most of the good-quality survey research ever carried out in Canada, making it possible for us to compare results across surveys.

Finally, the post-1968 period allows us to contrast the experiences of several generations of women over the same historical period. For example, take the Jones Employment Histories Survey, carried out in 1987-88. Women who were 60 at the time of the interview would have been 44-45 in 1971 and 54-55 in 1981; those who were 40 in 1987-88 would have been 24-25 in 1971 and 34-35 in 1981; those who were 30 in 1987-88 would have been 14-15 in 1971 and 24-25 in 1981. Another study, the Family History Survey, carried out in 1984, contains retrospective questions that discuss the earlier experiences of their respondents and also compares several generations at the same ages.

Canadian research on women's work has often relied on published official figures such as the census (cf. Armstrong and Armstrong, 1978); analysis of random samples from the Census Public Use Tapes (Nakamura and Nakamura, 1983); or large-scale government surveys, such as the Labour Force Survey, the Survey of Consumer Finances, and other special-purpose surveys (cf. Webber, 1982). These statistical and historical studies have been supplemented by smaller-scale interview studies, which usually focus on specialized issues such as time-budgets, 'networking', or re-entry to the work force (Pearson, 1979).

In the present research, Canadian census data are used to show the changes in female labour-force behaviour. Special tabulations from the Canadian Labour Force Survey are also used to show the changing nature of Canadian households and the diminishing effects of age, marital status, and parity. Various other Canadian surveys are analyzed to show differences between generations in fluidity and idiosyncracy. These include the Family History Survey (FHS), the Annual Work Patterns Survey (AWPS), the Social Change in Canada Survey (sometimes called the Quality of Life, or QOL, Survey), and the Women's Employment Histories Survey (the 'Jones survey').

MERITS OF DIFFERENT KINDS OF DATA

Cross-sectional versus over-time data

To study the timing and duration of household or labour-force events, follow-up data are needed to estimate model parameters. Cross-sectional surveys are still essential, but they cannot do justice to the increasing fluidity of social and economic processes. To paraphrase a common lament, what is needed is not so much a series of snapshots as some sort of 'moving picture'. At the same time we must bear in mind that longitudinal data are not much use without precisely formulated models of how social and economic processes work over time; we must decide on the extent to which Markov or semi-Markov assumptions are justified.

Where time and money are in short supply, retrospective questioning can be used to build up a history of family or work-related events. This approach was used in the British Women and Employment Survey, the Jones Ontario Survey, the Canadian Family History Survey, and the Canadian Fertility Survey. Outside Canada, it was also used in the Swedish Fertility Survey of 1981, the Norwegian Life History Study of 1971, and the Norwegian Life History Study for Women in 1980.

One problem with retrospective studies is the risk of measurement error. That is because people may be unable to remember exact dates or activities more than a decade old. Such errors are particularly damaging for estimates of movement from one status to another, and thus for all retrospective studies of social mobility (c.f., Macredie, 1983). Where longitudinal information is collected through retrospective questioning—as in Statistics Canada's Annual Work Patterns Survey, some Labour Force Surveys, and many academic studies—apparent changes in work status may actually be changes in self-classification (e.g., shifts in self-definition from 'unemployed' to 'not looking for work').

In follow-up studies, by contrast, data are collected almost immediately following the behaviour that is reported, and there should be no response errors due to faulty recall. Often, though, repeated interviews are required, and such follow-ups carry a tremendous risk of sample attrition through cumulative non-response. Difficult conceptual problems can also arise when the sampling unit is the household; households regularly disappear through normal processes of aging, divorce, 'empty nesting', and death.

National versus cross-national data

In principle, cross-national comparison can be useful. It extends the possibility of generalizing about some findings, and shows that others depend on their national contexts. In practice, a great deal of work must be done in order to establish equivalent meanings of occupational, social, and economic categories. Even within the same country, census definitions can change from one censal year to the next, and they may differ very widely from one country to another. For example, because of the way Sweden's leave system is funded, authorities there classify people on 'parental leave' as participating in the labour force. As a result, 86 per cent of women with children 0 to 6 years old were said to have participated in the labour force in 1986, even though only 56 per cent were at work during that year.

'Part-time work' also has widely varying definitions and legal implications in different countries. In the Netherlands, a part-timer works less than 25 hours a week; in Canada, less than 30; in the US, less than 35. Fortunately, a great deal of 'harmonization' of definitions has been brought about in the European Economic Community, where the Statistical Office (EUROSTAT) publishes comparable tabulations from the labour-force surveys of member countries. Gower (1988a) has recently made available a comparative Canada-US database adjusting Canadian data to the US definitions of part-time work.

It is also hard to use occupational or industrial classifications in cross-national comparisons. EUROSTAT has made progress using a harmonized industrial classification, but occupational classifications are still difficult to compare from one country to another, and women's occupations have their own classification problems, over and above the others.

Official versus non-official data

Government censuses and surveys typically have limited objectives—for example, to count the people or estimate the unemployment rate—and are expected to yield precise estimates of population characteristics. Therefore they use very large samples, but ask relatively few questions. Furthermore, the need for confidentiality usually means that Statistics Canada must suppress any result (a unique combination of characteristics, for example) that might conceivably identify an individual respondent.

In such surveys, the questions asked are factual in nature, and efforts are made to avoid both controversy and reliance on memory. (The latter is doubly important because in many surveys, the use of a proxy informant is permitted—for example, when the selected respondent is not available when the interviewer calls.) Finally, the concepts and categories used in many government surveys may differ widely from those commonly used by sociologists.

Longitudinal studies maintained by governments

In many countries, the central statistical office collects data on employment activity from a rotating panel sample. In such cases the panel is maintained for administrative convenience, not because of any primary interest in over-time data. Nevertheless, some special longitudinal analyses have been possible because of such panel data collection. Sundstrom's (1987) work in Sweden is a case in point. Members of the Swedish Labour Force Panel remain for two years and are interviewed every three months, for a total of eight interviews. By contrast, the Canadian Labour Force Survey interviews its members monthly and keeps them for only six months.

Some national statistical offices also maintain special panel samples that are not used for routine employment statistics. An example is the Dutch Central Bureau of Statistics which has kept a panel of about 4500 households since April 1984; interviews are carried out twice a year. One advantage of panels directed by the national government is that respondents are more likely to co-operate (Goyder, 1987). As a result, response rates and data quality will be higher than in studies directed by market researchers or university-based organizations. Even so, large financial incentives may be required to get satisfactory co-operation.

Record linkage

Linking records on a sample in earlier and later censuses is an attractive option, once procedures to protect confidentiality have been set in place. For example, the British Office of Population

Censuses has linked a sample of records from the 1971 and 1981 censuses with each other and with death registration data.

In Denmark, the entire system of national statistics is organized through record linkage of administrative registrations, and a sample of these data (with all identifying information removed) is available for academic and policy research through the University of Aarhus. Linked administrative records have also been used in Canada and elsewhere (Ham and Rae, 1987).

THE DATA USED IN THIS STUDY

Labour-market surveys

Statistics Canada is well-regarded by the international statistical community. Even so, its labour-market surveys give rise to severe problems if used for detailed research on women's employment. Simpson (1982) comments that the Census of Canada is not as useful as it might be, since although it gives information about household and family, it is infrequent, definitions sometimes change, and it gives no data on work experience beyond the previous year. Further, it yields no information on ability or work environment and no data on fringe benefits. The Labour Force Survey is frequent, but gives no data on work experience, wages, earnings, fringe benefits, union status, ability, or work environment.

Of course other government surveys are carried out in Canada, among them the Survey of Consumer Finances, the Annual Work Patterns Survey, the 1981 Survey of Work History, and the 1986 and subsequent Labour Market Activity Surveys. These have well-designed probability samples, large numbers of completed interviews or questionnaires, and high response rates. On the other hand, they frequently fail to ask questions of sociological interest.

Special tabulations, Labour Force Survey, 1976-1987

In order to obtain reliable population estimates of Canadian women's labour-force activity, we purchased special tabulations from Statistics Canada. These were estimates of annual averages of labour-market status for female heads of households (or spouses of household heads), by presence of spouse (spouse present or not), age (20-29, 30-39, 40-49, and 50-59), and family composition (no children aged 16 or less; with children under 6 years; without pre-school children, but with children aged 6 to 15). These estimates were obtained for the twelve years from 1976 to 1987. As usual with tables from Statistics Canada, estimates of less than 4,000 were not released.

The Annual Work Patterns Survey, 1977 and 1985

The Labour Force Survey (LFS) is designed to give a snapshot of the labour market at a single point in time; it cannot yield estimates of flows into or out of the labour market. In order to remedy this, Statistics Canada has conducted an Annual Work Patterns Survey (AWPS) every year since 1978. It usually supplements the January LFS, and collects retrospective data on labour-force status for each month of the previous year.

With these data one can examine movement into and out of the labour force and short-term shifts between full- and part-time work. Patterns of full-year and part-year work can also be examined. A disadvantage of this data source is that it includes little household information and no information on sociological variables such as ethnic origin or social class. For the present research, we purchased the 1977 micro-data tape and the one for 1985.

The Canadian Mobility Survey, 1973

One national study that focussed directly on female employment was the Canadian Mobility Study (Boyd et al., 1985). These data were collected in 1973, as a supplement to the Labour Force Survey. A self-completion questionnaire was dropped off at the selected household and mailed back by the respondent. The Canadian Mobility Survey, though an interesting historical source, has proved less useful than one might have hoped. Its questionnaire did not capture much detail on complex work-histories, or on withdrawal from the labour force to bring up children or to become a full-or part-time student. Further, the questionnaire had an improperly designed skip pattern, which resulted in failure to collect important data on part-time work.

The Quality of Life Survey, 1981

Another academic survey, the Social Change in Canada study (often referred to as the 'Quality of Life' survey), with interviews carried out in 1977, 1979, and 1981, includes many items of sociological interest. It even provides data on the last four years of the respondent's occupational history, at least for an urban subset of the cases. However, we have used the 1981 cross-section alone.

Little has been published on the panel component of these data, perhaps owing to problems of record linkage. A notable exception is work by Patricia Robinson (1986) which focusses on the effects of recent work interruptions on a woman's occupational status.

The Family History Survey, 1984

The Family History Survey (FHS) was carried out in February 1984 as a supplement to the Labour Force Survey. Interviews were conducted by telephone with a sample of roughly 14,000 respondents aged between 18 and 65. Proxy responses, regularly used in the Labour Force Survey, were not permitted. The interview schedule focussed on major family events, with many retrospective questions on marriages and child-rearing and a smaller number on work patterns. Questions on work interruptions focussed on those lasting one year or more, and included, *inter alia*, the year the interruption began and the number of years it lasted.

The Women and Employment Survey (Great Britain), 1980

In Britain, the Office of Population Censuses and Surveys (OPCS) carried out a survey of 5588 women aged between 16 and 59 in 1980. Each woman was questioned in some detail about her employment history up to that date (c.f., Martin and Roberts, 1984). The schedule reflects many of the preoccupations of policy makers and women's groups in the 1980s, covering (a) patterns of movement in and out of the labour market; (b) factors affecting labour-force participation; (c) recent and current employment activities; (d) consequences of not working and the process of job search; (e) factors affecting decisions about whether to work; (f) careers and occupational mobility; and (g) general attitudes to women and work. Theoretically, the project relates to sociological concerns about internal labour markets, female job ghettos, and the individualization of the female adult life course.

Women's Employment Histories Survey, 1987-88

The British interview schedule, adapted for Canadian use by Charles Jones, was administered to a sample of 600 southern

Ontario women (and 100 men) in 1987-88. City directories were used to select households randomly in the cities of Toronto, Kitchener-Waterloo, and Hamilton-Wentworth. Thus the sample is deliberately urban. The restriction to southern Ontario was the result of cost considerations. The eligible female population was defined as women born between 1922 and 1967, who would thus be aged between 20 and 65 at the time of the interview. The main aim of the study was to collect data on the employment histories of women, but a smaller sample of men was interviewed for comparative purposes. This was the first detailed survey of women's employment histories in Canada since a Department of Labour survey in 1957.

The interview schedule distinguished four types of labour-market spells: full-time paid work, part-time paid work, full-time education, and a residual category for those engaged in neither gainful employment nor full-time education. A spell was defined as a period of three months or more. Thus in comparison with the Family History Survey, the Jones survey measures the duration of spells more exactly, at best in months, at worst in quarters. Further, it distinguishes between full-time and part-time work in the employment history.

The Census Longitudinal Study (Great Britain), 1971-1981

In the British Census Longitudinal Study, a random sample of records from the 1971 Census of Population was linked with records for the same person in the 1981 census and with death registrations. This linkage allows examination of a mixture of age and period effects. One problem with these data is that employment trends must be interpreted with care, since 1981 found Britain in a deep economic slump. Research using this database has shown social-class and regional correlates of health and housing status.

LIMITATIONS OF OUR STUDY

In the present research, we have often felt that each of our sources of data lacked a different essential. Thus the Labour Force Survey tabulations are concerned with only a small number of variables, and confidentiality restrictions prevent us from having exact cell counts. The Annual Work Patterns Survey has enormous numbers of cases, but very few sociological variables. The Family History

Survey has more variables, but only sketchy information on the duration of different kinds of work. The Jones survey contains rich data, but they are retrospective, and the sample is restricted to southern Ontario. The list of complaints could go on.

What is lacking at present is a database that (a) is up-to-date; (b) is statistically representative of the Canadian population; and (c) contains a wide variety of variables of interest to sociologists. Ideally, such a database would contain repeated measures on the same people, to allow closer examination of trends and causal relationships.

Our present study uses many different kinds of data because the questions we want to ask are about historical change in the labour market: a large and complex national system. No single database exists with numbers large enough to answer these questions. Therefore we must take evidence from a variety of sources. We carry out many different kinds of analysis, partly because we have different kinds of data. In some cases, special tabulations from official government statistics (the Labour Force Survey) offer enormous numbers of cases, but only a small number of variables. In others, we have rich detail—hundreds of relevant questions—asked of a relatively small sample of women.

Nevertheless, so long as the different sets of data or kinds of analysis are free of error, when a hypothesis is supported by one analysis, or one kind of data, it will also be supported by another kind of analysis or database.

TECHNIQUES OF DATA ANALYSIS

Birth-cohort analysis

Our main tool for detecting trends with survey data is to divide a sample into generations, or what demographers call 'birth cohorts'. For example, using the Family History Survey we compare women born in the 1920s (1 January 1920 to 31 December 1929) with women born in the 1930s, the 1940s, and so.

Needless to say, there are problems with this approach. For one thing, the women born in the 1920s who were still in Canada to be interviewed in 1984 may not be a representative sample of all women born in the 1920s. As a sample, they will over-represent healthy, middle-class women, and women who did not emigrate. A second and more crucial problem is that women born in the 1920s, 1930s, or 1940s will have had much more time to experience the labour market than women born in the 1950s or the 1960s. For example, a woman aged 24 with two children the time of the survey may still have several pregnancies ahead of her, while a woman aged 44 at the time of the survey will not. If the 44-year-old has completed two pregnancies by the time of the survey, she will not have any more; of the 24-year-old, all we can say is that she has had *at least* two. Third, older generations of women will have experienced unique events—for example, the 1939-45 war—that younger generations will have missed.

Time trends are mixed up with the effects of growing older, and also with the effects of certain historical events. There is a problem distinguishing between, or identifying, cohort (or generation), age, and period effects in our data. Some possibilities of bias arise here, but in general we can interpret the findings with care, making reasonable judgements about the likely sizes of the various sources of bias. More specifically, we can reduce the confounding of age and generation by, for instance, comparing women only with respect to their patterns of household and labour-market activity over a standard part of the life cycle: say, over the first ten years after leaving school. Hence we can analyze the data of all women in our sample who were at least ten years out of school; or we can examine the number of employment spells each woman has had during her twenties, or between the ages of 25 and 34.

Different generations of women will have had this 'personal decade' at different historical times, so a comparison of generations will also be a comparison of historical periods. However, we expect birth-cohort effects to show a trend and we do not expect period effects to show trends. This analytic technique allows us to disentangle the effects of a woman's age from those of her birth cohort. Regrettably, historical-period effects are still confounded in our comparison of generations, since having the first ten years of your career in the 1980s is not the same thing as having it in the 1970s. The only way around this problem is to carry out a similar survey on the same population at a different time. By itself, then, a single longitudinal survey is unable to disentangle age, period, and cohort effects. What is required is a set of overlapping longitudinal surveys, but for reasons of cost this is rarely done.

A related approach is to assume that most of a woman's gender-related work interruptions have occurred by the time she has reached 45 years of age. Thus if we want to focus on trends in such interruptions, we can reasonably compare generations with respect to the first part of the life cycle (for example, school-leaving to age 45) for all those women in our sample who have reached the age of 45.

MERITS OF DIFFERENT KINDS OF ANALYSIS

Typologies

Typological analysis consists of defining a limited number of configurations of 'career' in both the household and the labour market. For example, Corcoran (1979) uses a five-fold typology: (a) continuous work; (b) delayed start; (c) one interruption; (d) delayed start with one interruption; (e) intermittent participation. She shows how the relative frequencies of these five types of career vary by race and other factors. Moen (1985), also using data from the Panel Study on Income Dynamics, divides women into (a) continuous full-time; (b) continuous part-time; (c) full-time and part-time mixture; (d) part-time and out of the labour force mixture; (e) full-time, part-time and out of the labour force mixture; (f) full-time and out of the labour force mixture; and (g) out of the labour force all year.

The general linear model

Multiple regression, analysis of variance, and multiple classification analysis are all different versions of a 'general linear model' for summarizing the effects of origin characteristics and career contingencies upon employment status or income. Multiple regression is a routine economist's or demographer's model, designed to assess whether or not any proposed independent variable has important influence, net of the effects of other predictors, that has been widely used in research on women's employment (Sweet, 1973; Corcoran, 1979; Denton, 1984; Boyd et al., 1985).

The model is flexible in that new variables, once appropriately coded, can easily be accommodated, and powerful methods for statistical hypothesis testing are available. Analysis of variance (ANOVA) is similar to regression, except that predictors should be categorical and their effects are conceptualized differently. With ANOVA it is particularly easy to test whether two or more predictors work even more strongly when combined. In the case of such 'interaction effects', the importance of one variable depends on the level of another.

Dependent (criterion) variables may be properly continuous or they may be dichotomous (for example, currently participating in the work force or not). There are technical problems involved in using a dichotomy as a dependent variable in regression analysis. The correct analytic technique in this case is logistic regression, discussed below.

A more important problem is how to handle the data when most or all of the predictors are categorical in nature. It is always possible to do this within the framework of multiple regression, by making up 'dummy variables' to replace categorical predictors. However, the technique of dummy-variable regression can sometimes produce results that are difficult to interpret. Hence an alternative approach called multiple classification analysis (MCA; Andrews et al., 1973) is often preferred and is frequently used in this study. MCA gives equivalent results to those of multiple regression, including 'R-squared' as a measure of explained variation; but it handles categorical variables much more easily. The scores on the criterion variable are broken down into an overall mean (the grand mean) and positive or negative components due to the effects of the categories of each predictor.

R-squared and 'explained variation'

We can test a theory by predicting the value of a dependent measure such as income or labour-force status. We are usually interested in the relative influences of several predictors. For example, studies of economic discrimination use human-capital and social-background variables to explain why people have different levels of employment income. From a technical point of view, the calculations are performed by multiple regression analysis, in which the best possible set of weights is found for combining a set of quantitative variables for the prediction of the criterion.

The weights are called 'partial regression coefficients', and when suitably standardized they are sometimes called 'beta weights'. 'Betas' indicate the relative importance of independent variables in predicting the criterion. Each weight is calculated in a way that removes the linear effects of the other predictors. This works even when the predictors are themselves intercorrelated, though it breaks down when correlations among predictors are very high. The overall success in prediction is measured by 'R-squared', the proportion of variation in the criterion that is perfectly correlated with the optimally weighted set of predictors.

R-squared varies between zero and one, and in general, a higher value is better, since it indicates that a smaller proportion of the variation remains unaccounted for. R-squared should be interpreted with care, however, since certain varieties of data—econometric time series, for example—routinely produce very high values, while micro data on individuals typically produce low values of R-squared. As Blau and Duncan (1967) remark, it would be a strange world indeed—and not the one we know—where a handful of variables could predict the individual behaviour nine times out of ten; so we cannot expect that level of predictive power. And in any event, evidence of correlation alone is never proof of causation.

Logistic regression

In this book we report several multiple regression and multiple classification analyses where the dependent variable is dichotomous. Such analyses are inappropriate from the point of view of statistical inference; specifically, the approach gives incorrect estimates of the standard errors. Further, the predicted probabilities are not restricted to the 0,1 interval. The correct statistical procedure, in this instance, is logistic regression.

In this approach, a transformation is applied to the proportions generated by the dichotomous dependent variable. Once this has been done, the tests of statistical significance on the partial regression coefficients are correct, and the predicted values for proportions cannot lie outside the limits of 0,1 (Hanushek and Jackson, 1977). The results are estimated by a non-linear method, and no indicator of 'explained variation' is defined. Fortunately for us, results generated in this way do not appear—in most cases—to differ much from results produced by the less-correct multiple regression and MCA techniques.

Event history analysis

In what has been called 'Event History Analysis', the time-bound aspects of a career become an explicit part of the analytic model. The dependent variables become transitions between states: for example, job-to-job, or job-to-non-job transitions (Felmlee, 1984), or the length of time spent in certain kinds of employment or non-employment. Such models focus on the 'waiting time' until a certain transition takes place.

The 'event history' paradigm (Tuma and Hannan, 1984) can be used to answer such time-dependent questions as: net of other factors, do younger generations of women return to the work force after a shorter child-bearing withdrawal period than the one taken by earlier generations? Some work bearing on similar problems has been reported by researchers using Canadian government surveys (Magun, 1983; Lemaître, 1984; Ham and Rae, 1987). However, none of these researchers has focussed on women's employment.

We report event-history analyses of the length of time women have spent in the four labour-force statuses of full-time work, part-time work, full-time education, and non-employment. We regard these labour-force statuses as 'repeatable events', since any woman may may enter and exit them more than once. Several strategies have been proposed for the analysis of such repeatable events. For example, each woman's work history is simply broken down into the 'spells' she has had in any of the four states, and then the spells for all the women are pooled into a single data file for analysis of transitions between the spells.

The first problem with this approach is that different women contribute varying numbers of spells to the analysis, and thus women with many spells are over-represented. The second problem is that statistical tests assume the spells are independent of each other, which may not be the case if two or more states come from the same woman and we failed to include measured variables that account for the dependency. This phenomenon of *state* dependence is common with all sequential data. In the context of 'event history' analysis, two main sub-types are distinguished: *occurrence dependence*, the effect of the number of previous spells; and *lagged duration dependence*, which is the effect of the length of previous spells. The best way to proceed is to include as predictors all the relevant variables that will summarize the individual's prior work history. If we are successful in this, then the residual amount of state dependence will be trivial.

Characteristic features of event-history data are the fact that durations cannot be negative, and right-censored observations (that is, cases where no transition has taken place by the time of data collection) are present. Some methods for statistical analysis require that the researcher know the true population distribution of durations or 'waiting times'. Standard distributions include the Exponential, the Weibull, and the Gompertz. Given assumptions about the population distribution of waiting times, regression-like models can be estimated for the effects of several predictors. It is also possible to estimate similar models by using Cox's 'proportional hazards' method, which avoids specifying the form of the population distribution.

Selectivity problems

Studies of employment income are necessarily restricted to the sub-sample of gainfully employed persons. Similarly, studies of part-time work or unemployment rates are necessarily restricted to the sub-sample of the economically active. Within these selected groups, the cases have different mean values from the general population, both on variables measured in the study and on variables that may be important but went unmeasured.

Within selected sub-groups, the measured predictors can be used to explain a criterion variable. However, it is also important to include these predictors in explaining how a case was selected into the subset where the criterion variable is predicted. In addition, any predictors that were important but unmeasured cannot be used in the calculations, and their effects will end up in the error terms of the regression equations. Since the effects of the same unmeasured predictors end up in the error terms of more than one regression equation, error terms may become correlated with one another, when this is inconsistent with the theory being tested. As Heckman first pointed out, regression analysis using a selected subset of cases may produce biased estimates of the model parameters unless the calculations are corrected by using results from a 'probit' analysis, which predicts whether or not a respondent was in the selected subset of cases.

Predicted values from the probit analysis are used to estimate the hazard of being selected, as a function of the variables that predict selection. The hazard rate is then treated as an instrumental variable for estimating the relationship between the predictors and the criterion, within the selected subset of cases. In most labour-market studies, this correction makes only a small difference to the estimated partial regression coefficients.

For our purposes the selection equation developed in Robinson's study is of some interest. This predicts the probability of being employed from the respondent's education, current marital status, mother's education, presence of a young child, age, age squared, spouse's wage, and the provincial unemployment rate. In turn, respondent's education was determined by father's education, mother's education, father's occupation and number of siblings (Robinson, 1986: 328). Note that the mother's educational level influences probability of employment directly and also through its effect on respondent's educational level. This predictor has special interest for those women who become mothers in their turn.

Censoring problems

Tabulations from the Family History Survey show that about 60 per cent of Canadian women who ever worked have interrupted work histories, but the average number of interruptions is low. By the time of the interview, of those women who have had any work interruption, about 75 per cent have as yet had only one. Only 28 per cent of all women have as yet had two completed employment spells: a working period, followed by a non-working period, followed by a second working period, followed by a non-working period that might not yet be finished.

Crude percentages such as these reflect the 'censored' nature of the data, because some of the women will have further interruptions during that part of their lives which occurs after the survey interview. Similarly, we can measure the length of time a person has been in a given employment status—full-time work, part-time work, or out of the paid work force. However, each person who is interviewed before the end of his or her working life will be interviewed part-way through a period of full-time work, part-time work, or non-employment. Thus some of the durations must be considered as being 'at least x months', rather than 'exactly x months'.

When censored data are correctly analyzed, the results of the analysis are not biased. However, the information conveyed by censored cases is less than the information conveyed by non-censored ones. Since important aspects of our model focus upon the length of time spent in various states and the probabilities of transition between such states, it is important to be sensitive to the possibilities of selectivity bias and censoring (Heckman and Singer, 1986). The underestimates and distortions introduced by censoring are largely remedied by a life-table or event-history analysis of work histories (cf. Krishnan, Penning and Kurian, 1981).

References

Abella, Rosalie Silberman
  1984   *Equality in Employment, A Royal Commission Report*. Ottawa: Supply and Services.
Acton, Janice, et al.
  1974   *Women at Work: Ontario, 1850-1930*. Toronto: Women's Press.
Adams, Owen, and Dhruva Nagnur
  1989   'Marrying and divorcing: a status report for Canada'. *Canadian Social Trends*, Summer: 24-7.
Akyeampong, Ernest B.
  1987   'Involuntary part-time employment in Canada 1975-1986'. *Canadian Social Trends*, Autumn: 26-9.
Allison, Paul D.
  1984   *Event History Analysis*. Beverly Hills: Sage University Papers.
Althauser, Robert P., and Arne L. Kalleberg
  1981   'Firms, occupations and the structure of labour markets: a conceptual analysis'. Pp. 119-52 in Ivar Berg, ed., *Sociological Perspectives on Labor Markets*. New York: Academic Press.
Anderson, Doris
  1988   'Status of Women'. Pp. 2072-4 in *The Canadian Encyclopaedia*. 2nd ed. Edmonton: Hurtig.
Andrews, Frank, J. Morgan, J. Sonquist, and L. Klein
  1973   *Multiple Classification Analysis*. 2nd ed. Ann Arbor: University of Michigan.
Archibald, Kathleen
  1970   *Sex and the Public Service*. Ottawa: Queen's Printer.
Armstrong, Patricia, and Hugh Armstrong
  1978   *The Double Ghetto*. 1st ed. Toronto: McClelland and Stewart.
  1983   *A Working Majority: What Women Must do for Pay*. Ottawa: Canadian Advisory Council on the Status of Women and Ministry of Supply and Services.
  1984   *The Double Ghetto*. Rev. ed. Toronto: McClelland and Stewart.
  1988   'Taking women into account: redefining and intensifying employment in Canada'. Pp. 65-84 in Jenson et al. (1988).
Baines, Beverly
  1988   'Women and the law'. Pp. 157-83 in Sandra Burt et al., eds, *Changing Patterns of Women in Canada*. Toronto: McClelland and Stewart.
Baker, Maureen, and Mary-Anne Robeson
  1981   'Trade union reactions to women workers and their concerns'. *Canadian Journal of Sociology* 6 (1): 19-32.

Balakrishnan, T.R., and Carl F. Grindstaff
 1988   'Early adult behaviour and later life course paths'. Report
         presented to the Review of Demography and its Implications
         for Social and Economic Policy. London: University of Western
         Ontario.
Banks, J.A.
 1954   *Prosperity and Parenthood: A Study of Family Planning Among the
         Victorian Middle Classes*. London: Routledge and Kegan Paul.
Barrère-Maurisson, Marie-Agnès
 1984   'Du travail des femmes au partage du travail: une approche des
         régulations familiales face aux évolutions du travail: le cas de
         la France depuis 1945'. *Sociologie du travail* 26 (3): 243-54.
Barrett, Nancy S.
 1984   'Part-time work will increase, bringing change to social mores
         and standards of compensation'. Pp. 120-1 in *Work in the 21st
         Century*. Alexandria, Va.: American Society for Personnel Ad-
         ministration.
Bartholomew, David J.
 1982   *Stochastic Models for Social Processes*. 3rd ed. London: Wiley.
Bartos, Rena
 1989   *Marketing to Women Around the World*. Boston: Harvard Business
         School Press, Wiley.
Baruch, Grace, Rosalind Barnett, and Caryl Rivers
 1983   *Lifeprints: New Patterns of Love and Work for Today's Women*. New
         York: Signet.
Beach, C.M., and S.F. Kaliski
 1987   'The distribution of unemployment spells: Canada 1978-82'.
         Industrial and Labour Relations Review 40: 254-67.
Beaujot, Roderic
 1978   'Canada's population'. *Population Bulletin* 33: 25-39.
 1985   'Changing patterns of marriage and childbearing'. London,
         Ont.: Dept. of Sociology, University of Western Ontario.
 1987   'The family and demographic change: economic and cultural
         interpretations'. London, Ont.: Dept. of Sociology, University
         of Western Ontario.
op de Beke, Julius M.J.
 1987   'Endogeneous extrapolation of labour force participation rates
         of married women'. Paper presented at Fontevraud Conference
         on Analysis of the European Labour Force Surveys.
Belloc, Brigitte
 1987   'Le travail à temps partiel'. *Données sociales*: 112-19. Paris: La
         Documentation française.
Bergmann, Barbara R.
 1986   *The Economic Emergence of Women*. New York: Basic Books.

Bernard, Jessie
  1973   *The Future of Marriage.* New York: Bantam Books.
Bernhardt, Eva, and Britta Hoem
  1985   'Cohabitation and social background: trends observed for
          Swedish women born between 1936 and 1960'. *European Journal
          of Population* 1: 375-95.
Best, Fred, and Barry Stern
  1976   'Lifetime distributions of education, work and leisure: research,
          speculations and policy implications'. Institute for Educational
          Leadership, Postsecondary Education Convening Authority.
          Washington, DC.
Bianchi, Suzanne M., and Daphne Spain
  1986   *American Women in Transition.* New York: Russell Sage Foundation.
Bibby, Reginald W., and Donald C. Posterski
  1985   *The Emerging Generation: An Inside Look at Canada's Teenagers.*
          Toronto: Irwin.
Blau, Peter M.
  1964   *Exchange and Power in Social Life.* New York: John Wiley.
Blau, Peter M., and Otis Dudley Duncan
  1967   *The American Occupational Structure.* New York: John Wiley.
Blitz, Rudolph C.
  1974   'Women in the professions, 1870-1970'. *Monthly Labour Review,*
          May.
Bloom, David E., and Todd Steen
  1988   'Why child care is good for business'. *American Demographics* 10
          (8) (August): 22-59.
Boothby, Daniel
  1984   'The continuity of married women's labour force participation
          in Canada'. *Canadian Journal of Economics* 17 (3): 471-80.
Bott, Elizabeth
  1957   *Family and Social Network.* London: Tavistock.
Boulet, J.-A., and L. Lavallée
  1984   *See* Economics Council of Canada (1984).
Boyd, Monica
  1985   'Education and occupation attainments of native-born
          Canadian men and women'. Pp 229-95 in Boyd et al. (1985).
Boyd, Monica, Margrit Eichler, and John R. Hofley
  1976   'Family: functions, formation and fertility'. Pp. 13-52 in Cook,
          ed. (1976).
Boyd, Monica, and Edward T. Pryor
  1989   'Young adults living in their parents' homes'. *Canadian Social
          Trends.* Summer: 17-20.
Boyd, Monica, and C. Taylor
  1986   'The feminization of temporary workers: the Canadian case'.

International Migration 24 (4) (December): 717-34.

Boyd, Monica, et al.
1985   *Ascription and Achievement: Studies in Mobility and Status Attainment in Canada.* Ottawa: Carleton University Press.

Bradbury, Bettina
1984   'Pigs, cows and boarders: non-wage forms of survival among Montreal families, 1861-91'. *Labour/Le Travail* 14 (Fall): 9-46.

Braverman, Harry
1974   *Labor and Monopoly Capital: The Degradation of Work in the 20th Century.* New York: Monthly Review Press.

Breton, Raymond, W. Isajiw, W. Kalbach, and J. Reitz
1990   *The Social Incorporation of Ethnic Groups.* Toronto: University of Toronto Press.

Brodie, Janine
1985   *Women and Politics in Canada.* Toronto: McGraw-Hill Ryerson.

Büchtemann, Christoph
1987   'Structural change in the labour market and atypical employment: the case of part-time work in the Federal Republic of Germany'. IIM/LMP, Wissenschaftszentrum, Platz der Luftbrücke 1-3, 1000 Berlin 42.

Burch, Thomas K.
1985   *Family History Survey: Preliminary Findings.* Ottawa: Statistics Canada. Catalogue 99-955.
1987   'Age-sex roles and demographic change: an overview'. *Canadian Studies in Population.* 14 (2): 129-46.

Burch, Thomas K., and A.K. Madan
        Union Formation and Dissolution. Statistics Canada. Catalogue 99-963.

Burt, Sandra, Lorraine Code, and Lindsay Dorney, eds
1988   *Changing Patterns, Women in Canada.* Toronto: McClelland and Stewart.

Cain, Glen C.
1984   'Women and work: trends in time spent in housework'. Discussion Paper 747-84, University of Wisconsin, Institute for Research on Poverty.

Campbell, Angus
1979   *The Sense of Well-being in America: Recent Patterns and Trends.* New York: McGraw-Hill.

Canada
1970   *Report of the Royal Commission on the Status of Women.* Ottawa.
1988   *Canada Year Book 1988.* Catalogue 11-402E. Ottawa: Supply and Services.

Canadian Labour Market and Productivity Centre
1988   'The quality of new services jobs'. *Labour Research Notes* 2.

Canadian Social Trends
   1986   Preliminary issue. Catalogue 11-008E, Summer. Ottawa: Statis-
             tics Canada.
Canadian Women's Educational Press
   1974   *Women at Work: Ontario 1850-1930*. Toronto: Canadian Women's
             Educational Press.
Casale, Anthony M., with Philip Lerman
   1986   *USA Today: Tracking Tomorrow's Trends*. Kansas City: Andrews,
             McMeel and Parker.
Chenier, Nancy Miller, and Dorothy Labarge
   1985   *Towards Universality: An Historical Overview of the Evolution of
             Education, Health Care, Day Care and Maternity Leave*. Report for
             the Task Force on Child Care. Series 2. Catalogue SW 43-1/2
             1985 E. Ottawa.
Chiplin, Brian, and Peter J. Sloane
   1976   *Sex Discrimination in the Labour Market*. London: Macmillan.
Clark, K.B., and Summers, L.H.
   1981   'Demographic differences in cyclical employment duration'.
             Journal of Human Resources 16: 61-79.
Cleverdon, Catherine L.
   1974   *The Woman Suffrage Movement in Canada*. Toronto: University of
             Toronto Press.
Coale, Ansley J.
   1969   'The decline of fertility in Europe from the French Revolution
             to World War II'. Pp. 3-24 in S.J. Behrman, L. Corsa, and R.
             Freedman, eds, *Fertility and Family Planning*. Ann Arbor:
             University of Michigan Press.
Cohen, M.
   1985   *Women's Work, Markets, and Economic Development in Nineteenth-
             Century Ontario*. Toronto: University of Toronto Press.
Cohn, Samual Ross
   1985   'Clerical labor intensity and the feminization of clerical labor in
             Great Britain, 1857-1937'. *Social Forces* 63 (4) (June): 1060-8.
Collins, Randall
   1982   *Sociological Insight: An Introduction to Non-obvious Sociology*. New
             York: Oxford University Press.
Connelly, Patricia
   1978   *Last Hired, First Fired: Women and the Canadian Work Force*. Toron-
             to: Women's Press.
Cook, Gail C.A., ed.
   1976   *Opportunity for Choice: A Goal for Women in Canada*. Statistics
             Canada in association with the C.D. Howe Research Institute.
             Catalogue IC 23-15.Ottawa: Information Canada.

Cooke, Katie, et al.
   1986   *Report of the Task Force on Child Care*. Ottawa: Status of Women
           Canada.
Cookingham, Mary E.
   1984   'Working after childbearing in modern America'. *Journal of
           Interdisciplinary History* 14 (4): 773-92.
Corcoran, M.E.
   1979   'Work experience, labour force withdrawals and women's
           wages'. In C.B. Lloyd, et al., eds, *Women in the Labor Market*. New
           York: Columbia University Press.
Coxon, Anthony P.M., and Charles L. Jones, eds.   *Jones*
   1975   *Social Mobility*. London: Penguin.
Cuneo, Carl J.
   1985   'Have women become more proletarianised than men?'
           Canadian Review of Sociology and Anthropology 22 (4): 465-95.
Daniel, W.W.
   1980   *Maternity Rights: The Experience of Women*. London: Policy
           Studies Institute Report no. 588.
Davidson, M.J., and C.L. Cooper
   1984   *Working Women: An International Survey*. Toronto: Wiley.
Davies, Margery
   1974   'A woman's place is at the typewriter: the feminization of the
           clerical work force'. *Radical America* 8 (4) (July-Aug.): 1-28.
Davis, James A.
   1987   *Social Differences in Contemporary America*. New York: Harcourt,
           Brace, Jovanovich.
Davis, Kingsley, et al., eds
   1987   *Below-Replacement Fertility in Industrial Society: Causes, Conse-
           quences, Politics*. New York: Cambridge University Press.
Degler, Carl N.
   1980   *At Odds: Women and the Family in America from the Revolution to
           the Present*. New York: Oxford University Press.
Delacourt, Marie-Laurence, and Jacques A. Zighera
   1988   'Situation au regard de l'emploi des femmes chefs de ménage
           ou conjointes de chef de ménage pour dix pays de la
           Communauté Européene en 1985'. Centre d'Analyse Statistique
           des Structures et des Flux, Université de Paris X-Nanterre à
           Nanterre.
Denton, Frank T., and Byron G. Spencer
   1987   'Population change and the Canadian economy: a survey of the
           issues'. Discussion Paper 87.A.2. Ottawa: Institute for Research
           on Public Policy.
   1987   'Population change and the future labour force'. Discussion
           Paper 87.A.3. Ottawa: Institute for Research on Public Policy.

Denton, Margaret A.
1984 'Industrial sectors and the determinants of earnings: male-female differences'. PhD thesis, McMaster University.
Dept. of Labour
1959 *Occupational Histories of Married Women Working for Pay in Eight Canadian Cities.* Ottawa: Queen's Printer.
Dex, Shirley
1984 'Work history analysis, women and large scale data sets'. *Sociological Review* 32 (4): 637-61
1987 *Women's Occupational Mobility: A Lifetime Perspective.* London: Macmillan.
Dex, Shirley, and S. Perry
1984 'Women's employment changes in the 1970s'. *Employment Gazette April*: 151-64 (and corrections, *Employment Gazette* May: 243).
Dex, Shirley, and Lois B. Shaw
1986 *British and American Women at Work: Do Equal Opportunities Policies Matter?* London: Macmillan.
Données sociales
1987 Paris: La Documentation française.
Dooley, Martin D.
1988 'An analysis of changes in family income and family structure in Canada between 1973 and 1986, with an emphasis on poverty among children'. McMaster University: QSEP Research Report no. 238.
1989 'Changes in the market work of married women and lone mothers with children in Canada: 1973-1986'. McMaster University: QSEP Research Report.
Duffy, Anne, Nancy Mandell, and Norene Pupo
1989 *Few Choices: Women, Work and the Family.* Toronto: Garamond.
Dumas, J.
1984 *See* Statistics Canada (1984)
Easterlin, Richard A.
1987 *Birth and Fortune: The Impact of Numbers on Personal Welfare.* 2nd ed. Chicago: University of Chicago Press.
Economic Council of Canada
1984 *The Changing Economic Status of Women.* By J.-A. Boulet and L. Lavallée. Ottawa: Supply and Services.
Economist
1987 'Falling out of love with men'. 21 Nov.: 44.
1988 'Japanese women: a world apart'. 14 May: 19-22.
Ehrenreich, Barbara
1983 *The Hearts of Men: American Dreams and the Flight of Commitment.* Garden City, NJ: Anchor.

Eichler, Margrit
    1976   'The prestige of occupation housewife'. In Patricia Marchak, ed., *The Working Sexes*. University of British Columbia: Institute of Industrial Relations.
    1981   'The inadequacy of the monolithic model of the family'. *Canadian Journal of Sociology* 6 (3): 367-88.
    1988   'Families: Evolving structures in a changing context'. In James Curtis and Lorne Tepperman, eds, *Understanding Canadian Society*. Toronto: McGraw-Hill Ryerson.

Employment and Immigration Canada
    1989   *Planning Environment Assessment Document: Trends and Perspectives*. Catalogue MP 43-230. Ottawa: Supply and Services.

England, Paula
    1981   'Assessing trends in occupational sex segregation 1900-1976'. Pp. 273-95 in Ivar Berg, ed., *Sociological Perspectives on Labour Markets*. New York: Academic Press.

Erneling, Christina
    1987   'Equality between women and men in Sweden: myth or reality'. *Canadian Woman Studies/Les Cahiers de la femme* 9 (2): 14-8.

Espenshade, Thomas J.
    1984   'Markov chain models of marital event histories'. Project Report. Urban Institute: Washington, DC.

EUROSTAT
    1987a   *Labour Force Survey*, Results 1985. Theme 3, Series G. Luxembourg: Statistical Office of the European Communities.
    1987b   *Demographic Statistics*. Theme 3, Series G. Luxembourg: Statistical Office of the European Communities.

Felmlee, Diane
    1984   'A dynamic analysis of women's employment exits'. *Demography* 21: 171-83.

Foot, David K.
    1982   *Canada's Population Outlook: Demographic Futures and Economic Challenges*. Canadian Institute for Economic Policy Series. Toronto: Lorimer.

Fox, Bonnie J., ed.
    1980   *Hidden in the Household: Women's Domestic Labour Under Capitalism*. Toronto: Women's Press.
    1988   'Conceptualizing Patriarchy'. *Canadian Review of Sociology and Anthropology* 25 (2) (May): 163-82.

Fox, Bonnie, J., and John Fox
    1987   *Occupational Gender Segregation of the Canadian Labour Force 1931-1981*. York University: Institute for Social Research.

France, République Française
    1987   *Population active, emploi et chômage depuis 30 ans*. Les collections

de l'Institut National de la Statistique et des Études Économiques (INSÉÉ). No. 563, série D, no. 123.

Freeman, Richard B.
1976   *The Over-Educated American*. New York: Academic Press.

Fuchs, Victor R.
1983   *How We Live: An Economic Perspective on Americans from Birth to Death*. Cambridge, Mass.: Harvard University Press.

Garrison, Dee
1972   'The tender technicians: the feminization of public librarianship, 1876-1905'. *Journal of Social History* 6 (2) (Winter): 131-59.

Gee, Ellen M.
1986   'The life course of Canadian women: an historical and demographic analysis'. *Social Indicators Research* 18: 263-83.

Glenn, Norvall D.
1987   'Continuity versus change: sanguineness versus concern: views of the American family in the late 1980s'. *Journal of Family Issues* 8 (4) (December): 348-54.

Gower, David
1988a   'The labour market in the 80s: Canada and the United States'. *The Labour Force*. Statistics Canada Catalogue 71-001 (June): 87-113.
1988b   'Annual update on labour force trends'. *Canadian Social Trends* (Summer): 17-20.

Goyder, John C.
1981   'Income differences between the sexes: findings from a national Canadian survey'. *Canadian Review of Sociology and Anthropology* 18 (3): 321-8.
1987   *The Silent Minority*. London: Polity Press.

Granovetter, Mark
1973   'The strength of weak ties'. *American Journal of Sociology* 78: 1360-80.

Gregory, A
1987   'Le travail à temps partiel en France et en Grande Bretagne'. *Revue française des affaires sociales* 41 (3): 53-60.

Gustafsson, Siv
1985   'Institutional environment and the economics of female labour force participation and fertility: a comparison between Sweden and West Germany'. IIM/LMP 85-9, Wissenschaftszentrum, Platz der Luftbrücke 1-3, 1000 Berlin 42.

Gutmann, Amy
1980   *Liberal Equality*. Cambridge: Cambridge University Press.

Hagan, John
1986   'Gender and the structural transformation of the legal profession in the United States and Canada'. Paper presented in the

Distinguished Lectureship Series, Dept. of Sociology, Notre Dame University, Indiana. (To be published in Maureen Hallinan, ed., *Change in Societal Institutions*. New York: Plenum Press.)

Hagan, John, Marie Huxter, and Patricia Parker
1988   'Class structure and legal practice: inequality and mobility among Toronto lawyers'. *Law and Society Review* 22 (1): 28-55.

Hajnal, John
1965   'European marriage patterns in perspective'. Pp. 101-43 in D.V. Glass and D.E.C. Eversley, eds., *Population in History*. London: Edward Arnold.

Hakim, Catherine
1979   'Occupational segregation: a comparative study of the degree and pattern of the differentiation between men's and women's work in Britain, the United States and other countries'. London: Dept. of Employment Research Paper no. 9.
1987   'Trends in the flexible workforce'. *Employment Gazette* (November): 549-60.

Halsey, A.H., ed.
1988   *British Social Trends Since 1900: A Guide to the Changing Social Structure of Britain*. Basingstoke: Macmillan.

Ham, John C., and Samuel A. Rae Jr
1987   'Unemployment insurance and male unemployment duration in Canada'. *Journal of Labour Economics* 5 (3): 325-53.

Hamil, Ralph E.
1987   'The arrival of the 5-billionth human'. *The Futurist* 21 (4) (July-Aug.): 36-7.

Hamilton, Roberta, and Michele Barrett, eds
1987   *The Politics of Diversity, Feminism, Marxism and Nationalism*. Montreal: Book Center.

Hanushek, E.A., and J.A. Jackson
1977   *Statistical Methods for Social Scientists*. New York: Academic Press.

Harvey, Edward, Lorna Marsden, and Ivan Charner
1975   'Female graduates: their occupational mobility and occupational attainments'. *Canadian Review of Sociology and Anthropology* 12 (4): 385-485.

Hatfield, Elaine, and Susan Sprecher
1986   *Mirror, Mirror: The Importance of Looks In Everyday Life*. Albany: State University of New York Press.

Heckman, James J.
1980   'Sample selection bias as a specification error'. *Econometrica* 47: 153-61.

Heckman, James J., and G. Borjas

1980 'Does unemployment cause future unemployment? Definitions, questions and answers from a continuous time model of heterogeneity and state dependence'. *Econometrica* 47: 247-83.

Heckman, James J., and Burton Singer, eds
1986 *Longitudinal Analysis of Labour Market Data.* New York: Cambridge University Press.

Hewlett, Sylvia A.
1985 *A Lesser Life: The Myth of Women's Liberation in America.* New York: Macmillan.

Hobart, Charles W.
1984 'Interest in parenthood among young Anglophone and Francophone Canadians'. *Canadian Studies in Population* 11 (2): 111-33.

Hochschild, Arlie
1989 *The Second Shift.* New York: Viking Penguin.

Hoem, Jan, and Britta Hoem
1987 'The impact of female employment on second and third births in modern Sweden'. Stockholm Research Reports in Demography no. 36.
1988 'The dissolute Swedes'. Paper presented at the International Union for the Scientific Study of Population (IUSSP) conference, Paris.

Hogan, Dennis P.
1981 *Transitions and Social Change: The Early Lives of American Men.* New York: Academic Press.

Holden, Karen C., and W. Lee Hansen
1985 'Part-time work, full-time work and occupational segregation'. Center for Demography and Ecology Working Paper 85-3, University of Wisconsin.

Hollingsworth, Laura, and Vappu Tyyska
1989 'The hidden producers: women's household labour during the great depression'. *Critical Sociology* (Spring): 2-39.

Homans, George C.
1974 *Social Behaviour: Its Elementary Forms.* Rev. ed. New York: Harcourt, Brace and Jovanovich.

Hotz, V.J., and R.A. Miller
1988 'An empirical analysis of life cycle fertility and female labour supply'. *Econometrica* 56 (l): 91-118.

Huckle, Patricia
1982 'The womb factor: pregnancy policies and the employment of women'. Pp. 144-61 in Ellen Bonaparth, ed., *Women, Power and Policy.* New York: Pergamum Press.

Humphreys, Jane, and Jill Rubery
1988 'Recession and exploitation: British women in a changing workplace 1979-85'. Pp. 85-105 in Jenson et al. (1988).

Intergovernmental Committee on Women in Employment
1980   *Maternity Leave in Canada*. Ottawa: Women's Bureau of Labour Canada.

Jenson, Jane, Elisabeth Hagen and Ceallaigh Ready, eds
1988   *Feminization of the Labor Force: Paradoxes and Promises*. New York: Oxford University Press.

Johnson, Bob, and Laura Johnson
1982   *The Seam Allowance: Industrial Home Sewing in Canada*. Toronto: Women's Press.

Johnson, Lynell
1987   'Children's visions of the future'. *The Futurist* 21 (3) (May-June): 36-40.

Joshi, Heather
1987   'The cash opportunity costs of childbearing: an approach to estimation using British data'. London: Centre for Economic Policy Research.
1989   'The changing form of women's economic dependency'. Pp. 157-76 in Joshi, ed., *The Changing Population of Britain*. Oxford: Basil Blackwell.

Joshi, Heather, and Elizabeth Overton
1984   'The female labour force in Britain 1971-1991'. Centre for Population Studies Research Paper 84-1.

Katz, Michael B.
1975   The People of Hamilton, Canada West. Cambridge, Mass.: Harvard University Press.

Kerr, Virginia
1973   'One step forward—two steps back: child care's long American history'. Pp. 157-71 in Pamela Roby, ed., *Child-Care—Who Cares?: Foreign and Domestic Infant and Early Childhood Development Policies*. New York: Basic Books.

Kettle, John
1980   *The Big Generation*. Toronto: McClelland and Stewart.

Keyfitz, Nathan
1988   'On the wholesomeness of marriage'. Pp 449-62 in Lorne Tepperman and James Curtis, eds, *Reader in Sociology: An Introduction*. Toronto: McGraw-Hill Ryerson.

Kiernan, Kathleen E.
1988   'The British family: contemporary trends and issues'. *Journal of Family Issues* 9 (3) (Sept.): 298-316.

Kitagawa, Evelyn M.
1981   'New life-styles: marriage patterns, living arrangements and fertility outside of marriage'. In C. Taeuber, ed., *America Enters the Eighties: Some Social Indicators*. Special issue of *The Annals of the American Academy of Political and Social Science* 453 (January): 1-27.

Kohl, Seena B.
1976   *Working Together: Women and Family in Southwestern Sas-katchewan*. Toronto: Holt Rinehart and Winston.
Krishnan, Parameswara, Margaret Penning, and Lizy Kurian
1981   'Working life tables for females in Canada 1971'. *Population et famille* 52 (1): 153-66.
Labour Canada
1983   *Part-time Work in Canada. Report of the Commission of Inquiry into Part-time Work.* Joan Wallace, Commissioner. Catalogue L 31-45. Ottawa: Supply and Services.
1985   *Canadian Women and Job Related Laws 1984* . Catalogue L 38-35.
Lambert, Ronald D., and James Curtis
1985   'The racial attitudes of Canadians'. *Past and Present* (Feb.): 2-4.
Land, Hilary
1978   'Who cares for the family?' *Journal of Social Policy* 7 (3): 257-84.
Langlois, Simon
1989   'Le travail à temps partiel: vers une polarisation de plus en plus nette'. Institut québécois de recherche sur la culture, 14 rue Haldimand, Québec, G1R 4N4.
Laurier, Claudine, André Archambault, and André-Pierre Contan-driopoulos
1986   'Differences between the practices of men and women pharmacists'. *Journal of Social and Administrative Pharmacy* 3 (4): 136-43.
LEAF (Women's Legal Education Action Fund)
1989   LEAF Letter no. 7 (Summer): 3.
Le Bourdais, Céline, and Hélène Desrosiers
1988   *Trajectoires démographiques et professionnelles: une analyse longitudinale des processus et des déterminants.* Université du Québec: INRS-Urbanisation.
Leckie, Norm
1988   'The declining middle and technological change: trends in the distribution of employment income in Canada 1971-1984'. Economic Council of Canada. Discussion paper no. 342.
Lee, John Alan
1976   *The Colors of Love*. New York: Prentice-Hall.
Lehrer, Evelyn, and M. Nerlove
1986   'Female labour force behaviour and fertility in the United States'. *Annual Review of Sociology* 12.
Lemaître, G.
1984   'Flows into unemployment: the job loser component'. *The Labour Force* (Dec.): 149-59.
Leprince, Frédérique
1987   'La garde des jeunes enfants'. *Données sociales*. Paris: La

Documentation française.

Leslie, Gerald R., and Sheila K. Korman

1985 *The Family in Social Context*. 6th ed. New York: Oxford University Press.

Lewenhak, S.

1977 *Women and Trade Unions*. London: Ernest Benn.

Lowe, Graham S.

1980 'Women, work and the office: the feminization of clerical occupations in Canada 1901-1931'. *Canadian Journal of Sociology* 5 (4): 363-84.

1987 *Women in the Administrative Revolution: The Feminization of Clerical Work*. Toronto: University of Toronto Press.

Lucas, R.A.

1971 *Minetown, Milltown, Railtown: Life in Canadian Communities of Single Industry*. Toronto: University of Toronto Press.

Lupri, Eugen, and James Frideres

1981 'The quality of marriage and the passage of time: marital satisfaction over the family life cycle'. *Canadian Journal of Sociology* 6 (3): 283-305.

Luxton, Margaret

1980 *More than a Labour of Love: Three Generations of Women's Work in the Home*. Toronto: Women's Press.

McGill, Elsie Gregory

1981 *My Mother, the Judge*. Toronto: Peter Martin.

McLaughlin, Steven D., et al., eds

1988 *The Changing Lives of American Women*. Chapel Hill: University of North Carolina Press.

McKie, Craig

1986 'The law—a changing profession'. *Canadian Social Trends*, preliminary issue: 28-34.

Mackie, Marlene

1983 *Exploring Gender Relations, a Canadian Perspective*. Toronto: Butterworths.

Macredie, Ian

1983 'The impact of response errors in the estimation of labour market flows'. Statistics Canada, Labour Force Activity Section.

Magun, S.

1983 'Unemployment experience in Canada: a five year longitudinal analysis'. *Monthly Labour Review* 106 (4): 36-8.

Mann, Michael

1986 *The Sources of Social Power*, Vol. 1, *A History of Power from the Beginning to AD 1760*. New York: Cambridge University Press.

March, James G., and Herbert A. Simon

1958 *Organizations*. New York: John Wiley.

Marini, Margaret M.
1984   'The order of events in the transition to adulthood'. *Sociology of Education* 57: 63-84.

Marsden, Lorna R.
1979   'Agitating organizations: the role of the National Action Committee on the Status of Women in facilitating equal pay policy in Canada'. Pp. 242-60 in Ronnie S. Ratner, ed., *Equal Employment Policy for Women.* Philadelphia: Temple University Press.

Marsden, Lorna R., and Joan Busby
1990   'Feminist reciprocity: women's movement representations to parliament and women senators—the case of divorce'. *Atlantis.* forthcoming.

Marsden, Lorna R., and Edward Harvey
1972   'Access to post-secondary education in Ontario: some influences of social class and sex'. *Interchange* 2 (4): 11-26.

Marshall, Katherine
1989   'Women in professional occupations: progress in the 1980s'. *Canadian Social Trends,* Spring: 13-6.

Martin, Jean, and Ceridwen Roberts
1984   *Women and Employment: A Lifetime Perspective.* London: Her Majesty's Stationery Office.

Mason, Greg
1982   'Longitudinal micro-level data in research on women and the Canadian economy: an evaluation of MINCOME data'. Institute for Social and Economic Research, University of Manitoba.

Mason, K., and W. Mason
1982   *Detroit Area Study 1974: A Study of Women's Labour Force Participation.* International Consortium for Political and Social Research study 7901. Ann Arbor, Mich.

Meissner, Martin
1981   'The domestic economy: now you see it, now you don't'. Pp. 345-66 in Naomi Hersom and Dorothy E. Smith, eds, *Women and the Canadian Labour Force: Proceedings of a Workshop.* University of British Columbia.

Michelson, William
1985a   *From Sun to Sun: Daily Obligations and Community Structure in the Lives of Employed Women.* Totowa, NJ: Rowman and Allenheld.
1985b   'Divergent convergence: the daily routines of employed spouses as a public affairs agenda'. Public Affairs Report 26 (4): 1-9.

Mincer, Jacob, and Haim Ofek
1982   'Interrupted work careers: depreciation and restoration of human capital'. *Journal of Human Resources* 17 (1): 3-24.

Mintz, Steven, and Susann Kellogg

1988 *Domestic Revolutions: A Social History of American Family Life.* New York: Free Press.

Miron, John R.
1988 *Housing in Postwar Canada: Demographic Change, Household Formation and Housing Demand.* Kingston and Montreal: McGill-Queen's University Press.

Moen, Phyllis
1985 'Continuities and discontinuities in women's labour force activity'. Pp. 113-55 in Glen H. Elder, ed., *Life Course Dynamics: Trajectories and Transitions.* 1968-1980. Ithaca, NY: Cornell University Press.

Moloney, Joanne
1989 'On maternity leave'. *Perspectives on Labour and Income,* preview edition. Catalogue 75-001E: 27-46. Ottawa: Canadian Government Publishing Centre.

Le Monde
1987 'L'emploi de femmes: une grande vulnerabilité'. 15 sept.: 40.

Moore, Maureen
1989a 'Female lone parenting over the life course'. Ottawa: Statistics Canada.
1989b 'Dual earner families: the new norm'. *Canadian Social Trends,* Spring: 24-6.

Morgan, Nicole
1988 *The Equality Game: Women in the Federal Public Service (1908-1987).* Ottawa: Canadian Advisory Council on the Status of Women.

Morissette, Diane
1987 *Growing Strong, Women in Agriculture.* Ottawa: Canadian Advisory Council on the Status of Women.

Moynihan, Daniel P.
1965 *The Negro Family: The Case for National Action.* Washington, DC: Office of Policy Planning and Research, US Department of Labor.

Myles, John
1987 'The expanding middle: some Canadian evidence on the deskilling debate'. *Canadian Review of Sociology and Anthropology* 25 (3): 335-64.

Myles, John, W. G. Picot, and T. Wannell
1989 'Wages and jobs in the 1980s: changing youth wages and the declining middle'. Statistics Canada, Analytical Studies Branch, Research Paper no. 17.

Nagnur, Dhruva, and Owen Adams
1987 'Tying the knot: an overview of marriage rates in Canada'. *Canadian Social Trends,* Autumn: 2-4.

Nakamura, A., and M. Nakamura
    1983   'Part-time and full-time work behaviour of married women: a model with doubly truncated dependent variables'. *Canadian Journal of Economics*: 229-57.

Nakamura, A., M. Nakamura, and Dallas Cullen
    1979   *Employment and Earnings of Married Females*. Census Analytic Study. Ottawa: Statistics Canada.

National Council of Women
    1900   *Women of Canada, Their Life and Work*. Ottawa.

Nett, Emily M.
    1981   'Canadian families in socio-historical perspective'. *Canadian Journal of Sociology* 6 (3).

OECD
    1983   *Employment Outlook 1983*. Paris: OECD.
    1985   *The Integration of Women into the Economy*. Paris: OECD.
    1987   *Statistiques de la population active 1965-1985*. Paris: OECD.
    1988   *Employment Outlook 1988*. Paris: OECD.

Ontario Task Force on Employment and New Technology
    1985   *Final Report, Employment and New Technology*. Toronto: Government of Ontario.

Oppenheimer, Valerie K.
    1976   *The Female Labour Force in the United States: Demographic and Economic Factors Governing its Growth and Changing Composition*. Westport, Conn.: Greenwood Press.
    1982   *Work and the Family: A Study in Social Demography*. New York: Academic Press.

Ornstein, Michael
    1983   'Job income in Canada'. Pp. 41-75 in R.V. Robinson and D.J. Treiman, eds, *Research in Social Stratification and Mobility*. Vol. 2.

Parliament, Jo-Anne B.
    1989   'Women employed outside the home'. *Canadian Social Trends*, Summer: 2-6.

Paukert, L.
    1984   *The Employment and Unemployment of Women in OECD Countries*. Paris: OECD.

Pearson, Mary
    1979   *The Second Time Around: A Study of Women Returning to the Work Force*. Canadian Advisory Council on the Status of Women. Ottawa: Supply and Services.

Peitchinis, Stephen G.
    1989   *Women at Work: Discrimination and Response*. Toronto: McClelland and Stewart.

Peron, Yves, Evelyne Lapierre-Adamcyk, and Denis Morissette
    1987   'Le changement familiale: aspects démographiques'. *Recherches*

sociographiques 28 (2-3): 317-39.

Picot, W. Garnett
    1986a   'Modelling the lifetime employment patterns of Canadians'. Research paper no. 4. Statistics Canada Analytical Studies Branch.
    1986b   *Canada's Industries: Growth in Jobs Over Three Decades: 1951-1984.* Ottawa: Supply and Services.

Pierson, Ruth R., and Marjorie Cohen
    1986   *'They're Still Women After All': The Second World War and Canadian Womanhood.* Toronto: McClelland and Stewart.

Pineo, Peter C.
    1985   'Family size and status attainment'. Pp. 201-28 in Boyd et al. (1985).

Platt, John
    1987   'The future of AIDS'. *The Futurist* 21 (6): 10-17.

Pool, Ian, and Maureen Moore
    1986   *Lone Parenthood: Characteristics and Determinants. Results from the 1984 Family History Survey.*Statistics Canada, catalogue 99-961, Ottawa: Supply and Services.

Porter, John
    1985   'Canada: the societal content of occupational allocation'. Pp. 29-65 in Boyd et al. (1985).

Portner, Joyce, and Larry Etkin
    1984   'The work-family connection in the year 2020'. Pp. 207-25 in Lester A. Kirkendall and Arthur E. Gravatt, eds, *Marriage and the Family in the Year 2020.* Buffalo, NY: Prometheus Books.

Powell, Douglas R.
    1987   'Day care as a family support system'. Pp. 115-32 in Sharon L. Kagan et al., eds, *America's Family Support Programmes: Perspectives and Projects.* New Haven and London: Yale University Press.

Prentice, Alison, Paula Bourne, Gail C. Brandt, Beth Light, Wendy Mitchinson, and Naomi Black
    1988   *Canadian Women: A History.* Toronto: Harcourt Brace Jovanovich.

Prentice, Susan
    1989   'Daycare organizing in Toronto: 1946-1951'. Paper presented at the Canadian Sociology and Anthropology Association Meetings, Quebec City.

Reitz, Jeffrey
    1980   *The Survival of Ethnic Groups.* Toronto: McGraw-Hill Ryerson.

Rhyne, Darla
    1984   *Marital Satisfaction in Canada: A Descriptive Overview.* Toronto: Institute for Behavioural Research, York University.

Robinson, Patricia
  1986   'Women's occupational attainment: the effects of work inter-
          ruptions, self-selection and unobservable characteristics'. *Social
          Science Research* 15: 323-46.
  1987   *Women's Work Interruptions.* Statistics Canada, catalogue 99-962.
Romaniuc, Anatole
  1984   *see* Statistics Canada (1984).
  1986   'Fertility in Canada: a long view'. Presented at the colloquium
          'The Family in Crisis: A Population Crisis?', organized by the
          Federation of Canadian Demographers, University of Ottawa,
          28-9 November.
Rose, Sonya
  1966   'Gender at work: sex, class and industrial capitalism'. *History
          Workshop Journal* 21.
Ross, David, and Richard Shillington
  1989   *The Canadian Fact Book on Poverty 1989* . Canadian Council on
          Social Development.
Rueschemeyer, Dietrich
  1986   *Power and the Division of Labour.* Cambridge: Polity Press.
Ruggie, Mary
  1984   *The State and Working Women.* Princeton, NJ: Princeton Univer-
          sity Press.
Russell, Cheryl
  1987   *100 Predictions for the Baby Boom: The Next 50 Years.* New York:
          Plenum Press.
Scarce, Rik
  1987   'Women of tomorrow: issues and alternative futures'. *Futures*
          19 (6): 701-6.
Schultz, George
  1962   'A nonunion market for white collar labor'. Pp. 107-55 in *Aspects
          of Labor Economics: a conference of the Universities National Bureau
          Committee for Economic Research.* Princeton, NJ: Princeton
          University Press.
Scott, Joan W., and Louise A. Tilly
  1975   'Women's work and the family in nineteenth-century Europe'.
          Comparative Studies in Society and History 17 (1): 36-64.
          (Reprinted as pp. 45-70 in Elizabeth Whitelegg et al., eds, *The
          Changing Experience of Women.* The Open University. Oxford:
          Basil Blackwell, 1984.)
Seward, Shirley B.
  1987   'Demographic change and the Canadian economy: an
          overview'. Discussion paper no. 87.A.O. Ottawa: Institute for
          Research on Public Policy.
Shaw, Lois B.

1983   'Causes of irregular employment patterns'. Pp. 45-60 in Shaw, ed., *Unplanned Careers: The Working Lives of Middle-Aged Women*. Lexington, Mass.: Lexington Books.

Simpson, Wayne
1982   'An evaluation of existing Canadian databases to support research into women and work'. Paper delivered at the 1982 Conference on Women and the Canadian Economy, University of Winnipeg.

Smith, Pam
1988   'Working life and unemployment tables for males and females Canada 1981'. Discussion paper no. 55. University of Alberta Population Research Laboratory.

Social Trends 19
1989   Tom Griffin, ed. London: Her Majesty's Stationery Office.

Sorenson, Aage B.
1975   'Estimating durations from retrospective questions'. Working paper 83-26. University of Wisconsin-Madison: Center for Demography and Ecology.
1977   'Estimating rates from retrospective questions'. Pp. 209-23 in D.R. Heise, ed., *Sociological Methodology* 1977. San Francisco: Jossey-Bass.

Sorensen, Annemette, and Sara Mclanahan
1985   'Married women's economic dependency: 1940-1980'. Working paper 85-24. University of Wisconsin-Madison: Center for Demography and Ecology.

South, Scott J., and Glenna Spitze
1986   'Determinants of divorce over the marital life course'. *American Sociological Review* 51: 583-90.

Spence, Alan
1988a   'The development of new methods of forecasting activity rates'. Unpublished paper, Dept of Employment, room 450, Caxton House, London SW1H 9NF.
1988b   'Labour force outlook to 1995'. *Employment Gazette* March: 117-29.

Sproat, K., et al.
1985   *The National Longitudinal Surveys of Labour Market Experience*. Toronto: Lexington Books.

Stafford, F.P.
1985   'Women's use of time converging with men's'. *Monthly Labor Review* 103 (December): 57-9.

Stasny, E.A.
1986   'Estimating gross flows using panel data with non-response: an example from the Canadian Labour Force Survey'. *Journal of the American Statistical Association* 81: 42-7.

Statistics Canada
    1982   *Vital Statistics, Vol. ll: Marriages and Divorces.* Catalogue 84-205. Ottawa: Supply and Services.
    1983   *Historical Statistics of Canada.* 2nd ed. F.H. Leacy, ed. Ottawa: Supply and Services.
    1984a   *Fertility in Canada from Baby Boom to Baby Bust.* By A. Romaniuc. Ottawa: Supply and Service.
    1984b   *Report on the Demographic Situation in Canada 1983.* By J. Dumas. Ottawa: Supply and Services.
    1984c   *Women in the World of Work.* Catalogue 99-940. Ottawa: Supply and Services.
    1985a   *Family History Survey: Preliminary Findings.* Catalogue 99-955. Ottawa: Supply and Services.
    1985b   *Population Projections for Canada, Provinces and Territories 1984-2006.* Catalogue 91-520. Ottawa: Supply and Services.
    1985c   *Population Projections for Canada, Provinces and Territories 1984-2006.* Ottawa: Supply and Services.
    1987a   *Interim Household and Family Projections for Canada, Provinces and Territories to 2006.* Ottawa: Supply and Services.
    1987b   *Population Estimation Methods,* Canada. Ottawa: Supply and Services.
    1987c   *Current Demographic Analysis: Report on the Demographic Situation in Canada.* Catalogue 91-209E. Ottawa: Supply and Services.
    1987d   *Historical Labour Force Statistics—Actual Data, Seasonal Factors, Seasonally Adjusted Data. 1986.* Catalogue 71-201. Ottawa: Supply and Services.
Stone, Leroy O., with the assistance of Frances Aubry, Susan Fletcher, and Andrew Siggner
    1978   *The Frequency of Geographic Mobility in the Population of Canada.* Census Analytical Study, catalogue 99-751 E. Ottawa: Supply and Services.
Strong-Boag, Veronica
    1976   *The Parliament of Women: The National Council of Women of Canada, 1893-1929.* Ottawa: National Museums of Canada.
    1988   *The New Day Recalled: Lives of Girls and Women in English Canada 1919-39.* Markham, Ont.: Penguin.
Strong-Boag, Veronica, and Anita Clair Fellman
    1986   *Rethinking Canada, The Promise of Women's History.* Toronto: Copp Clark Pitman.
Sundstrom, Marianne
    1987   *A Study in the Growth of Part-time Work in Sweden.* Stockholm: Almqvist and Wicksell International.
Sweet, James A.
    1973   *Women in the Labour Force.* New York: Seminar Press.

Swidinsky, Robert
1983 'Working wives, income distribution and poverty'. *Canadian Public Policy* 9 (1): 71-80.

Sydie, Rosalind A.
1987 *Natural Women, Cultured Men: A Feminist Perspective on Sociogical Theory*. Toronto: Methuen.

Tegle, Stig
1985 *Part-Time Employment: An Economic Analysis of Weekly Working Hours in Sweden 1963-1982*. Lund: University of Lund.

Tennov, Dorothy
1979 *Love and Limerence*. New York: Stein and Day.

Tepperman, Lorne
1975 *Social Mobility*. Toronto: McGraw-Hill Ryerson.
1988a 'Social Mobility'. Pp. 2030-1 in *The Canadian Encyclopaedia*. 2nd ed. Edmonton: Hurtig.
1988b *Choices and Chances, Sociology for Everyday Life*. Toronto: Holt, Rinehart and Winston.

Thélot, Claude
1987 'Les formes particulières d'emploi en France'. Institut National de la Statistique et des Études Économiques.

Thernstrom, Stephan
1973 *The Other Bostonians*. Cambridge, Mass.: Harvard University Press.

Tilly, Louise A.
1977 'Urban growth, industrialization and women's employment in Milan, Italy, 1881-1911'. *Journal of Urban History* 3 (4) (August): 467-84.

Tivy, Louis
1972 *Your Loving Anna: Letters from the Ontario Frontier*. Toronto: University of Toronto Press.

Townson, Monica
1987 'Women's labour force participation, fertility rates and the implications for economic development and government policy'. Disucssion paper 87.A.11. Ottawa: Institute for Research on Public Policy.

Tuma, Nancy B., and Michael T. Hannan
1984 *Social Dynamics: Models and Methods*. New York: Academic Press.

United Nations
1967 *Manual IV: Methods of Estimating Basic Demographic Measures from Incomplete Data*. New York: Dept of Economic and Social Affairs of the UN.

Vaneck, Jann
1974 'Time spent in housework'. *Scientific American* 231: 117-20.

Veevers, Jean E.
   1980   *Childless by Choice.* Toronto: Butterworths.
   1989   'Permanent availability for marriage: considerations of the Canadian case'. Unpublished paper, Department of Sociology, Simon Fraser University.

Veevers, Richard
   1986   'Results from the Annual Work Patterns Survey: 1984 and 1985'. *Labour Force Survey,* March: 85-98. Catalogue 71-001.

Vlassoff, Carol
   1987   'Fertility and the labour force in Canada: critical issues'. Discussion paper 87.A.12. Ottawa: Institute for Research on Public Policy.

Vogelheim, Elizabeth
   1988   'Women in a changing workplace: the case of the Federal Republic of Germany'. In Jenson et al. (1988).

de Vries, John, and Frank G. Vallee
   1980   *Language Use in Canada.* Census Analytical Study. Catalogue 99-762E. Ottawa: Statistics Canada.

Waite, Linda J.
   1981   'US women at work'. *Population Bulletin* 36 (May): 62.

Waite, Linda J., Gus W. Haggstrom, and David E. Kanouse
   1985   'Changes in the employment activities of new parents'. *American Sociological Review* 50 (April): 263-72.

Walby, S.
   1986   *Patriarchy at Work.* Cambridge: Polity Press and Oxford: Basil Blackwell.

Wallace, Joan
   1983   *See* Labour Canada (1983).

Wannell, Ted
   1989   'Losing ground: wages of young people 1981-1986 '. *Canadian Social Trends* Summer: 21-3.

Wattenberg, Ben J.
   1987   *The Birth Dearth.* New York: American Enterprise Institute, Pharos Books.

Webber, M.
   1982   *The Labour Force Survey and its Supplements as a Data Source for Research into Women and The Economy.* Unpublished Report. Statistics Canada.

Weber, Max
   1958   *From Max Weber: Essays in Sociology.* Translated and edited by Hans Gerth and C. Wright Mills. New York: Oxford University Press.

White, Julie
   1983   *Women and Part-Time Work.* Ottawa: Canadian Advisory Coun-

cil on the Status of Women.

Wolfson, Michael
  1986   'Stasis amid change—income inequality in Canada 1965-1983'.
           Canadian Statistical Review February: 6-27.

Wright, Robert, and Andrew Hinde
  1989   'The dynamics of full-time and part-time female labour force
           participation in Great Britain'. In T.J. Trussell, ed., *Demographic
           Applications of Event History Analysis*. London: Oxford Univer-
           sity Press.

Yankelovich, Daniel
  1981   *New Rules: Searching for Self-fulfillment in a World Turned Upside
           Down*. New York: Bantam.

Yeandle, Susan
  1982   'Variation and flexibility: key characteristics of female labour'.
           Sociology 16 (3) (August): 422-5.

Young, Michael, and Peter Willmott
  1975   *The Symmetrical Family*. Harmondsworth: Penguin.

Zighera, J., et al.
  1975   'Analysis of the results of sample surveys of the labour forces
           in EEC countries: male and female employment rate by age,
           structure and evolution, 1973, 1975, 1977'. Centre d'Analyse
           Statistique des Structures et des Flux, Université de Paris X-
           Nanterre. Study number 79-17.

Subject Index

Author Index